D0953005

waymaker

waymaker

FINDING THE WAY TO THE LIFE
YOU'VE ALWAYS DREAMED OF

ANN VOSKAMP

W PUBLISHING GROUP

AN IMPRINT OF THOMAS NELSON

Published in Nashville, Tennessee, by W Publishing Group, an imprint of Thomas Nelson.

Published in association with William K. Jensen Literary Agency, 119 Bampton Court, Eugene, Oregon 97404.

Thomas Nelson titles may be purchased in bulk for educational, business, fund-raising, or sales promotional use. For information, please email SpecialMarkets@ThomasNelson.com.

"Red Sea Road," Ellie Holcomb, Nicole Marie Witt, Christa Nichole Wells, writers. © 2015 Full Heart Music (ASCAP) (adm. at CapitolCMGPublishing.com). All rights reserved. Used by permission.

The Weight of Glory by C. S. Lewis © C. S. Lewis Pte. Ltd. 1949. *Pilgrims Regress* by C. S. Lewis © C. S. Lewis Pte. Ltd. 1933. *The Great Divorce* by C. S. Lewis © C. S. Lewis Pte. Ltd. 1946. *The Four Loves* by C. S. Lewis © C. S. Lewis Pte. Ltd. 1960. *Mere Christianity* by C. S. Lewis © C. S. Lewis Pte. Ltd. 1942, 1943, 1944, 1952. Extracts reprinted by permission.

Unless otherwise noted, Scripture quotations are taken from the Holy Bible, New International Version®, NIV®. © 1973, 1978, 1984, 2011 by Biblica, Inc.® Used by permission of Zondervan. All rights reserved worldwide.

Scripture quotations marked cev are taken from the Contemporary English Version. © 1991, 1992, 1995 by American Bible Society. Used by permission. Scripture quotations marked esv are taken from the ESV® Bible (The Holy Bible, English Standard Version®). © 2001 by Crossway, a publishing ministry of Good News Publishers. Used by permission. All rights reserved. Scripture quotations marked hnv are taken from the Hebrew Names Version. Public domain. It has also been known as the World Messianic Bible (WMB) and the World English Bible: Messianic Edition (WEB:ME). Scripture quotations marked kjv are taken from the King James Version. Public domain. Scripture quotations marked msg are taken from THE MESSAGE. © 1993, 2002, 2018 by Eugene H. Peterson. Used by permission of NavPress. All rights reserved. Represented by Tyndale House Publishers, a Division of Tyndale House Ministries. Scripture quotations marked nasb are taken from the New American Standard Bible® (NASB). © 1960, 1971, 1977, 1995, 2020 by The Lockman Foundation. Used by permission. www.Lockman.org. All rights reserved. Scripture quotations marked nasb1995 are taken from the New American Standard Bible® (NASB). © 1960, 1971, 1977, 1995 by The Lockman Foundation. Used by permission. www.Lockman.org. All rights reserved. Scripture quotations marked nkjv are taken from the New King James Version®. © 1982 by Thomas Nelson. Used by permission. All rights reserved. Scripture quotations marked nlt are taken from the Holy Bible, New Living Translation. © 1996, 2004, 2015 by Tyndale House Foundation. Used by permission of Tyndale House Ministries, Carol Stream, Illinois 60188. All rights reserved.

Any Internet addresses, phone numbers, or company or product information printed in this book are offered as a resource and are not intended in any way to be or to imply an endorsement by Thomas Nelson, nor does Thomas Nelson vouch for the existence, content, or services of these sites, phone numbers, companies, or products beyond the life of this book.

ISBN 978-0-3103-5222-8 (ITPE)

Library of Congress Cataloging-in-Publication Data

Names: Voskamp, Ann, 1973- author.
Title: Waymaker : finding the way to the life you've always dreamed of / Ann Voskamp.
Description: Nashville, Tennessee : W Publishing Group, [2022] | Includes bibliographical references.
Identifiers: LCCN 2021049412 (print) | LCCN 2021049413 (ebook) | ISBN 9780310352198 (hardcover) | ISBN 9780310352204 (ebook)
Subjects: LCSH: Trust in God—Christianity. | Dreams—Religious aspects—Christianity. | Christian life.
Classification: LCC BV4637 .V67 2022 (print) | LCC BV4637 (ebook) | DDC 234/.2—dc23/eng/20211029
LC record available at https://lccn.loc.gov/2021049412
LC ebook record available at https://lccn.loc.gov/2021049413

Printed in the United States of America

22 23 24 25 26 LSC 10 9 8 7 6 5 4 3 2 1

To Shiloh
My heart is tied to your heart,
always and forever,
no matter what,
because, in a thousand ways,
the WayMaker split the seas and made the Way through to
the wonder of you,
to the miracle of Love,
to the dream come true
that is nothing less than the lovingkindness of His arms,
and in Him, no matter the way,
we are all,
always,
soul-safe.
Trust.

CONTENTS

Part One

Part Two

Contents

Part One

chapter one

IN THE BEGINNING

Where am I? Who am I? How did I come to
be here? What is this thing called the world?
How did I come into the world? Why was I not
consulted? And if I am compelled to take part
in it, where is the director? I want to see him.
—SØREN KIERKEGAARD

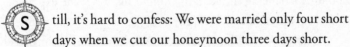

Still, it's hard to confess: We were married only four short
days when we cut our honeymoon three days short.

I close the bathroom door of our lime-green, shag-carpeted
motel room, turn the shower tap to hot, let it thrum loudly,
drown out the heart fracturing. I slide down the wall, crumple a bit on the chipped tile floor, and cry like a baby who

3

wants her mama, tears mingling with steam. He's a deeply kind man. Doesn't he want to grab my hand and gather me close, more than he wants to go home, grab his work boots, and feel the curve of some tractor's steering wheel in his hands? It's not about needing to be living some dream script—I just need the script running in my head to say I'm wanted, that I won't be abandoned, that I'm somehow seen and known and safe.

If you don't know you're really wanted in the beginning, you can end up somewhere you never wanted—somewhere you never dreamed. Neither one of us knew that then. Then, he just knew he wanted to get back to the farm and get back to the rhythm of work. And now, if I'm crying-out-loud honest on a bathroom floor, I wonder if I actually wanted to find a way out too. To find my own exodus, out of me, out of this story I didn't sign up for. Where is the exodus—the way out of the things that hurt beyond words—to a promised, expansive way of life?

Water drums in the empty shower. We may think we know what we want, but what we really want is to be known. Heard. Seen. Safe. My disillusion spills soundlessly all over the floor. How do you hope to find a way out of all that's going wrong in your one and only life? Everyone's just trying to find their own way, to their own dream come true. The dream isn't ever truly about experiencing miraculous things, but about the experience of feeling miraculously known.

After our wedding, after our reception, after we'd driven slowly down the gravel laneway and away from the white tent in the backyard of my parents' farm—me waving to the knots of guests still mingling with their plastic cups of lemonade punch out on the lawn between the barn and the gnarled old apple trees of my childhood summers—I'd turned to him, the man whose name I now shared. I'd smiled long and happy in the dark.

This was the beginning.

In the beginning, in our beginning, there was hope. There was a honeymoon. There was a used Ford Taurus, and there was a gym bag of his t-shirts in the trunk alongside the suitcase I'd bought for my first year of university. Now it was packed with the silk robe and lingerie my mama and I had picked out and folded up carefully for this honeymoon of dreams come true, a time once meant to be a whole month long, as long as it takes for the moon to wane and wax anew.

Sure, we were just two dirt-poor kids who didn't have the luxury of any two pennies to rub together, who couldn't even dream of running away to some rustic mountain hideaway or some posh, sun-drenched resort. Not only because we were scrounging every dime for a down payment on a place of our own, but also because some wise mentor, who sat in the back pew of Sunday chapel with his bride of a half-century, had told us that if a honeymoon was ultimately about seeing some beautiful place, it might distract from the beauty of ultimately seeing the person. So we'd made up our minds—and our frugal pockets sealed the deal. We'd just drive forty-five minutes of gravel country roads up to the lake. The same lake where, as kids, we'd known Sunday afternoon picnics of fried chicken— the same lake we'd known our whole lives. We'd sit at the water's edge and begin our life together there. We'd book some motel that was easy on the wallet, that was still near the water, and maybe if we slid open a janky window and craned our necks, we'd even hear the lake—the promise of waves, coming again and again all night long to kiss old wounds and wash all things clean, and we would begin to become one.

But I had absolutely no idea that every honeymoon—one with a mate, a job, a child, a dream, a hope—murmurs an earnest warning of its own. Every moon wanes. The moment the moon is finally full, it immediately begins to wane. This is the way things are; this is the rhythm of being; these are things you can never change. Like the moon, our dreams, our loves, our hopes wax and wane, ebb and flow, rise and fall. Life comes in waves, and the way to live is to find a way to ride waves.

Under the stillness of stars on the twenty-fifth of June, right there under the rising and falling and waving shape of Cassiopeia, we drive away from our farmyard reception. I'm wearing silky and pearled white, and he's wearing tuxedoed black, and we're both wearing our engraved gold bands and the shy smiles of this tender bonding—and the moon orb over our matrimonial heads and the bowed heads of the wheat fields to the west is already waning gibbous.

We marry. We honeymoon on a waning moon.

THE PLANS OF MICE AND NEWLYWEDS

As he drives toward the waves of the Great Lakes, I pull up just the hem of my wedding dress, the scalloped embroidery grass-stained from our backyard reception. I curl my bare feet up under me, turn a bit on the front seat of that Ford Taurus, and lay my head on his leg. He runs his big Dutch farming hands through my hair slowly, whispers it, the line of a song they used to play on the radio: "I think we're alone now."

He traces the nape of my neck.

"You couldn't be more beautiful. I couldn't be happier."

I guffaw as he curls my hair around his fingers. Would we be the honeymooners who sleep close in islands of lunar light, like the lunatics who believe that dreams can last and never wane?

I can feel his gentle smile in the dark. And I must have closed my eyes only for a moment, but it's enough to drift away into dreams of bringing home babies we never bury, and our parents aging into softly worn, silver-crowned glories who hold hands on front porch rockers while they hold the tiny humans our love has made. And the whole road ahead of us endlessly reroutes in our imaginations, avoiding head-on collisions with suffering, and we find ourselves in our own kind of promised land.

My own mama, she had four children, four and under, and she held her swaddled three-week-old babe in her arms when she stood over an open grave to bury her two-year-old daughter. It's my very first memory, just after my fourth birthday—standing beside Mama as she screamed bloody horror, watching as an oblivious service truck driver struck down our little Aimee, crushing her in our farmyard right outside the kitchen window as we washed dishes at the sink, and then blithely driving on out our lane. How can a delivery driver not feel the wholeness of your child under the tires of his truck when she holds your whole heart?

My mother-in-law, she'd stood over two of her children's graves, burying first her four-year-old son with different abilities, to whom she had been a 24/7 primary caregiver. Then only six years later her firstborn, her seventeen-year-old son, pulled out directly in front of a truck he couldn't see in the blinding blaze of a glorious Friday evening sunset, on his way to a church youth group meeting. He'd been a mere two miles from home. She buried him on a Tuesday afternoon, then came home with her six younger children to get dinner on the table before they all had to go to the barn for the six p.m. milking of the cows.

If she stated it once, my mother-in-law told me literally two hundred times: "Three things." She held up her thick fingers over the bean leaves, her plain gold wedding band wearing a pressed red ring right into her skin. I was a gangly, spectacled kid of seventeen, dating her boy, the youngest of her nine, and she and I were out in her kitchen garden, both hunched over a row of yellow string beans, heaping our wooden baskets full.

"There were only three things I was certain about when I was twenty years old: I never wanted to marry a farmer. I never wanted to leave the Netherlands. I never wanted to have a big family."

She stood up, straightened in a patch of lazing sun. Said it slow, so I wouldn't miss the summary of her life story: "And? I ended up marrying a farmer. I left my home country—my mother, my family—the day after I married. And then I had nine kids—and ended up burying two."

She was still standing.

Still standing in the beans. Still standing, softened and worn into the beauty of real, after nothing turned out the way she had dreamed for the only life she would ever have. What was she trying to tell me? Was this strong Dutch woman in an apron asking for pity? Doubtful. She may have been trying to tell me: Detours are the way dreams and destinies actually come true.

The destiny we all ultimately dream of is a destination where we are ultimately seen, safe, soothed, and secure.[1] Even nightmares of loss and tragedy and grief can still become an unexpected awakening to tender dreams, if there are ways—even in the dark places—to be seen and known, safe and secure. Dreams are brave laughter that lingers long into the night, hands finding ours, warming light finding our faces—and the possibility of being known even here grows our hearts achingly large. Wherever we are always accepted and never alone, never abandoned, our deepest dreams can come true—even in the midst of nightmares. I had high hopes of waking to a dream different from both of our mothers'. No graves. No slammed doors or cold wars, no lightning-bolt diagnosis or stalking depression, no abandonment or estrangement, no cascading job loss or piling bills or empty arms. No trauma from the straight-out-of-nowhere tragedy, the unlikely addictions, the turned distractions, the knife-in-the-back betrayal, the flat-out rejection, or the entirely suffocating personal failure you can't escape because you can't escape out of your own skin. Why do we think that our life will be the one that finds a way to easier roads? Why in the world did I? It's when we expect life to be easy that it becomes hard.

Buy the lie that your life is supposed to be heaven on earth, and suffering can be a torturous hell. But life is suffering, and suffering is but the cross we bear, part of earth's topography to cross on our way to heaven. I wouldn't know it for years: Screens sell pipe dreams. Every screen is trying to sell the lie to you—from Hollywood to Netflix to Instagram—the lie that all you have to do is buy this, work out like this, wear this, style it like this, believe this, pursue this, get a career like this, find someone like this, and you, too, can find the way to a perfect life, just like this. But buy any perfectly filtered and marketing-framed illusion, and you end up painfully disillusioned. Regardless of what Instagram or all the glossy ads are shilling, your suffering isn't some unique anomaly; suffering is the universal experience of all humanity. Suffering doesn't mean you're cursed; suffering means you're human. The question isn't "Why is there suffering in my life?" but "Why *wouldn't* there be suffering?" Because such is life in a broken world. The question is "What way will you bear your suffering?" I didn't know it then, and I am still learning this now: Life is really hard because that is the reality of being alive. Life is hard in a thousand ways, and what comes the easiest to us is getting lost.

DANGEROUS EXPECTATIONS

I stir as he slows the Ford Taurus to make a right turn in the dark. I catch the headlights swinging across trees.

"Where—where are we?"

It's one Edenic question, whispered in the dark. An echo of history's first good question: *Where are you?* And perhaps in response, all of us through history have had our own EPS—an internal Expectational Positioning System—with expectations of where we think we should be by now on the road, of where the road is supposed to go, expectations of how we'd be loved, of how long we'd all have together, of the way everything is expected to work out in the end.

Expectations can slay any relationship, especially with God. And an Expectational Positioning System has never failed to eventually position the soul in a bit of a hell of its own making—with its expectations to at least keep pace with, or better yet surpass, someone else, anyone else. Strange, how you cannot feel content in your heart whenever it feels like someone else is ahead of you. Whenever you measure the seeming distance between where you are and where someone else is, discontent fits into your soul. Measuring sticks are self-harming. Comparison is soul-maiming. And likening your journey to anyone else's is a way to hate your own soul. I still bear tender scars.

"We're almost there." He whispers it in the dark, leaning ahead, looking for a street name. I try to find my shoes. It would take me decades to look back and see where I really was.

Life is never made unbearable by the road itself but by the way we bear the road. It's not the hard roads that slay us; what actually slays us is the expectation that this road isn't what we hoped it to be.

"I think it's right here." He slows to turn into the hotel parking lot. I exhale, reach for his hand, feel that strange gold band right there wound round his virgin ring finger. Us. Together, bound.

HONEYMOON

I don't remember check-in. Or what the clerk at the desk thought of the fresh-faced kid in his tuxedo with the nervous megawatt grin. I do remember him opening the door to our motel room and the shade of the green shag carpet and how I steadied my knees when I stepped in.

We stand at the edge of the bed. His fingertips brush the nape of my neck again as he gathers my hair and fumbles to help me with the zipper of my dress. I am now more vulnerable than waymaker

I have ever known. Newborns begin in vulnerability, and with every breath, we only keep growing into greater vulnerability, or we let parts of ourselves die.

He turns out the lights. Turns to try to find me in the dark under sheets.

Bare inner arch of his naked foot finds the bridge of mine, us finding our ways across the space between us, the shy entangling of a new and tender grace.

"You okay?"

What do I even say? I'm awkward, like a nervous introvert finding herself on a dance floor. I'm kinda desperate to hide. He lifts my chin to find his eyes, as if the rhythm can find and move even the most nervous. Hollywood plotlines be cursed. We aren't living in some movie; we are living our own miraculous stories. He enfolds me close. Dreams come true on their own timelines.

We won't rush this, force this. The only way to make real love anywhere ever is vulnerably, and trust needs time to unfurl into a fig leaf that protects. I tell myself that we have time. I've got absolutely no idea if that's true, but I tell myself that we have a whole tender and waiting lifetime to navigate because you have to tell yourself stories that roar like the Lion of Judah against all the other lying beasts in the dark.

Shafts of moonlight fall across the floor, across our sheets.

All these songs and screens, shaping our expectations of what should happen next, how the waves should come, and we rise, and then fall into the depths of each other, followed by the easy afterglow of pillow talk—all are an evasive mirage. One plus one should equal one. But here we are, still two.

I'm heart-crushed, disappointed in my paralyzing fears. I

don't try to imagine his disappointment. I keep fingering the strange new gold band there on his left hand. His breath is heavy and slow with sleep, right there at the curve of my ear. Light rings the moon hanging far above the draped motel window. Will I always be the dreamer who follows shafts of moonlight, who trusts there's always a way through the dark, even though the moon wanes?

I reach for his hand around my waist, interlace my fingers through his, band touching band. Wherever we choose to connect, we disconnect from more pain.

Late the next morning, in a swaddling of sheets, a sliver of sun pries through a crack in the green tapestry drapes.

"You and I . . . It's—kinda like the garden of Eden, isn't it?" I stir. Turn.

"This?" I laugh, embarrassed—and in a split second all the inexperienced floundering of last night washes over me again, and I can feel shame's heat visibly rising up my neck like a scarlet letter of its own and I try to pull the coverlet higher.

"Hey." He grins, tugs teasingly at the sheet. "Where are you going on me here?"

"What do you mean—where—am I going?" I laugh, nervous, as he leans in closer.

"I mean—I like Eden, don't you?" His leans his forehead against mine.

"Yes," I whisper.

Who doesn't expect their own return to Eden? If each life begins out of what is meant to be an act of intimacy, don't we all expect to find a way to remain—to live—in an enfolding of intimacy? Whatever way we think we want, oneness—the kind that destroys aloneness—is always the dream. Because humanity is ultimately created out of intimacy, humanity's destiny is ultimately intimacy.

We are all created out of intimacy, for intimacy.

Whatever road we expect to be on, the way we want most to find—is a way to be wanted and not left alone.

Who—who doesn't have expectations of consummation? We all fill our heads with dreams of a life of fulfillment. Honestly, my naive Expectational Positioning System had these honeymoon expectations of tracing faces with gentle fingertips, eyelids brushed with lips, vulnerability cupped with tender caresses—the consummate heavenly bliss. And here I am, waking up—in a kind of disorienting wilderness. He has bad breath, I have bedhead, and we both are trying to swallow down a sickening sense of failure. And it's already happening to us, just like it happened to my Dutch mother-in-law who had never wanted to leave the thatched roofs and whirling windmills of Voorthuizen, Holland. Yet there she found herself, the day after her wedding, waking up on a ship headed straight across the ocean to a foreign land, nauseatingly green from the rock of the waves.

Despite the piece of paper you sign on your wedding day, you end up turning around and saying, "I didn't sign up for this."

Moons wane faster than you ever dreamed.

You can book a ticket for the promised land—and wake up in the badlands of some wilderness. Is there a way to make badlands into promised lands?

I turn and try to memorize his eyes. Kind. Still kind. We aren't here to live up to each other's expectations. We are here to live with each other, be for each other. (Who could have known how hard finding a way to do that could be?) He kisses my forehead, like he's reading my mind.

EXODUS

When he tells me on Wednesday evening of our unconsummated honeymoon that he wants to go home, I don't care how many evenings he took me down to the water's edge to a little hole-in-the-wall restaurant, the Lakeside Cafe, for secluded candlelight dinners—prime rib, medium rare, and chicken, cordon bleu. I don't care that I laughed and said I wanted to lick my plate, then he'd laughed, leaned over, and kissed my lips tasting like the warmth of wine. I don't care that we'd run down to the beach at sunset, run right into the ebbing, rose-gilded waves, and he had caught me up in the surround of his arms, and I felt beautiful. All I care about is the fact that my brand-new husband wants to exit our honeymoon three days early and I'm embarrassed—ashamed—and wildly desperate for some kind of exodus of my own.

Get out of this bathroom, get out of this cheap motel room, just any way to get out of here. I turn off the shower. Wash my face, wash away all the vulnerability of tears. I don't want him to know. We don't know each other like Adam knew Eve, and I, as sure as heaven and a month of Sundays, don't want him to know that I feel scorched with rejection. I reach for a towel to quickly dry my face then quietly open the bathroom door. He's packing his bag, folding his beach towel. He looks up, smiles gently, completely oblivious to how exiting a honeymoon paradise early may leave a tender, twisted scar.

"Hey, I'm just gonna grab some air for a minute. Headache." Why mention that my head isn't throbbing nearly as badly as my heart's fracturing?

I reach the door before he can say anything, reach the beach before he can follow, reach the water's edge and the water crashing cold across toes, water from somewhere else in the world, full of stories that found a way to keep going. Somehow.

"Where are we going here? How in the world did we get here already?" I'm choking it back, walking too quickly through a fringe of ragged waves. If he wants a way out of our honeymoon to get back to work, can I try to find my way out too? If we can't even get a taste of the milk and honey in the honeymoon phase, what do the rest of the blasted phases of our moon look like together? The waves keep crashing against my legs.

"Where *are* you?" Where is the One who promised if we did it His way, everything would turn out all right?

"Where are you?" (Genesis 3:9). It's God's first recorded question in all of history, the shortest question of the entire Hebrew Bible, and it hasn't stopped echoing across the topography of time. Only three words: *Where are you?* The most life-changing questions always are the shortest. In Hebrew it's actually only one word: *ayekah*. That one word God is speaking into this moment, even right now: *"Where are you? Where are you? Where are you?"* Where are you going with your life? Where is your soul on the way? Where you are—is this truly where you want to be?

No, I am not where I expected to be, not where I imagined I'd be, none of this is the way I thought it would be. Is that my Expectational Positioning System's alarm wildly going off?

When an all-knowing God asks a question—*"Where are you?"*—isn't He only asking so *you* will begin to know the answer? The God who knows how to choreograph the sun and moon and stars across the skies, who moves these waves, who knows where Adam hid, who knows where the head's at, where the soul aches, where the heart's fractured. God isn't asking for Adam's or anyone's coordinates—He's asking me to seek out and coordinate my own heart with His. The disappointments and disillusions, the dreams and desperate hopes, these are already known to an all-knowing God. He asks you where you are in your life because He wants you to name the place, see the place, acknowledge it, sit with it—even *befriend* it.

Befriend here? All I want to do is scream it across waves: I want a way out of here!

Ayekah means God understands everything going on inside and doesn't want a soul to hide. Not to hide from the feelings, not to hide from the hoping, not to hide from the dreaming, not to hide from the grieving. Like Adam and Eve, the temptation is to flee. To cover who I am and how this feels because I'd rather wander lost than sit with the fear of fully feeling, the fear of being transparent and known, only to experience the flooding shame of rejection and abandonment.

But here's what no one tells you: When you hide who you are, what you ultimately are hiding from is yourself. This is a haunting, exhausting kind of lost. And if evil can keep you distracted from taking the time to ask your soul where you really are, he can take you every day further from the life you envisioned.

When we find the courage to be transparent, we find ourselves found. Only when you ask where you are every day can you find your way. The God who asks where you are, He's large enough to hold you—however, wherever, you are.

Where in the world am I really?

Search me, O God, and know my heart!
Try me and know my thoughts!

> And see if there be any grievous way in me,
> and lead me in the way everlasting!
> (Psalm 139:23–24 ESV)

Do I really want to locate where I am in this story? I know, I know: Refuse reflective questions, and you refuse the self-reflection that has the power to change your very reflection. But all I want to do is ask God where He is in all of this. Do I want to say where I am to I AM? "God speaks to Adam and halts him in his flight. Come out of your hiding place . . . out of your self-torment . . . Confess who you are, do not lose yourself in religious despair, be yourself. Adam, where are you?" beckoned theologian Dietrich Bonhoeffer.[2]

This is the age of Adams—we evade the arms of God. Stay alone and you stay lost.

But when aloneness ends, lostness ends, and we have a God who names Himself the One who is with us.

The setting sun is painting the waves shades of blush, and how can life ache so much?

It's striking that He used the word *ayekah* when He could have used the more common, generic word for "where" in Hebrew, *eifoh*, which simply means to locate.[3] *Eifoh* is the word Saul used when seeking David, when Naomi asked about Ruth's whereabouts, when Joseph was trying to track down his brothers. *Ayekah*, on the other hand, expresses a heart motivation beyond mere location, and *ayekah* conveys expectations: "Where have you gone? Where are you if you are not here with me?"

When Adam and Eve turned away from intimacy with God, God cried *ayekah* because He was asking more than simply, "Where are you?" He was asking, "Where are you in relation to

Me? Where have you gone that's taken you further away from Me? Where are you when the expectation is that you and I would always be together?"

God cries because there is distance between Him and His lover, and God's first known question of history asks you to orient to the topography of intimacy, to locate yourself in the Landscape of Love.

God knows what it's like for there to be trouble in paradise, for paradise to go all wrong, for the perfect way to fall away, for there to be distance. For all the times nothing is turning out the way I've dreamed, and I've howled at God, "Where are you?" He's howled His own very first question of all time with that one word, *ayekah*, that howls:

> *Where are you when it was once all about you and Me—and now it's all about you and that damned lying snake? Woe is Me; where have you gone? I just want you here with Me.*

For the Lord your God is looking for you, means to be "always with you. / He celebrates and sings because of you" (Zephaniah 3:17 CEV).

The triune God isn't disappointed in you, isn't rebuking you, isn't rejecting you, but the triune God delights in you, smiles over you, seeks to be with you, revives you with His kiss of grace and can't stop singing love songs because of you. God knows that it always takes three to make the realest love out of anything, never only two. In the space between two people, only God can make a love that transcends the disappointments. The way that God wants the most is the way that keeps us close to Him. Right from the beginning, God has ached over any space and distance between us. When we were looking for a way out, God's woe over any distance between us drove Him to make a way to us. To be with us.

The cross points to the Way with open arms.* Because our fall was detachment from God, our restoration is found only in attachment to God. If our first sin was to turn from God, detach the fruit from the tree, and savor it, then our return to wholeness is to turn, attach to God, and savor Him. Though our fall broke our attachment to God, He makes a way to us, slips His arms around us, and whispers all will be well now because He is Immanuel, God with us. Our story can only know restoration if our attachment to God is restored. The very symbol of the faith, the intersection of the cross, expresses how God purposes us for connection. God has always been a WayMaker, making more than merely a way *through*. The WayMaker is *making a way to you*.

> Because our fall was detachment from God, our restoration is found only in attachment to God.

What if the only thing that will heal our hearts is to let Him fuse His broken heart with ours?

REROUTING

Far off on the horizon to the west, I can see how a sailboat rides right into the sun and seems to ignite, and maybe after everything

---

* The first followers of Jesus were known as followers of "the Way" (Acts 9:2; 19:9, 23; 22:4; and 24:14, 22).

burns away, this is all that's left: Well-being is a function of controlling your sail well.

You can't control the way the wind blows. You can't control the way the currents run. You can't control the way of waves. There is tender mystery in God's ways. Lovers fail to love. People disappoint. Plans implode. Bodies struggle. Expectations go awry. Pain is all-encompassing and none of us are immune.

You can't control the way of waves—but you can control the way of your sail.

You can turn the sail to fill with the wind of the Spirit, you can move forward in the current of His love, you can reroute through waves.

Turn your sail toward the Spirit, and it turns out you can get out of the boat and walk on waves right back to Him.

Unlike Adam, when Abraham heard God calling for him, Abraham answered: *Hineni.* "Here. I am here" (Genesis 22:1, my paraphrase). *I am here, my WayMaker, whatever Your way.*

How in this ever-hurting world did David keep putting one step in front of the other after being betrayed by his son Absalom? How did Martha find a way forward after Lazarus and all her hopes were bound in grave clothes and laid in the cooling dark? How did Moses find any real way forward after messing up at Meribah? How did Hagar find her way through when death stalked, dreams shattered, and she felt abandoned by all sense of hope? All the universe is echoing with His *ayekah*—and all we have to do is keep whispering the shortest one-word answer: *hineni*, here. Not in the sense of a roll call *here*, but in the sense of *I am all here.* Spoken only eight times in all of Scripture, and every time, a transformative turning point.

I am here, hineni, all here, turn me right around, turn me toward You.

I am here, my WayMaker, whatever Your way.

Hineni, this is my location.

Hineni, I am fully paying attention.

Life is about location, location, location—attention, attention, attention.

God, this locating, this attending, this whispering your honest hineni *can hurt.*

But no matter how brutally hard it is, unless we keep locating our soul—we'll keep losing our way. Be brutally honest and say your *hineni* out loud because there is no other way to be found. And who can afford to lose their way? Any old way will do if you don't care where you're headed. But where are you really, and where is your head, if any old way will do?

Any old way will *not* do with your only life. *This is your only life. You have to brave the waves.* When there seems to be no way, reroute through waves. *It's never about the storm—it's always about your sail.* When there seems to be no way, I can reroute my EPS, my Expectational Positioning System: If I am upset that he hasn't responded the way I'd hoped, I can reroute and look for the ways he's trying to connect. True, he didn't gather me up and hold me long in the morning before getting out of bed. But also true, he did make the bed and get me a steaming cup of tea. When there seems to be no way, I can reroute and gently explain the ways I need to be heard and held, seen and made safe. When there seems to be no way, I could reroute and thank him for the ways of love I've felt. True, dreams didn't happen. Hope hit a roadblock. Plans didn't come through. And also true, reroute, reroute, reroute. There are real ways to simultaneously decrease your pain and increase the number of ways you have to navigate through the pain, and there is a real way through. Actively, bravely trust. Reroute all this thinking about this disappointment—toward a different possibility. Every day, you can make it your way of life to find one way to reroute. You can make it your way of life to see.

What is in the way is actually making another way.

Ayekah?

Hineni.

I am here, my WayMaker, whatever Your way.

Rerouting.

chapter two

THE ART OF THE TURN

We all want progress, but if you're on the
wrong road, progress means doing an about-
turn and walking back to the right road; in that
case, the man who turns back soonest is the
most progressive.

—C. S. LEWIS

Oh, return to me,
for I have paid the price to set you free.
—ISAIAH 44:22 NLT

ttentive to the road stretching straight ahead of us, we
leave all we dreamed behind, and he turns right, off

Bluewater Highway and onto Gore Road, making our winding way toward home, past windmills surrendered to wind, and old bank barns with doors open like a welcome to whatever comes. I don't exactly know why he's chosen the route home that he has. We could have taken the way by the water's edge, staying close to the shore, passing through little dozing villages of white light-houses and rickety boardwalks, all lulled to sleep by the relentless rock of the waves. But maybe it's easier to just leave the lake behind us entirely now that we are abandoning the whole lakeside honeymoon early. Or maybe he just needs to find the old roads, tried and true, and head out cross-country toward home, passing all the patchwork of farms on his hankering way to get back to the farm where he'll keep tending old mama sows and working the willing earth with my dad. And we'll set up our new home there on the farm—right there in the farmhouse basement, under the planked floors of my childhood.

Farmer Husband has his window rolled down, a cassette tape in the Ford Taurus blasting Petra praise music through crackling speakers, and he's humming, wind in his hair, turned to drink in the passing fields of flowering soybeans.

His hand reaches over to find my hand, laces his fingers slowly through mine.

I don't pull my hand away, just turn my head away. No one likes anyone seeing spilled milk or tears. A straggle of white Charolais cattle, chewing their cud in a line, all along a barbed-wire fence by the roadside, blur by in a liquid grief. How do you let yourself feel any love when you're drowning in rejection? You can't waste your days waiting until things are painless to finally be joyful. You have to find a way to believe: Love lives at peace with pain, and the two will never divorce. Because to love is to be tender enough to know suffering, to be vulnerable enough to know hurt, and the only way to divorce your way from any pain is to divorce yourself from any love. The way to love always knows roads of pain—because there is no other way to ever know love. I let his hand hold mine.

Sometimes, just because you don't feel chosen doesn't mean that you aren't chosen. All feelings are not facts, but all emotion is the language of the soul's motion, the language of the pilgrim, the language of the soul's movement toward God. God, though, these feelings feel like I'm dying inside.

How in the world can God be good and actually love me when He isn't writing this story in a way that makes any sense, in a way that feels like He's chosen me? And who can't say that for a thousand different things? Are we truly chosen if our heart feels broken? Wheat fields wave past my window like whole watery oceans through tears that keep falling. I don't look over at him, don't say anything, just close my eyes and try to stop wave after wave of sadness that keeps coming, and I can't stop seeing it replay all over again, me as a sixteen-year-old kid sitting beside him for the first time in a car and how wildly hopeful I felt that storming December night.

His hand was there on the stick shift, close to my knee, and I had felt this heat of possibility, and can still see it, the way he kept grinning from ear to ear, like the kid who swallowed a dream.

SWEET SIXTEEN

He could have asked any girl to go with him to the high school youth Christmas banquet. But he'd come half-sprinting round the first corner of that forgotten back high school hallway, trying to make homeroom before the bell, and he'd about run into me. My heart kinda lurched straight into my throat, shoving all this heat up to my cheeks, when he stopped short and blurted it out. "Hey, I was gonna ask you . . ." He'd grinned, sticking his hands in his Levi's.

"The Christmas youth banquet? On the sixteenth? You wanna go?"

He talked fast, and I stared through my smudged horn-rimmed glasses down at my laced-up black leather orthopedic shoes, feeling too awkward to look him in the eye.

"Sure?"

Wait.

"Uh—" My face ignited in flame, and I was a fireball of shame, but I had to ask because I'd just said yes to something I was sure I hadn't heard right—there wasn't a snowball's chance in Hawaii that I could have heard him right. Clarification is always worth the embarrassment.

How can you believe you're chosen if you would never choose you?

"Uh, sorry, what—what did you just ask?" *Just let the earth below me open up and swallow my bungling gawkiness whole.*

He grinned, his eyes gentle, the blue stillness of a sea at dawn, sure and undisturbed.

"The Christmas banquet." He stepped closer, so I could hear the calm of his reassurance. "I'd like to take you."

"Oh. Take—me?"

"Yes."

Yes, please.

Take me.

waymaker

Pick me.

Choose me. Take me wherever you choose.

When you trust that you're chosen by someone good, you can trust that you're always being taken to good places. The chosen are simply the ones approached by an enamored God who can't stop thinking about you. This is worth returning to. This turns and reorients a life.

"I could pick you up at 6:30 on the sixteenth?" Farm Boy flashed this ten-thousand-watt swoon smile.

And I lit with the epiphany: Where there's chosenness, there isn't aloneness. Feel wanted—and you want for little else. Whatever the dream is, the dream is to feel special. When you feel special, the whole world becomes special to you. Chosenness isn't about being better—it's about making everyone know they belong. Know your chosenness—and you choose to make everyone know they're chosen too.*

When I was eight, my mama walked into a psych ward and they locked the door behind her, and there was a wall between me and the first person who ever held me and loved me. If you're one of God's chosen, how come things you would never choose happen to you?

When my brave and busted dad told us kids that we couldn't tell a soul where Mama was—and that meant Grandma and Grandpa too—there seemed to be no way to live with a secret

---

* "We have not chosen God; He has chosen us. There is no concept of a chosen God but there is the idea of a chosen people . . . We do not say that we are a superior people. The 'chosen people' means a people approached and chosen by God. The significance of this term is genuine in relation to God rather than in relation to other peoples. It signifies not a quality inherent in the people but a relationship between the people and God." Abraham Joshua Heschel, *God in Search of Man: A Philosophy of Judaism* (New York: Farrar, Straus & Giroux, 1955), 425–26.

that strangling. So I just let the secret burn a hole in the wall of my gut and ended up diagnosed with an ulcer in grade three, a kid trying to sear a way right out of her life. If you're one of God's chosen, how come you're not shielded from what no one would ever choose?

I'd like to forget how long it took for me to realize it: When you find yourself on a way you wouldn't choose, and can't change, choosing to believe that you're still chosen for a good way is the only way through.

That sixteen-year-old girl lifts her eyes to linger in that sixteen-year-old boy's. "Yes, the sixteenth. That would be— perfect." His smile feels like buoyant hope, like a lifting out of deeps.

I am chosen. I have chosen?

Being chosen *is* being found.

Ayekah? Where are you, the one I want, the one I choose?

Hineni. I am here.

I am found and chosen—*rerouting.*

PLAN A TO PLAN Z

The actual night of the youth Christmas banquet, he'd driven through a flurry of white, turned off snow-packed Main Street of a town we two farm kids hardly ever drove through, turned onto Barn Swallow Drive, and said it as soft as all the snow coming down, more to himself than to me—"I think it's right up here?"—like he wasn't quite sure of where we were.

"At least . . . I thought it was right down this street. I'm sure that's what my brother said—right at the end of Barn Swallow

Drive?" Farm Boy's leaning up against the steering wheel, peering out through the windshield, out through the heavy snow. Farm Boy shifts the Volkswagen into reverse. I look down at the time. That long anticipated youth Christmas banquet? Commences in exactly four minutes.

And I can only imagine how it's decked out in strands of Christmas lights, and all the kids from the neighboring church youth groups far and wide are swarming the foyer, coiffed city girls in holiday gowns giddy to find their seats in the banqueting hall next to all the guys in their choking ties.

I don't dare to ask him the obvious: "Hey? Are we—really lost here? Did you just flat-out miss a sign somewhere along the road that would have pointed out a better way?"

It's the cosmic question that every WayFarer asks along the way:

> Did you choose to take me but not really know the best
>   way to take?
> If you chose me to go with you, aren't you making sure
>   there's a safe way to go?
> How can someone choose you and then seemingly not even
>   know the tried-and-true way through?

Welcome to life, where Plan A transforms into Plan Z to transform *you*.

I think I've always expected . . . *more*.

I mean, maybe that's always been the story, right from our collective beginning. The whole of the rest of the garden of Eden wasn't enough; we wanted—expected—more. Though we were chosen to bask in the bliss, we weren't satisfied until we could choose our own way, pick our own dreams, take a bite out of our own choosing, and have all of it. But to be dangerously frank, the way God chose for us in the garden can seem misguided at best, and foolishly illogical at worst: Don't eat this fruit. Why in the name of all things holy does He choose to forbid . . . *fruit*? What in the world is immoral about savoring a bit of the proverbial apple? Why obey a commandment not to sink your teeth into the sweet, an edict that seems, from any human perspective, more than a bit random and bordering on frivolous?

But maybe this points the way to a surrendered trust without horizons in Him whose holy ways are higher than ours. We want things to go the way we choose—and God wants us to choose to trust His ways. We expect more—and God expects us to trust Him more. The ways God chooses for His chosen are ways that beg us to choose trust. It's impossible for us to please God unless we trust God with the impossible (Hebrews 11:6). There is no pleasing God without trusting God. Trusting God is no small thing: To God, it is everything. God wants to be chosen too.

I turn to look over at that sixteen-year-old Farm Boy, read his face, the headlights of oncoming traffic lighting his eyes. He feels my eyes tracing his face—and he flashes that grin that melts me every time. I smile slowly in a Volkswagen car lost in the snow going—somewhere, anywhere. We're just together, aren't we?

So what if this is the first date and we're lost? So what if we're missing the banquet and all the slicked-back guys in ties have led their satin-swathed ladies to the candlelit tables and the evening's program has commenced? So what if the expectation of all my imaginary dreams just blew away in a gust of cold December wind?

The banquet wasn't his dream. I was. If we made it to the

banquet, fabulous. If we stayed lost in the car, maybe more fabulous. To be chosen is the ultimate dream, communion the ultimate destination, and you don't have to keep looking for a way, because God is looking for you, to be with you, and your chosenness destroys all aloneness.

It can look like we are lost on the way—but if we are with Someone who loves us, we are never lost.

OFF THE MAP

Years later I would be standing at a kitchen sink, suds up to elbows, and I would be thinking about how being chosen is the dream because even when chosenness doesn't mean you get your way, what you get is the way of witness that destroys aloneness. And Holy Spirit Wind would part the chambers of my heart in that moment with a word I didn't even clearly know.

Hesed.

And I'd dry my hands and go read it very slowly in the thin pages of the Word, the thinnest place to experience glimpses of His bare heart:

> It was not because you were more . . . that the LORD set his [*hashaq*] love on you and chose you, for you were the fewest of all peoples, but it is because the LORD [*hesed*] loves you. (Deuteronomy 7:7–8 ESV)

No matter how hopeless you feel, or how abandoned you've felt, you were chosen because of *hesed*.

You don't have to be the most brilliant, the most beautiful, or the most breathtakingly successful to be chosen because, let's face facts, the grass withers, and what your face looks like and what your hands can accomplish will all fade away. But the *hesed*-love of the Lord chooses you because He can't not choose to be with you. Chosenness isn't about a life of perfectness but a life of withness.

It's true that the lines of His holy love letter to us often translate *hesed* as "lovingkindness," a word literally invented in an attempt to translate the all-encompassing Hebrew word *hesed*,* but "lovingkindness" apparently doesn't fully convey how *hesed* is an entirely different stratosphere of love. Used nearly 250 times in Scripture, in such a powerful manner that some theologians have suggested it may be the most important word in Scripture,[1] *hesed* is the forever covenantal, always unconditionally, unwaveringly loyal, kind love of inseparable bonding, of divine family, of eternal attachment. That's what *hesed*-love is: "*Hesed* is attachment love."[2]

Hesed is an entirely singular kind of love that says: You are chosen because God simply and forever chooses to perfectly *hesed*-attach Himself *to you*. You are not merely endured, you are not hardly tolerated, you are not barely accepted—but *you*—your very being, your actual presence, your whole soul, all of the miracle that is you is wanted—picked, chosen, delighted in, special—simply because your lungs expand to take in His love and exhale with love, the kiss of existence. God wants to

---

* "Loving-Kindness . . . is a biblical word, invented by Miles Coverdale . . . and is one of the words he used in the Psalms (23 times, plus Hosea 2:19) to translate the Hebrew *chesed* when it refers to God's love for his people." Norman H. Snaith, A Theological Word Book of the Bible, ed. Alan Richardson (New York: MacMillan, 1951), 136–7, reproduced in Michael D. Marlowe, "The Meaning of 'Chesed' in the Hebrew Bible," Bible Research, accessed November 14, 2021, http://www.bible-researcher.com/chesed.html.

inhale you, move with you, curl like kindness around your every thought. Believing this is to be really living.

God chooses to love you simply because He chooses you to love, God wants to be with you because He wants to be with you, He *hesed*-loves you because He *hesed*-loves you, and this is the perfect circular logic of Love. You are captivating to the point that God bound Himself to you, making His heart captive to yours to liberate you from every lie that you are forsaken.

Hesed is when the fissures of your broken heart become fused with the Heart beating at the center of everything; *hesed* is when "the person from whom I have a right to expect nothing gives me everything."[3] Shards of dawn splitting November dark, warm May rains on eyelashes, fireflies blinking like gathering stars all through the woods, your very name written into the veined hands of God, the literal keys to the kingdom, this is everything, this is all for you. Expect nothing, but expect the everything that is *hesed*.

It's growing expectations that grow suffering. The moment you let go of your expectations, much suffering lets go of you.

Expect nothing but expect *hesed*. Expect God to knock at your door, expect God to rise on your horizon, expect hope and mercy and miracles and a glass of cold water, but just don't expect God to come looking any way you expect. Expect nothing but *hesed*, the lovingkindness of God—just not in the kinds of ways you'd ever dreamed. Pain will come, but name it a mystery, and find manna in it,

> Expect God to knock at your door, expect God to rise on your horizon, expect hope and mercy and miracles and a glass of cold water, but just don't expect God to come looking any way you expect.

and taste bits of miracle even in what you can hardly stand and don't understand.

"You okay?" Farm Boy had turned around that snow-globe December night, laughed a bit nervously, making another U-turn at the end of the street. "I know we're now kinda late—or actually really late."

But maybe, if we've already connected, we've already arrived. Whatever all the pixelated streams and screens laud as having finally arrived, as being the hit we hunger for, the destination we dream of, the verifiable truth is: Relationship is the only reward that is real, that lasts. Everything else is the journey, everything else is a fleeting mirage. Only relationship is the destination. And he's being kind, and I am being kind, and doesn't looking for moments of lovingkindness make a way out of all kinds of pain? A *hesed* moment, a persistent, unconditional, completely undeserved, dependable lovingkindness—that is what's falling all around us in the dark, like a luminous dusting of heaven.

Maybe: It doesn't matter how your road turns, but it matters who you turn and attach to. This is all I know: Presence heals pain. Withness binds up wounds. Bonding eases trauma.

"Kinda embarrassing—" Farm Boy winks, downshifts the Volkswagen to turn at the end of Barn Swallow Drive, cranes his head for any sign of the church. "I mean, maybe it only looks like we're lost?" How is he speaking in ways that make my heart all ear, to hear things inside of me I've never known?

"Yeah, I'm really okay." I nod, smile. And I am. Whatever can be said, there is *hesed*. There is the always *hesed*-love of withness, the always *hesed*-love that takes up the road with us, the always *hesed*-love that keeps pace with us, mile after hard mile, the always *hesed*-love that goes with us as long as the road goes on. Life isn't about arriving—it's about *hesed*-attachment. Our deepest dreams aren't about mere love, but deeply attached *hesed*-love; not about mere kindness, but the always kindness of *hesed*; not about an easy way, but the covenanted way of *hesed*-love through every hard thing. There are people you'd rather be lost with, than arriving anywhere without.

WHAT LIFE TURNS ON

I didn't realize then how it all was an omen, right then from that very first night: When he turned around at the end of Barn Swallow and swung us around in the snow, that was the harbinger of all there was to come.

There would be a December night thirty long years in the future—whole decades after our first date, after our honeymoon—that this same Farm Boy would ask me out and drive me down the exact same road that those two sixteen-year-old kids had turned around and around on, lost on a snowy night. And I'd turn and look over at the man I'd had that first date with some thirty years prior, and I'd see a glimpse of the Farm Boy who was, of the man who cut a honeymoon short, and see what I had never seen: Life is the art of the turn.

The turn to find each other, though you've lost each other a thousand times. Because every turn says I choose you all over again. I choose you over whatever is in front of me, choose you over distractions. I choose you over me.

I'd reach over to touch his hand thirty years later to the night, lay my hand on his leg and realize: Every day you lose the person you once were and who everyone around you was because this is what it means to grow. You are becoming, and your person is becoming, and somehow you have to keep turning and choosing to come closer to each other.

This, this would turn out to be everything.

The whole of life turns on the turn: The redirect, the reorient, the meeting, the seeing, the repentance, the rerouting. Turn and expect nothing but *hesed*. Turn and see the *hesed*-lovingkindness of God in the light on the leaves, in the holy joy of a smile, in the shimmer of pure glory in eyes looking into yours, and in someone reaching out, then trace up the arm of God that's encircling you right now. Turn and look for how *hesed* happens now. Turn and find the delight of God, whom we have no right to expect anything from, giving you everything you need for this moment, for nothing in return.

Turn and see that turns come tender and small in relationships and can't afford to be missed: It's me turning to tell him I'm terrified of the trajectory of one of our teens, and him turning to really listen to what I'm saying between the words, and me realizing that holding on to fears is to delay the comfort of God, and this listening tour can release us all to new understanding. It's him turning to brave, baring a bit of his heart about what the bank manager said about our year end, and me turning to hear the real courage he makes look commonplace. It's turning, time and again, to make each other feel—*cherished*. Chosen. We *get* to do this.

On that night of our first date, when he gets to the end of Barn Swallow Drive for the third time, still searching for the church, he notices a side street tucked in right at the very end—and he turns—and there it is! The church! The church and all its windows aglow casting long gold islands of light across the night, across a falling blanket of snow. All we had to do was turn. All we ever have to do is turn. Turn to the light, turn and look in a different direction, one that isn't looking to the left or the right but looking toward where the Love still is and always will be.

When he holds open the door of the church for me to step in from the snow-swirl night and into the quiet light of the foyer, it doesn't matter one iota that the party is already started in the banqueting hall and we're the last ones to arrive. He's laughing in the empty foyer, brushing snowflakes out of his sandy blond hair, watching me lift a few large lacy ones caught in my eyelashes, and we catch each other's eyes and every expectation melts away into this: The only way needed is to where we're seen and known, safe and not alone. *Wherever you are can be an arriving.* Hesed *always has you.*

Who knows if anyone even noticed or said anything about us slipping in on our own timeline, but no one is ever behind if they know they are beloved. I do remember us sitting in this dancing candlelight, feasting on grace and God, and how Farm Boy had a second helping of turkey and dressing, and I only wished for a second serving of the cheesecake drenched in sweet cherries. We sing "O Come, All Ye Faithful" at the top of our lungs and I laugh, embarrassed, when I trip up the chorus. His shoulder touches mine and I'm stilled and we both linger. He catches me twice memorizing the way his smile starts in the corners of his lips—and something in me flips in a flutter of butterflies on a cold December night.

It's just before eleven p.m. when we pull into our farm driveway heavy with snowfall. He lets the Volkswagen idle. His cologne a hint of cedarwood and earthy musk, and I inhale him like an arriving home.

"Thanks." I smile, scared and smitten—scared of saying the wrong thing, scared of what comes next in a dark car, or scared of what doesn't, scared that tonight will evaporate into a memory, a mirage of a dream that could have been. I wring my hands with all kinds of hopes and fears.

"It . . . was really . . . everything . . ." And in its own strange and unexpected way, it really was. My heart is pounding, deafening loud in my ears. I'm reaching for the door handle, my voice betraying me with the slightest quake.

"In spite of a rocky start and a few speed bumps . . ." He smiles, his eyes lit by the soft light of the dashboard.

"Just—yeah, thanks again—for . . ." I want to say "thanks for choosing me, for taking me with you," but all I say is, "Just—thanks for everything." Is that what we will always end up saying in the end? And I'm standing out in the cold snow, calling back into the car, closing the door gently behind me, escaping the risk and the awkwardness of getting the next couple of moments wrong, but who knows if even this—if this isn't the right turn? I run up the walk, through the snow, up the stairs, open the door, turn into the pitch-black living room, and watch his red taillights drive down the road through the falling white. Will he ever choose me again? Would I, him? Would we live it out, a bit like Bob Dylan crooned, would our future be a mirage in our past, would our first love end up actually being our last—or not?[4] Would we discover that there is a First Love to return to that would show us the whole way through to the end?

Can anyone else hear my heart slamming against my chest like a drum begging its own kind of please?

ALWAYS WE BEGIN AGAIN

It's sometime after four p.m. on a humid June afternoon midweek when our official honeymoon is over, and we drive up the same farm laneway that he'd first driven before and after the first lost-in-the-snow date four and a half years ago.

He parks the Taurus by the entrance to the basement apartment waiting for us in the house where I grew up and where his boss, my dad, lives with my mama and little sister and a few stray cats that linger round at the back door waiting for a way in.

He untwines his fingers slowly from mine in the heavy stillness.

I turn slowly from the window and all these passing scenes from that first night of chosenness, but I don't turn to find his eyes. Somehow you have to put one foot in front of the other and keep choosing each other. I don't know how to do this, or I don't want to do this, or I keep forgetting how to do this.

"You—ready to begin?" I can feel his eagerness, his smile falling gently on me—and I want to turn and scream: "What in the world do you mean *begin*? You just went ahead and ended our honeymoon early. It feels like the end before we even begin!"

But all I say is—

"Yeah—yeah, sure, we can begin." I try to sound like I mean it. Somehow there's always got to be grace to begin again. And I open the car door and will one step in front of the other and trust God's will always has a way. I head down to the basement apartment and the rest of our lives.

I'm kneeling in a stack of wedding presents when he tells me that he thinks he'd better check on the mama sows out in the barn, see if my dad needs any farmwork finished up today. And I nod bravely, this brand-new, fledgling wife who can't yet see how her fine man's just trying to provide in good and faithful ways—who sees now, at the root, our greatest fear is always that we will be left abandoned and unloved. Maybe we could always live unafraid if we knew we'd never be unchosen.

When he closes the door, I can hear him bound up the stairs and out to the barn—and I curl my knees up under my chin, wrap my arms around shins, and hold myself while the dam of everything tender and uncertain breaks.

You don't have to be afraid to let your heart break like a wave. You can curl forward, you can fracture into a thousand shimmering bits, you can shatter and scatter and fear nothing because you can break into light, catch all the light, you can return to whence you came from, you can fall into Him and not be afraid in all this ocean of grace. Your every heartbreak can be a wave breaking into light. This is a truth that gently embraces a whole world of heartache too: Make an idol out of any relationship and you become a dysfunctional relationship of pain. Whatever rock and tender place the bruised soul finds itself between, it's written there right into the face of the rock we're facing. There is no such thing as salvation by romance, or by achievement, or by dream life, or by any good behavior, or by self or anyone else.

In the midst of all these witnessing wedding presents, it comes, out of nowhere, this old lullaby to gather me up and mother me close, and I gently rock on the basement floor: "Hush, little baby, don't say a word. Mama's gonna buy you a mockingbird."

As if there is something that someone can give us to take away all the pain along the way. As if we are chosen, we will get a pain-free way of our choosing.

"And if that diamond ring turns brass, Mama's gonna buy you a looking glass."

Someone's gonna, someone shoulda, someone better . . . come and make this all right.

And Someone does, but not in any way I may expect or ever understand, and the mystery of our stories can taste both like pain and grace. The soul still knows from whence its help comes, the heart beats to the drum of the psalmist, and the soul rocks on the waves of the ancient lullabies: "Make your face shine on your servant; / save me in your steadfast [*hesed*-attachment] love" (Psalm 31:16 ESV).

Even when I don't feel it, I am Father-held, His everlasting arms around all my needs, and Someone's not gonna save me by being a genie in a bottle who's gonna make all my dreams come true, not gonna save me by wish fulfillment or carrying me off into some sunset—Someone's gonna save me by tenderly attaching His heart to mine like a fusing. *Salvation by* hesed.* "But I have trusted in your steadfast [*hesed*-love]; / my heart shall rejoice in your salvation" (Psalm 13:5 ESV). Can this save a life? Not in some infomercial way, but in a real marrow-of-your-bones, lining-of-your-lungs, I-can-actually-breathe way?

If God chooses to attach Himself to your soul, what can anyone say, or do, to shame you, to detach you from Love Himself? If God has covenanted lovingkindness to you, what crisis or catastrophe can ever break that kind of chosenness?

---

* Dr. James Wilder writes of Dallas Willard, "Dallas passed on, but not before urging the ongoing discussion of salvation as *hesed*. His understanding was that salvation should produce disciples who spontaneously exhibit the character of Jesus [but] too often [don't]. Dallas saw in attachment love a possible remedy." James Wilder, *Renovated: God, Dallas Willard, and the Church That Transforms* (Colorado Springs: NavPress, 2020), 8.

"Though the mountains be shaken
and the hills be removed,
yet my unfailing [*hesed*-love] for you will not be
shaken
nor my covenant of peace be removed,"
says the LORD, who has compassion on you.
(Isaiah 54:10)

This is actual comfort that traces your bruises and wounds with the slowest, tender assurance that you are going to be more than all right. You can feel this presence like a certain nurturing that girds your every breath, every step, every heartbeat. The assurance that you seek, the chosenness that you want, the grace that you crave, the hope that you need—it's there in His eyes tenderly and forever holding yours. *Hesed* is who God is. "The LORD, the LORD, the compassionate and gracious God, slow to anger, abounding in [*hesed*] and faithfulness, maintaining [*hesed*] to thousands" (Exodus 34:6–7). The Lord, abounding in *hesed*-attachment love, who is more than holy, more than awesome, more than good, the Lord who is unwaveringly kind chooses to bind Himself to me, one nail at a time on the cross, and I am saved and safe in real time.

Because all trauma is about detachment—detachment and loss of connection from our people, our bodies, our souls, our Maker*—what saves and heals us is *attachment*—attachment to our people, our bodies, our souls, our *God*.

---

* Dr. Peter Levine writes that "trauma is about a loss of connection—to ourselves, to our bodies, to our families, to others, and the world around us." Peter A. Levine, *Healing Trauma: A Pioneering Program for Restoring the Wisdom of Your Body* (Boulder, CO: Sounds True, 2008), 9.

"Help me, LORD my God; / save me according to your [*hesed*-attachment] unfailing love" (Psalm 109:26).

> What saves and heals us is *attachment*—attachment to our people, our bodies, our souls, our *God*.

Hush, hurting soul, don't fear your tears. You can hug your knees and feel yourself contained and safe within the arms of God and trust: Chosenness doesn't mean you get wish fulfillment, but that you get *hesed*-attachment. Because wish fulfillment doesn't ultimately fulfill like *hesed*-attachment fills us with communion that begins to heal trauma. Because your papa's never gonna stop singing it over you in ways that resonate like an enfolding in all the empty places:

> "Behold, [you're the one] whom I uphold;
> My chosen one in whom My soul delights."
>> (Isaiah 42:1 NASB)

> "[You're] the one I chose,
> and I couldn't be more pleased with [you]."
>> (Isaiah 42:1 MSG)

You are chosen not because of any of your choices but because the very God chooses you. And no choice you or anyone else makes has the power to make you unchosen. No matter how rejected you feel, you are chosen for *hesed*-attachment because no matter how it may seem, what you want most deeply is to be deeply wanted as a person, valued and needed, seen and safe and known. This is the way of *hesed*; this is the way our Father heals our trauma. He will make a way through to what we need the most. "Turn, LORD, and deliver me; / save me because of your unfailing [*hesed*-attachment] love" (Psalm 6:4).

That brave newlywed holding her knees on the floor doesn't know that one day she'll sit over a toilet and weep over the blood of a miscarried baby she'd never hold, and she'll find herself still held. One day, decades from that moment, that newlywed will read a text from someone she loves that sucker-punches her nauseous, and her whole world will shatter like a rain of glass. She'll find herself in a story she never wanted and doesn't know how to live through. She can feel numb and nothing and that doesn't mean that she isn't still being held close enough that His heart attached to hers is what is keeping hers beating.

One day, after too many dark days and nights of the soul, she'll fight the temptation to follow through on a plan to end it all. And still underneath will be the actual everlasting arms of God, whose *hesed*-attachment goes on without end, making a way right through to forever: For His *hesed*-lovingkindness "is great toward us" (Psalm 117:2 NKJV). His "lovingkindness is better than life" (Psalm 63:3 NKJV). His *hesed*-lovingkindness is better than every kind of dream, or hope—or even life itself.

But this day is not those days, not yet. On this day that tender newlywed is gathered and soothed by His presence that she experiences as the mothering comfort of a lullaby.* And when she is gathered and pulled together enough, she doesn't dare brush

---

* Isaiah 66:13: "As a mother comforts her child, / so I will comfort you"; and also Psalm 131:2: "But I have calmed and quieted myself, / I am like a weaned child with its mother; / like a weaned child I am content."

away the tears, but touches them slowly with her fingertips, like you can absorb your grief and it can become you, like it can make you more becoming.

Lament can be tears that water new life, if you let it come.

God knows that we don't need a way to something as much as we need a way to be healed—and healing comes through the closeness of *hesed*-attachment because He knows how close we need Him to actually experience His healing touch.

> I will be glad and rejoice in your [*hesed*-
> attachment] love,
> for you saw my affliction
> and knew the anguish of my soul.
> (Psalm 31:7)

I lay my head down on the corner of an unwrapped wedding present, damp cheek sticking to the sheen of the paper.

There's no way I could have expected him to take that route home from a honeymoon cut short, there's no way I could have expected getting lost en route on our first date, there's no way, no way, no way.

And the voice of the Spirit, *hesed*-joined to the very chambers of the heart, beats sure: *Hineni*. Here I am. Here I am. All the universe echoing: *I AM. I AM. I AM.*

I am here for you. You are chosen. Choose Me. "Every person the Father gives me eventually comes running to me. And once that person is with me, I hold on and don't let go" (John 6:37–38 MSG). There's a romance for the ages, just waiting for a turn.

My fingers find the edge of a piece of tape on the corner of the box, and I turn back the paper, unwrapping the next present slow, with no expectation of what comes next. *Expect nothing but* hesed—*because this turns out to be everything.* Behind every kind act of God is the *hesed*-lovingkindness of God. "Thank the miracle-working God, / His [*hesed*-attachment] love never quits" (Psalm 136:4 MSG).

When I hear the Farmer come back in from the barn, I'm still unwrapping presents, unwrapping hope. "Hope is a good thing, maybe the best of things."[5]

I turn—and find his eyes.

He's grinning, and I love him. I really love him.

"Well, what'd we get?"

I reach out my hand for his, wanting him close.

"I have no idea. But I am sure it's all . . . —truly good and kind."

chapter three

COME LET ME LOVE YOU

Make him the source, centre, and circumference
of all thy soul's range of delight.
—CHARLES SPURGEON

ross that hearth of ours, he carried me like a timeworn choreography. But I hadn't known that this cleaving of souls could feel more like an axe severing you off from hope.

Unless you slow, and take the time, to learn the steps of a great ancient dance.

My dad had walked me to the altar on the eve of his and Mama's twenty-third wedding anniversary. Then he'd turned, kissed me gently goodbye in front of Farm Boy, and slipped into the pew beside my mama.

I think on some level, when Farm Boy and I chose to get married on the twenty-fifth of June, I somehow thought getting married the day before my parents' wedding anniversary would be a signpost, that our marriage could mirror theirs. I had no way of imagining how very nearly our story could have been theirs in aching ways I'd never dreamt.

I'd hoped, like them, we'd find a way to weather all the financial flattenings of trying to eke out a living as farmers, we'd find a way to avoid any widening, diverging of roads through the lengthening years, find a way to survive together even if there were mocking coffins, a walking away from the churned dirt of a grave.

Who among us isn't a thread of hope desperately looking for a way through the eye of a needle, looking for a sliver of lightning possibility along a wall of impossible, a trace of a trail that is the less-traveled way through?

But what our preacher man said during our marriage ceremony should have been my premonition—for all of us.

Pastor Dixon, with his shock of white hair reminiscent of Albert Einstein, looked over his glasses at me during our ceremony and said what we didn't expect to frame our vows: "Ann. Ann-girl. I don't know if you know that John Denver song. 'Annie's Song'?"

How could he have known that listening to John Denver crooning "Annie's Song" on a skipping vinyl record was my dad's favorite way to spend a howling winter's evening?

I glanced past my veil to Dad brushing away tears, my mama, tendrils falling from her upswept chignon, squeezing his other hand.

"Did you know that John Denver had written those lyrics

for his wife, Annie, a song about how the senses of a man can fill with the love of a woman, like a waving ocean can keep coming to caress the shore, filling him, touching him, moving him, again and again?"[1]

Did Pastor Dixon know that Mama would sit down at the piano on dusky Sunday evenings and play the haunting notes of "Annie's Song" across keys in desperate need of a tuning, but none of us even noticed for the glory of it, Mama's long fingers reaching for the next note, reaching for more. I could see Dad lying tired on the living room couch on a Sunday night, asking her to play it all over again, and again, like a haunting longing for something he ached for but couldn't ever quite find. His every heartbeat like a begging knock on the door of God, but he just doesn't know it. Like an "inconsolable" longing, the kind that C. S. Lewis wrote of, for all his senses to be filled like a waving deep ocean, like Lewis described as a "desire for our own far-off country . . . for something that has never actually appeared in our experience"[2]—"that unnameable something, desire for which pierces us like a rapier at the smell of a bonfire, the sound of wild ducks flying overhead . . . the morning cobwebs in late summer, or the noise of falling waves."[3]

Maybe all that good ole boy John Denver ached for, what he sensed in the rain and the stars and the sky and the waves, wasn't ever anything that his Annie could fulfill. His yearning was actually more *Sehnsucht*, that German term describing a yearning for the inexpressible that Lewis spoke of—this sense of the lost that longs to be found. "If I find in myself a desire which no experience in this world can satisfy, the most probable explanation is that I was made for another world,"[4] wrote Lewis.

From the beginning, this world's stars and soil, heavens and earth, have been locked in love, giving us glimpses of that other world. *Heaven* is a masculine noun in Hebrew, and *earth*, a feminine noun, and from the beginning, the sacred story opens with a cosmic couple. Waving seas and dry shore sand, roving animals and forest stands, this whole spinning universe is a created complementary world designed to dovetail into the wholeness of one. The universe is a metaphor for union. For the metaphor that is already and almost. If we find ourselves with a passion to be loved that can't be fully satisfied by anything in this world, the most probable explanation is that we are made for another otherworldly love.

That Farm Boy I'm looking at all starry-eyed, who I am about to kiss with my forever, can he find a way to fill me up with everything, with all the passion and love I am like cupped hands for? Can he read in my eyes that not seventy-two hours before, I had dialed Grandma on the rotary phone in the upstairs hallway, in the middle of the night, because I am a question—and who else to speak the words out loud to: "What if—what if I'm making a—mistake?" I try to get it all out before Grandma says anything. "What if he—isn't the right one? What if—I've gotten this all wrong?" What if we are a map turned the wrong way, and how do you find out before it's too late?

"Oh dear." Grandma quietly sighed on the other end of the line. "Oh, Ann. Listen, dear."

I slumped down to the dark hallway floor outside my half-open bedroom door, all craning cochlea to phone receiver, not wanting to miss whatever calm Grandma would wrap around this quake of an almost-bride.

THE RIGHT WAY

Do I tell her there was once another guy? I'd been dating Farm Boy almost four years when Third-Year Latin Guy, who lived in the same bilingual dorm, started walking me back across the shadowed campus after evening class. I thought he was the consummate gentleman, headed the same way, looking out for the shy farm girl at a big-city university. And then, the day before spring break, in front of said farm girl's dorm-room door, I found the longest-stem rose I'd ever seen—with a carefully creased and wax-sealed, four-page handwritten letter that ended with the poem of his heart: "If you knew the way I saw you, you'd know your dreams were coming true, and you'd make a way for there to be us."

Would I pray: Was there any way?

My hands trembled folding the pages back up smooth, like I could somehow smooth out this nauseating wrinkle. Is there a way to go back to being friends after you've witnessed the way a soul unfolds into more?

Sure, Third-Year Latin Guy may have loved all the same things—literature and language, poetry and history, but was he the way to go? I ended up going for a wandering walk along lamplit campus paths, spilling all the questions and doubts and dreams to the Maker of stars. What if one way seems like a fairytale dream come true—and another way is fair and true? There is a way that *looks* right—and another way that *is* right. There was once a tree at the center of a garden that looked like a beautiful yes, but when we see the way God placed a protective no at the very center, we can see our way right through. There is a way that can seem right to the senses that leads nowhere good for the soul.

I dropped the rose into a garbage can. And went home to Farm Boy for spring break.

You only have to see one star in your night sky to see your way home.

Had I made the right choice, Grandma? Was I going the right way right now?

"Listen. Never let cold feet make you either coldhearted or hotheaded." Grandma's gently gathering-me-up with words lilted like a cradling. This is why I called Grandma; this is how wise women soothe.

Live in the space between stars and you grow cold. Move toward the light, toward the Morning Star, and whatever's cold will always ignite all over again. Because at the center of the universe is the spinning dance of the communion of Father, Son, and Spirit in this selfless, giving, sacrificial orbit of Oneness. Before even the first shimmer of flaming star danced across space, an all-fulfilled, all-relational triune God, fully complete in the spin of the selfless, giving dance of communion, chose to create a world for the singular purpose of us sharing in His communion, orbiting in His selfless, giving love.

What matters is not that anybody makes you spin on the inside, but that the spinning, selfless, giving dance of the Trinity is what drives your commitment to an encircling love that has no end.

All I can tell you is what I know now: Love is more than an emotion; love is commitment set in motion.

I never got a chance to tell Grandma: God is love, but if we get it turned around, and make being loved into our god, we get lost in self. Death of self is always the pulse that keeps love alive.

From the beginning, one man and one woman leave their worlds and cleave to one another in a constellation of oneness, and a marriage becomes a metaphor of more.

> All I can tell you is what I know now: Love is more than an emotion; love is commitment set in motion.

Standing there at the altar, in front of Farm Boy with a ring in his pocket, I could glimpse Grandma out of the corner of my eye, sitting there in her sage-green dress on the other side of Dad, gently patting the arm of his gray suit, comforting her son, nodding at me, like she's nudging me to go on, go on.

"And then John Denver would sing to his Annie," Pastor Dixon's voice thundered through the sanctuary.

I looked up into Farm Boy's eyes, and I knew "Annie's Song" by heart, and it was all my heart: How do I get to love you, how do I get to come to you and give you my life?

How much did my heart realize in that moment that to give your life to someone—Someone—is the work of a lifetime? There is no easy way to give your life to someone. Every wedding aisle is a narrow way. Love is always the narrow way that limits one's options but expands and fulfills one's soul.

And to give your life to someone every day for the rest of your life means giving intentionally every day. Every forever is made up of the everydays.

Farm Boy held my hands in his hardworking ones, looking down at me, his thumbs gently stroking the backs of my hands.

"Romance won't keep a marriage together." Pastor Dixon's

bass voice with this rolling English accent reverberated through the sanctuary.

My heart pounded, like the church bells tolling *Come, this is the moment, come.*

"You are both going to sorely disappoint each other." *Wait. Why is he taking our marriage ceremony this way?*—"Because you both are marrying a sinner."

Pastor Dixon turned to me and punctuated every word with his finger.

"Ann, you think you are marrying Prince Charming." *Yes, yes, now we are back on track here.* I gazed up into Farm Boy's eyes and that swooning, mile-wide smile of his. But Pastor Dixon was not finished. "But the truth is, Ann, you are really marrying the decidedly undreamy frog."

I failed to smother a guffaw and the sanctuary erupted with howling guests, and Farm Boy's little nephew, sitting on his mama's lap back in the third pew, started ribbiting on cue like a frog, and Farm Boy threw his head back in blushing laughter and I was tipsy drunk happy with the surprise of the moment.

Pastor Dixon was far from done.

"And you," he said and pointed to Farm Boy, "you think you are marrying Cinderella, but—you are really marrying the ugly stepsister."

The sanctuary rioted with laughter; all I could feel was the blushed heat of my cheeks and the swirling delight of the chapel, and I willed myself not to glance over my shoulder to the only bridesmaid standing beside me: my beautiful sister.

"But what you are doing here today is making a promise, a vow, a covenant." The sanctuary pulled itself together, steadied and settled as Pastor Dixon pressed on into the center. "What you are doing is promising to love each other regardless of the ways things go, you are promising—" He held up a worn old book.

"'Submit to one another out of reverence for Christ.' Pastor Dixon's voice dropped soft and tender, like a beckoning: "'For this reason a man will leave his father and mother and be united to his wife, and the two will become one flesh. This is a profound mystery—but I am talking about Christ and the church.'"* Step into the mystery of marriage and the earth falls away to the strangeness of holy ground and a new, reorienting world.

A DEEP MYSTERY

I may only have been a nervous twenty-year-old bride standing at the altar that day, but it is true of every marriage: Marriage is a metaphor for the profound mystery for the very meaning of being.

Years later I would read from another pastor:

That's the goal of creation. Everything was designed that the Son might [have] a bride—beautified in splendor . . . Christ came to create a beautiful bride out of a hard-hearted rebel people—you and me.

This blood-bought, beautified bride will be God's delight forever . . . [the one over whom he can't stop singing:] "She's going to be my joy forever. It's what I've been about all these thousands of years."[5]

---

* Ephesians 5:21, 31–32.

Just behind me, two candles flickered like a testimony, one lit by my mama, one lit by Farm Boy's mama—and one candle still waiting in the center to be lit by the two becoming one. We were becoming an otherworldly metaphor, and this mattered. It matters still. I memorized the face of the young man in front of me. My cheeks ached with the joy.

"The strong affection which a husband ought to cherish towards his wife is exemplified by Christ, and an instance of that unity which belongs to marriage is declared to exist between himself and the Church," attested the theologian John Calvin of the same text Pastor Dixon read before us at the wedding altar. "This is a remarkable passage on the mysterious intercourse which we have with Christ."[6]

A profound mystery. I, a blushing bride, holding a bouquet of white roses at the front of a farm-town chapel wedding altar. He, a flushed farm boy, squaring his shoulders. And all of us that day held in a cosmic mystery that began at the foot of the cross.

"Has He not said to thee," asked England's best-known minister, Charles Spurgeon, "'I will betroth thee unto Me in righteousness, and in judgment, and in lovingkindness'? Have not His own lips said it, 'I am married unto thee, and My delight is in thee'?"[7]

"There is a closer union in this holy marriage [with the Lord] than there can be in any other," assured the Puritan preacher Thomas Watson:

> In other marriages, two make *one flesh*, but Christ and the believer make *one spirit*: "But he who is joined to the Lord is *one spirit* with Him" (1 Cor. 6:17) . . . This spiritual union brings in more astonishing delights and ravishments than

57

any other marriage relationship is capable of. The joy that flows from the mystical union is unspeakable and full of glory (1 Peter 1:8).[8]

When I am a middle-aged woman sitting in a therapist's office one day, I will look at the timeline of my life written on a whiteboard across his wall, and when he asks what was the happiest day of my life, I will point to this one. My wedding day. To the astonishment of this moment. To imagine an even happier day? Unspeakable. *Glory, glory, glory.*

"Indeed, the union by which [God] binds us to himself when he receives us into the bosom of the church is like sacred wedlock," wrote Calvin.[9] And elsewhere: "Therefore that joining together . . . that indwelling of Christ in our hearts—in short that mystical union—are accorded by us the highest degree of importance."[10]

I GIVE YOU ME

"You are here today, to pledge your troth to one another"—Pastor Dixon paused, continued—"to pledge your utter fidelity, to say you can rely on me in the toughest times." He smoothed out his handlebar mustache for effect.

"You both are here today to make a solemn vow to be committed to each other not when it's easy—but when it'd be easiest to walk away."

In a humble chapel, the pews full of Dutch farmers with worn hands, sitting beside wives wrangling toddlers in laps, Pastor Dixon with the Albert Einstein hair and handlebar mustache was preaching a wedding sermon, but something sacred echoed and reverberated like an invitation off the walls we all find ourselves up against: This "marriage is a sign of all things in heaven and on earth coming together in Christ,"[11] directed N. T. Wright.

All the married are signposts.

This is what every marriage is: We are signposts pointing the way to the union that is forever and as real as feeling His fingers slip through yours and the palm that birthed the stars pressing warm against yours.

And Farm Boy began to nervously recite vows that he'd written, that he memorized by heart, that he inadvertently stumbled on right at the beginning: "I give you this Ann, ring."

Guests chuckled. Farm Boy closed his eyes and laughed with this endearing embarrassment. And all I wanted was to reach out and caress that cheek of his and say, "Come here."

It was like he read my eyes. He stepped closer. And began again, like we always get to breathe deep and begin again. And he vowed words that he's promised to me again countless times over the last two and a half decades: "I promise to dig deep channels of communication the rest of my life between my soul and yours."

Promises made, and then we'd have to breathe life into them with our days. Two fresh-faced kids, but still we vowed, in essence, promises as holy-wind-wild as this:

There will certainly be an ocean of impossible that lies between us, and I promise to dig deep channels of communication between us, knowing the only way to dig those deep channels of communication is with shards of a broken open heart.

There will certainly be life-ambushes that will press us up between a rock and a hard place, and I promise courage

to break open my heart in vulnerability—so we can walk
out into a deeper intimacy.

There will certainly be anxiety and stress, and in the midst, I
promise to be careful, and care-full, and full of care with
your heart—because *giving your hand in marriage means
handling another soul with the deepest care.*

There will certainly be letdowns, and fallouts, and I promise
to destroy shame and never you—because shame says
things can never change. Shame beats down and grace
lifts up, and shame is a bully and grace is a shield, and
cruciform love makes a way through.

There will certainly be wrong turns, yet I promise to live
forgiveness because nothing else is life-giving. Because
forgiveness gives oxygen to the soul.

And no matter the days we feel like we're lost in a wilderness, I promise to keep stumbling back to wear a habit
of gratitude—because thanksgiving gives us a way out
of entitlement and judgment and control management,
and gratefulness makes for a greater life.

We don't have any inkling of the shattering reality when we
say those vows. All marriage vows are made by broken people who
break promises, and this can break a heart, but this is always the
mysterious way of marriage. Marriage breaks us and remakes us,
and out of wreckage can come resurrection. There always has to
be a dying for there to be loving. Look at Love Himself.

Farm Boy slipped the ring on my finger, and Pastor Dixon
asked, "Ann, do you take this man as your lawful wedded husband?"

"I do."

And I quietly began my own memorized vows, looking up into his eyes as I tentatively recited the words of Ruth, and felt the holy gravity of the *hesed* words my lips were forming, the "one-way love" that is the essence of *hesed*:[12]

Out of wreckage can come resurrection. There always has to be a dying for there to be loving.

"Where you go I will go, and where you lodge I will lodge. Your people shall be my people, and your God my God. Where you die I will die, and there will I be buried. May the LORD do so to me and more also if anything but death parts me from you." (Ruth 1:16–17 ESV)

I slipped the ring on his finger, and he took me, and Pastor Dixon proclaimed us husband and wife. "The bridegroom may kiss the bride." Pastor Dixon smiled.

And Farmer Husband leaned in, pulled me close, and I closed my eyes, and if in all our dark we can feel the kindness of a kiss, one can find the way to bliss. You can feel all the darkness open like waters parting, and you can feel yourself spinning with stars, and there was no shame in this proclaiming we were one in front of everyone, that this kissing was our arriving. The end of he and me and our beginning.[13]

Farmer Husband's hand slid gentle and kind down my bare arm, found the small of my back, and together we turned toward the unity candle. I took in hand my family's candle. He reached for his. And our two flickering flames met over the waiting candlewick . . . and I gave my light. He gave his . . . and then, in our self-giving, the third wick caught flame and there we ignited. One wave of brave light.

Then he extinguished his personal wick—and I blew out mine.

A TIME TO DANCE

All around these three candles with only one flame, around all of us even right now, dances the Trinity of God the Father, God the Spirit, and God the Word, Jesus Christ, in this intimate dance of interlaced communion, a trinity of givenness of three equally divine, distinct persons, a ring of selfless, giving relationship. Behold, I speak a mystery. Behold, our lungs expand right now with this mystery.

What existed even before creation was communion. And the goal of all creation, the way every soul is on, is to return to communion, to usher us into the profound mystery of the selfless, giving communion—the great dance of the Trinitarian relationship.

The trinity of candles made one behind me was an allegory, and the cross at the front of the chapel told the wide-open-armed story of oneness, and this is the Maker's sacred vow:

The triune God came for more than making us right with Him. He came to make us *one* with Him.
He came for more than cleaning us up and making us right. He came to marry us and make us *His*.
He came for more than making a way to what we want. He came to make a way for us to want *Him* most.

We who are to be little Christs are to be like the incarnated Christ, who literally embodied humanity, attaching with, and becoming one with God.*

What the triune God has joined together, let no way of thinking, dreaming, or living, tear asunder. Candles blaze. Souls exhale, believe, dance.

"[This] matters more than anything else in the world," wrote C. S. Lewis. "Each one of us has got to . . . [take his or her] place in that dance. There is no other way to the happiness for which we were made."**

There is no other way to happiness—but this way to the great dance of oneness.

Your life turns on the turn of the dance.

Farmer Husband took off his tuxedo jacket the minute we made our processional out of the chapel, claiming he was way too hot, and I raised an eyebrow and winked, and he laughed and turned to kiss me again.

The wedding cake my mama made, and my brother drove kinda haphazardly to the chapel, we found cracked right apart, fracture lines splitting right through the Mr. and Mrs., and I told myself it was fine, everything was fine, it wasn't like the writing was on the wall.

We ended up with a series of blushing photographs, knife in hand, lovely mementos of the hilarious fiasco: He and I cutting a wedding cake propped together with actual rolls of toilet paper

---

* "Every Christian is to become a little Christ. The whole purpose of becoming a Christian is simply nothing else." Also: "The Church exists for nothing else but to draw men into Christ, to make them little Christs. If they are not doing that, all the cathedrals, clergy, missions, sermons, even the Bible itself, are simply a waste of time." C. S. Lewis, *Mere Christianity* (1952; repr., New York: HarperOne, 2001), 177, 199.

** Lewis, *Mere Christianity*, 176.

stacked under the cake's cardboard base, a bouquet of ivy slyly trying to hide the hideous foundation trying to hold us together.

"Guess when things fall apart, you guys will have to figure out how to roll with it," some smart-aleck uncle quipped as he yanked on the toilet paper, and there may or may not have been eye-rolling. When we cracked and things fell apart, as all unions do, would we know the way to turn and roll around the other in an orbit of selfless, giving love? Would we learn the turns of the dance?

When the last of the cake was served, the last of the speeches that roasted us to a crisp wound down to rousing applause, the last of the glasses tinkled for yet one more lingering, electric kiss, just as the first stars blinked on, Farmer Husband grabbed my hand and led me out of the backyard wedding tent to witness what my brother and his friends had set up in the field. Wedding guests mingled behind us in the chill June evening air, hands stuffed deep into suit pant pockets, arms wrapped around wives for a bit of melded warmth. Farmer Husband stepped behind me, slipped his arms around my waist, pulled me into him like hearts could fuse, and we both tilted our heads back, looking up into the starry night sky, waiting.

My brother knelt in the field and lit the first fuse—and a black night sky over a wedding tent erupted like heart magma building, breaking, blooming into a million bits of white-hot lava, a volcanic awakening into meaning. The sky rhumbaed.

"Ann?" My aunt's voice was right there at my shoulder, Grandma right there beside her. Fireworks broke and spun over our heads, brilliant in their dying dance under stars.

"You chose the right one." My aunt whispered it right into my ear, pecked me quick on the cheek. Taken aback, I turned to see her smiling. And there was Grandma winking, reaching over to pat my arm. And I blinked it back.

Did they hear what Pastor Dixon said right after he recited those John Denver lyrics of "Annie's Song"?

"And then—John Denver divorced his Annie." I hadn't expected that turn in the story.

Love songs can bleed into laments and marriages may not survive, and if you expect another human to find a way to fill you, you will lose your way. Expect another human being to fill all your emptiness, and you can expect to divorce yourself from the only way through. Expecting another human being to fill up your senses, like the glorious awe of a lapping vast ocean or a raincloud breaking over desert, doesn't ultimately make any sense—because a mere human can't fill up our senses like God. Mountains in early May only fill up our senses because what is filling them is the glory of God. Longing for our senses to fill up like a dark night in the deep woods is longing for more than love—it's longing for Love Himself.[14]

What we're all looking for is a way to look into the eyes of One who is always looking for us, and there is only One.* And the dark night over us spins with embers of light, like the eyes of God dance when He looks into ours, takes us in arms, and we sway, swept into the oneness of the Great God Dance.

---

* "We all are born into the world looking for someone looking for us, and that we remain in this mode of searching for the rest of our lives." Curt Thompson, *The Soul of Shame: Retelling the Stories We Believe About Ourselves* (Downers Grove, IL: InterVarsity Press Books, 2015), 138.

chapter four

HOW TO BE KNOWN

~⁓

The knowledge of God is very far from the love
of Him.

—BLAISE PASCAL

What comes into our minds when we think
about God is the most important thing about us.

—A. W. TOZER

evelations like "you can't figure out the way to consummate your marriage" can very well land you in therapy.
Ask me how I know. Cleaving is hard.

And yet . . . not cleaving into one can split your heart right
in half.

When he reaches to caress me under the crease of newlywed

cotton sheets, I try to not visibly stiffen, tighten, with this wild fear of being seen, known, explored, a new land being discovered. He pauses his hand, rests.

"You—don't want me?" He whispers it wounded at my ear.

"I do—I do want you." I turn to kiss him gently, like a vow all over again. "It's just—me. I just want to be someone different than—me. For you."

When I sit in the corner chair in the office of Shalom Counseling, I repeat that same thing to my therapist.

"Look." My therapist tucks a strand of her white hair behind her ear. "When you're all wrapped up in you, it's going to be hard to wrap around him—or let him wrap you up in his arms."

I smile weakly, nod, trying not to imagine what kind of visual she's imagining in her head.

She leans forward like she's about to pack one of my wounds with gauze and wisdom.

"Do you know what research has discovered to be some of the keys of happiness?" She starts numbering the instances on her fingers. "We are the happiest when we are standing before some natural wonder like the Grand Canyon. We are the happiest when we are in a deeply creative zone, what they call the flow.[1] And? We are the happiest when we are deeply intimate with our spouse." Her eyes glint with divine delight, with the knowing.

"And when they analyzed what was similar about each of these experiences . . ."

I shift awkwardly, embarrassed in my chair.

"In each of these instances of complete happiness—what is happening—is that we completely forget ourselves."

Before I can stop myself, one eyebrow shoots up, giving away my doubt.

She's smiling, like she's beckoning that this is safe, that this is all safe.

"When you're gazing out at the Grand Canyon, when you're gazing into your spouse's eyes, forgetting yourself, giving yourself to your partner whom you are absorbed with, that experience of awe, is what we call 'a diminished sense of self.' That diminished sense of self, that smallness, in the face of something larger and greater, creates a deep sense of bonding and connection."

I'm nodding, trying to connect the dots of what she is saying to where I want to go: Wherever there is self-forgetfulness, there is happiness.[2]

Where we forget ourselves—we find exactly what we are looking for: *joy.*

I try to make this large mental note straight across my cerebrum: *Self-forgetfulness is the essence of happiness. A diminished sense of self can grow a greater sense of connection.*

"But this is a journey, a long journey of forgetting yourself to find real joy."

After the close of our session, I simply sit out in the car in the parking lot, staring up at the Shalom Counseling sign, and let what she's just said percolate, like an elixir through my veins. Thinking of self less—is how we find more joy. Why doesn't anyone tell you that self-fulfillment is perhaps a gross misnomer and fulfillment is a function of self being made small with awe? Turns every hackneyed notion of self-fulfillment right on its head. That's what the research had said: When you let awe make you feel small, you feel a larger sense of

> *Self-forgetfulness is the essence of happiness. A diminished sense of self can grow a greater sense of connection.*

connection.³ You're in the zone of happiness—only when you leave the zone of self. Wildly counterintuitive, countercultural.

I drive leafy country roads home, tree limbs stretching across the road to move my soul to worship, thinking of how the therapist said, "This is a long journey."

It was Thomas Aquinas who first said that our core identity as human beings is as "homo viator," pilgrims on the journey, humans on the way, "human wayfarers," the homo viator on the way to life in patria, "in the fatherland"—in our Father.⁴ Augustine so often referred to humanity as homo viator that all of life itself in the medieval age became known as "in via"—on the way—and heaven was referred to as "in patria"—in our Father.⁵

I am not staying here; I am on the way. I am a WayFarer, wrestling, pressing, climbing, stumbling, falling, flailing, rising, not staying here in this place in my head, in my relationships, in my thinking, in my understanding, in my marriage, in my self-orientation, in my relation to God. All roads lead through Gethsemane, surrender to this—but there is one road who is the Way, who leads us on to God. Accept Gethsemane roads, accept the offer of God's shoulder, accept still being on the way—to awe, to glory, to worship, to a remaking, a restorying and restoring of your soul, to resurrection, to smallness, to largeness, to connection. Internal landscapes can reshape, topographies of souls can shift, self-focus, interior fears, sharp failures can all change, and where I was yesterday, who I was yesterday, is not who or where I will be tomorrow. "Now we look inside, and what we see is that anyone united with the Messiah gets a fresh start, is created new. The old life is gone; a new life emerges!" (2 Corinthians 5:18 MSG).

My therapist may be right: This is a long journey of losing myself, of finding more than myself, and I am more than in

> All roads lead through Gethsemane, surrender to this—but there is one road who is the Way, who leads us on to God.

process—I am "in via"—*in the Way Himself*. It's the WayFarers *in via*, on the way, who know they are never behind, but relax into knowing they are always on their way to rising dawns, and God with skin on, and wide-open fields and being touched by Jesus through someone's loud, carbonated laughter out of nowhere, and hope always coming to meet us like the stream with a song that goes on and on without end. This, too, will be part of the journey: There will be miles in the valley, but in Christ, we are *in via*, on our way. In Christ, the Way, there's power in us, to not get bogged down in the valleys, but to keep walking through the valley of all the haunting shadows.

When I drive in the farm laneway, park in front of my childhood home, walk down the farmhouse's back steps into our newlywed basement apartment, the Farmer's already in from evening barn chores, already showered and the scent of my soul's home, already standing in a warming patch of light, setting out our plates, meat right off the grill steaming on a platter.

When he hears me at the door, he looks up, smiles, summer evening sloping gold across his face.

How do you know the moment when you love someone the most?

I used to think it was that snow-shake of a December night when he pulled over on Reesor's side road, pulled open a red velvet box, and there ain't a container in this whole ole world that can hold that kind of joy.

How a man proposes isn't what makes him romantic. It's

how a man purposes to lay down his whole life that makes him romantic.

The Internet age may try to sell you something different, but real romance isn't measured by how viral any wedding proposal goes—and viral is closely associated with sickness—but it's the moments of self-forgetfulness: Setting the table at the end of a long day and rustling up some hearty dish for those who have your heart, and then—without any cameras rolling or soundtracks playing—clearing the plates to make your own love perfectly clear—this is the way of robust romance.

> How a man proposes isn't what makes him romantic. It's how a man purposes to lay down his whole life that makes him romantic.

He sets the pitcher of water down on the corner of the table and winks in all this coming gold light.

"Glad you're finally home." He smiles.

The way home is more winding and steeper than you think, and you have to find how to navigate disappointment on the way to dreams because it's when your life isn't going the way you want it that you can most know the Way. The way will be long, and the WayFarers will lose more than they imagined, and find more meaning than they ever imagined, and the real romantics know that the journey, the wrinkles in the story, in the dreams, in us, is deepening into something sacred.

HOW TO MAKE THE REALEST LOVE

"Counseling go okay?" His arms find my waist. His eyes are waiting on words from mine.

I trace his lips and nod.

"You figuring things out?" He tilts my chin up.

"Yeah . . . yeah, I am." I grin. "Wanna skip dinner and just go straight to dessert?"

His eyes glint, dance. He lifts me a bit off the floor, laughing.

"Yeah . . . I've lost my appetite for dinner." He nuzzles my neck, and I laugh, and butterflies lift and swirl, and he's carrying me away.

There are no standing lovers: The only way to love is to lay down.

Lay down plans.

Lay down agendas.

Lay down self. Think of self less.

Love is always the laying down.

Love lets go of self—to hold on to the other.

This is how to make love out of a marriage: Love lays down its own wants to lift up the will of another.

Later, in the candlelight, he lifts my chin again, finds my shy eyes.

"You—okay, Ann?"

Cleaving, union, is hard, yes. But cleaving into one is also holy.

I close my eyes, let my slow, lingering smile say all that can't be expressed, slip arms around his neck, lacing fingers there at his nape: "Yes, Darryl."

This is how to make love out of a marriage: Love lays down its own wants to lift up the will of another.

We surrender. We cling. We cleave. The attaching of one man and one woman is divine metaphor. We lie there in each other's arms.

This is the passion of Christ. This is the mystery of the Oneness, a sacred and "great mystery, but I speak concerning Christ and the church" (Ephesians 5:31–32 NKJV). Our marital union is a sculpted image, a symbol of the sacred intimacy God means to have with us. The great mystery is that the Mystery Himself wants to marry us, know us, love us, be one with us, that we would be in Christ and Christ in us.

Ours is the romanced universe.

His fingertip traces my jawline, his eyes not leaving mine.

> For your Maker is your husband—
>   the Lord Almighty is his name—
> the Holy One of Israel is your Redeemer;
>   he is called the God of all the earth.
>   (Isaiah 54:5)

For your husband is your Maker, for the One who is committed to you is Christ, for God so loved, He gave, He lived a vulnerable givenness, a humble self-forgetfulness, the knowness of a tender communion.*

"As a bridegroom rejoices over his bride, / so will your God rejoice over you" (Isaiah 62:5).

As the lover has a glint in his eye, lights when you grace a room, breaks into a smile when he catches you looking his way, as the lover traces the contours of your face, like he can outline, map, intimately know the promised land of your soul—who knows that is how your WayMaker thrills to find you: "There she is! There she is!" smiling every time He sees you, never stops

---

* Philippians 2:1–11.

smiling over you, His heart, hurting with His joying and rejoying in *you*.*[6] Who knows how the triune God, in His sweet, swooning baritone,

> celebrates and sings
>> because of you,
> and he will refresh your life
>> with his love. (Zephaniah 3:17 CEV)

Who knows and is known by the tenderness of already being loved like this, how God breaks out into a serenading love song not just over you—God's singing *because of* you, because who you are, your beloved soul, moves your Maker to music? Who keeps coming back to this, to sit in a knowness, a love like this?

"That I get to know you like this," Darryl pulls me in closer, brushes my forehead with a kiss.

Known? *Known.* Is—is that what we are now?

"Now Adam knew [*yada*] Eve his wife" (Genesis 4:1 NKJV).

There is a knowing that is information, and there is a knowing that is intimacy. There is a knowness that is an intellectual knowness of acknowledgment, and there is an intimate *yada*-knowness

---

* "That we should delight ourselves in him, is very easy to understand; but that he should delight himself in us, oh! the very thought of it is ravishing to my heart. Even in the Old Testament Scripture, our Lord said to his chosen, 'Thou shalt be called Hephzibah,' that is, 'My delight is in her.' Is it really so, that the infinite God takes delight in his chosen people? . . . Think of it, my soul, that Jesus takes great delight in thee . . . He could not rest till he had found thee out, and had wooed and won thee . . . He has made a household whereof we twain are the companion parts, himself the Husband, and his church the spouse. Oh, who shall tell it all out?" Charles Haddon Spurgeon, "Christ's Love to His Spouse," Spurgeon Center, accessed November 14, 2021, https://www.spurgeon.org/resource-library/sermons/christs-love-to-his-spouse/#flipbook/. (More of Spurgeon's quote appears in the Notes section, as noted above.)

of attachment. *Yada* is "an act involving concern, inner engagement, dedication, or attachment to a person."[7] There is a knowing that is surface level, and there is a *knowing* that is skin to skin, soul to soul.

He has seen me, and now . . . he's *in via*, on his way, to knowing me, all of me. His eyes don't leave mine as he leans close, brushes my lips with this tender vulnerability.

"Beautiful." I don't close my eyes to shut him out; I close my eyes to try to stop the brimming. Try to turn my head away, embarrassed, not receiving what I can't imagine to be reality in any universe. He cups my chin gently, holds my eyes steady, sure, with his.

"You are beautiful." He says it again slowly, like he wants to draw each word out to bathe all my unbelieving, saturate to marrow and bone.

"And I will betroth you to me forever. I will betroth you to me in righteousness and in justice, in steadfast love [*hesed*-lovingkindness] and in mercy. I will betroth you to me in faithfulness. And you shall know [*yada*] the LORD" (Hosea 2:19–20 ESV).

God wants to wed us, His covenant people. From our garden beginnings, through the garden of Gethsemane, to the consummation of all things in the revelation garden of paradise, the way of God's whole story is for the two to become one, every female and male plant and animal of all of creation, the man and the woman, God and us. The story of God opens with the wedding of the first woman and man, and time draws to a close with the wedding of the church bride and Christ the Bridegroom at the marriage supper of the Lamb. Oneness is the whole story of God. God is making everything into a way for this: Communion, withness, attachment, bonding, oneness. In the image of the Trinity, we are made for diversity becoming unity.

And His covenant never stops swooning over us, never leaves us, never lets us go, never fails us, salvation by *hesed*-lovingkindness. Three times the Trinitarian God espouses the whole of Himself, saying, "I betroth, I betroth, I betroth," I do, I do, I do, through a forever marriage with His people because then "you shall know [*yada*] the LORD" for who I really am (v. 20 ESV).

That same word that's used to express intimately knowing God, *yada*, is also the very same word that's used to describe the intimacy of physical oneness.* To know your spouse, to "have relations" with them, is *yada*—and to have a relationship with God is nothing less than *yada*. Knowing marital oneness is a metaphor for knowing *God*. The covenant of love that's expressed physically is a metaphor for spiritually knowing *God's covenant of love for us*.

Stand back from God, like He's only some holy smoking mountain, and you can only know *about* this God. To *know* this God, you will have to stay close enough to touch Him. Close enough to touch, to trace every word, every line, from His Word,

---

* "But the most daring statement of all is the last one in verse 20: 'And you shall know the Lord.' To see what this means, recall the peculiar use of the word 'know' in the Bible. For example, Genesis 4:1, 'Adam knew Eve his wife, and she conceived and bore Cain.' And Matthew 1:25, 'Joseph knew her [Mary] not until she had borne a son.' In the context of a broken marriage being renewed with the fresh vows of betrothal, must not the words, 'and you shall know the Lord' (v. 20), mean, you shall enjoy an intimacy like that of the purest sexual intercourse." John Piper, "Call Me Husband, Not Baal," (sermon, Bethlehem Baptist Church, Minneapolis, MN, December 26, 1982), MP3, 34:52, Desiring God, https://www.desiringgod.org/messages/call-me-husband-not-baal.

from His lips, to lean the whole weight of your world upon Him and trust how He holds, to turn and caress His bare heart. Then, and only then, after you've touched Him, experienced God, encountered God, do you know God.

And I'm the scandalous woman who's touched Him, the sinner who loosed her hair and kneeled and let all of her cascade, and my wet cheeks have leaked all over His feet, and I have kissed His soles, and I am Doubting Thomas, touching, tracing, interrogating His tender wounds with stinging questions, and He hasn't flinched back, not even once, and I'm the woman who hasn't just touched the frayed edge of His hem, but I've yanked on His whole long cloak, dragged Him down into the sand, and He's scratched out a love note for me in the dirtiest parts of me with His very finger, then lifted my chin with His finger . . . and whispered,

> "Don't be afraid, I've redeemed you.
>
> I've called your name. You're mine.
>
> When you're in over your head, I'll be there
> with you.
>
> When you're in rough waters, you will not go
> down." (Isaiah 43:1–2 MSG)*8

---

* "Hence it is that the child of God carries on a secret intercourse with heaven. See him on his knees—he talks with God, he pours out his heart before the Lord. And in return—whether the world chooses to believe it or not, it is a matter of fact with us—in return the great Invisible Spirit pours into the praying heart a stream of sacred comfort, keeps it in its time of trouble and gives it to rejoice in its moments of sadness. . . . [T]o tell it to God . . . to lay bare his bosom, to let its inmost secrets be exposed to the great Searcher of Hearts, to pour out what one cannot say in words. . . . Is there a care which I dare not cast on Him? Is there a sin which I would not humbly and tearfully confess before Him? Is there a need for which I would not seek relief from Him? Is there a dilemma in which I would not consult Him? Is there ought so confidential that I may not divulge to man, which I may not breathe out to my God? . . . Then the Lord is pleased in return to manifest Himself unto His people." Charles Spurgeon,

Question and doubt, slam and smash, rail and flail with fury, but keep close enough to keep pounding His chest. Don't ever withdraw enough that you don't know Him, that you can't draw His heart by heart because what's hellish is:

"Not everyone who says to me, 'Lord, Lord,' will enter the kingdom of heaven, but only the one who does the will of my Father who is in heaven. Many will say to me on that day, 'Lord, Lord, did we not prophesy in your name and in your name drive out demons and in your name perform many miracles?' Then I will tell them plainly, 'I never knew you. Away from me.'" (Matthew 7:21–23)

Yada *God or you depart from God.*

Only those who obey and go the Way of God can say they know God. To know God like the back of your hand, your hands, your feet, your heart, you have to move with Him. To know God is to be so intimately attached to God that you move with God, and He moves through you. "Remember how the LORD your God led you all the way in the wilderness . . . to humble and test you *in order to know* [yada] *what was in your heart, whether or not you would keep his commands*" (Deuteronomy 8:2, emphasis mine). To obey God is our way of laying out the welcome mat for God to come know all the chambers of our heart intimately, to know how our heart is for Him. Still, turn, sit, hunger, linger, long to intimately *yada*-know God's heart, and let God *yada*-know all of your heart, and you

---

"Private and Confidential," in *The Metropolitan Tabernacle Pulpit: Sermons Preached by C. H. Spurgeon*, vol. 60, 1914, Christian Classics Ethereal Library, https://ccel.org /ccel/spurgeon/sermons60.xlii.html. (More of Spurgeon's quote appears in the Notes section, as noted on the previous page.)

explore the terrain of His heart, and He explores yours, and you find life isn't about a way to a destination but about a way to travel, a way to be wholly known and still wholly loved.*

It's splashing in the shallows, in all kinds of hell, to only know God from page, pulpit, pixelated memes, to merely have *informational knowledge*, when there's a way to dive deep, to look God in the eye and experience *relational knowledge*, this knowing reverberation of His assuring word ringing sure through the deepest chambers, the ones where the storehouses of shame and abandonment and grief and loss overflow, and you know that you know that you know that He is here, still right here, and He hovers over your deep, and you've known it, the warmth of His wing, the shadow that shields, and underneath everything that's underneath all the things, you've felt His steady arms that cannot ever give way.

> Life isn't about a way to a destination but about a way to travel, a way to be wholly known and still wholly loved.

Let us press on to [*yada*] acknowledge him.
As surely as the sun rises,
    he will appear;
he will come to us like the winter rains,
    like the spring rains that water the earth.
        (Hosea 6:3)

---

* Tim Keller defines the word *yada* as "the most deep and intimate and experiential word in the Hebrew language for knowledge. It is knowledge so passionate and so intense and so intimate that it's a synonym for sexuality when used in the book of Genesis." Tim Keller, "Creation Care and Justice," August 28, 2020, in *Gospel in Life*, podcast, MP3 audio, https://www.oneplace.com/ministries/gospel-in-life/listen/creation-care-and-justice-881138.html.

Press on, pursue hard after Him who is coming for you like the warming dawn across your face every day, who falls on your upturned face and your every parched place like gentle, resurrecting rains, who guides your way to thriving, which only comes from intimately knowing all of Him.

I don't turn away from him.

"I . . . just want us both to—feel loved. Wanted."

Known.

I circle-trace the white kiss of a scar that pecks his right eyebrow.

"If something ever happened to you?" I outline the side of his face, his neck, with the tip of my finger. "And somebody called for me to come? I know all the ways I'd know it was you."

I KNOW YOU, I *YADA* YOU.
I WOULD *YADA*-KNOW YOU ANYWHERE.
I KNOW YOUR HEART BY HEART, KNOW THE SWIRL
OF THE FINGERPRINTS OF YOUR SOUL.
I COULD MAP THE SECRET BACK PASSAGES
OF YOUR MIND, DRAW THE INNER LANDSCAPE
OF YOUR THOUGHTS BECAUSE I'VE DRAWN
CLOSE ENOUGH TO CALL THE WARMTH OF YOUR
BREATH MY SAFEST HOME.

I'm never going to stop soul-mapping him, learning him, not from ink and lines on paper, not by descriptors or commentators or secondhand, but by hand, by my own hand, my own intimate encounters, so I just have to close my eyes and I can hear the rhythm of his slow and steady voice, the way I can find him, that cadence, even from the back, in a crowd, the way I can feel the contours of his closeness in the dark, the way I've memorized him, all of him, how he says every night, "Better call it a day. Tomorrow morning comes early," how I can see his handwriting, these small, printed scratchy lines, all stacked there in that journal he keeps on his open Bible, how I know it's him just by the way he walks across the floor.

I can say this, and anyone can say, I try and I fall, I get lost and I turn around, and I self-forget and I self-preserve, and I unveil my soul and I reach for masks, but nothing would be worse than to say I don't know God, that I don't know God like I know part of me. Yada *God or you depart from God.*

> As long as Christ remains outside of us, and we are separated
> from him, all that he has suffered and done for the salvation
> of the human race remains useless and of no value for us . . .
> All that he possesses is nothing to us until we grow into one
> body with him.[9]

When God knocks and moves right in, dwells within, abides within, takes up residence and makes His home within, takes off His shoes, lights a candle, leans over and slips His arm around you, the Way has already found you, and you are home where you're emotionally known and forever soul-safe.

Why need a way to somewhere else when your interior world with the WayMaker is so lovely, so enfolded in a love where you are fully seen and deeply known and wholly safe, a world you can turn and return to, when there is nowhere else you want to be? "Then Christ will make his home in your hearts as you trust in him. Your roots will grow down into God's love and keep you strong" (Ephesians 3:17 NLT). Prayer only happens when we are unmasked and soul-bare before God, letting Him touch and know all the parts of us, letting all of us be wholly loved by Him, not as we pretend to be, but as we truly are.

It was paradise in the beginning only because He knew us—because He was with us. We can return to paradise anywhere because the home of God is wherever we are: *in us.* "You realize, don't you, that you are the temple of God, and God himself is present in you?" (1 Corinthians 3:16 MSG).

Turn and return to Eden: God is with us.

Darryl knew his wife.

I knew my husband.

It was like Eden, and there was no shame.

LIFE TO THE FULL

Ten and a half months after we *hesed*-covenanted for forever, I drive my swollen self down backcountry roads to the hospital, four weeks before my due date, before this twenty-one-year-old bride could naively imagine or grasp that her body was in actual labor, before Darryl drops planting farm fields and beats it in a pickup truck to the hospital, and yet on the eve of Mother's Day, I look right into Darryl's eyes looking into mine, gripping his arms so tight I bruise them, bear down, and birth our first son, Caleb, because Caleb was one who "had a different spirit and has followed Me fully" (Numbers 14:24 NASB).

Almost exactly twenty-four months later, Darryl would drop

his feed scoop in the barn before six a.m., leave his sows hungry and waiting, to fly through sleepy country towns, swerving around early morning clatter of Mennonite horse and buggies, to get his labor-heaving, heavy-breathing wife to the hospital, shaving a forty-minute drive down to twenty, and there he was, Joshua, the one God commanded to "be strong and courageous. Do not be frightened, and do not be dismayed, for the LORD your God is with you wherever you go" (Joshua 1:9 ESV). Joshua, who along with Caleb, "followed the LORD wholeheartedly" (Numbers 32:12). This was, and is, and always will be the prayer.

Joshua was born on a humid Saturday on the very last day of May, and I carried him in arm to the barn on Monday, me feeding sows, me feeding Joshua. A swaddled brand-new nursing babe in one arm, tending brand-new baby pigs with the other, and a two-year-old clinging to my leg, I work from dark to dark beside my man, barn to field to barn, and *yada*-know my husband's whole world.

The bottom falls out of the price of pigs. Thirty dollars to produce a piglet will only leave eight dollars back in our hands. Our pockets hemorrhage our dreams. Tensions rise, we fight. We forgive. We pray and surrender, give way to whatever is His way. The babies and I cry ourselves to sleep. Darryl holds me, and my belly swollen, through the nights he can't sleep.

Then one night in the dead of winter, as our dream of keeping the farm afloat is just about dead, he drives me to the city's YMCA just before close and, nine months heavy with child, I sausage into a swimsuit, float out into the pool only to teeter into a handstand, begging our third baby to turn under the pressures of the pool waters—turn, breech baby, turn. But five days later, and ten unexpected days early, in a little country hospital that has absolutely no way to perform a C-section for a baby coming breech, my weary Farmer, who's been desperately trying to keep us and all our dreams alive, finds my eyes and begs me in hard labor, begs for all of us, "You'll have to give your everything, Ann."

I *yada*-know his eyes and all the words he isn't saying, and I self-forget and focus on the happiness beyond me, and four roaring, herculean pushes later, we hold our first daughter, born breech, born naturally, and we pray to never stop giving her our everything, the girl we named Hope because "'I know the plans I have for you,' says the LORD. 'They are plans for good and not for disaster, to give you a future and a hope'" (Jeremiah 29:11 NLT).

And in the beginning a husband knew his wife and a wife knew her husband, and intimacy bears all kinds of fruitfulness, and time and again I swelled large and contracted and labored, and I nursed and leaked and sagged, and I grew stronger than I could have fathomed, and in a holy dance with the Trinity, we made half a dozen tiny humans and cocreated souls, and we delivered them into air and the story of God. Caleb, Joshua, and Hope would soon be followed by the miracle of Levi, Malakai, and Shalom.

When you *yada*-know the kindness of God, you can know there will be some kind of fruitfulness. Intimacy with God bears fruit for God. Intimate God-experience births God-obedience. Know the Way, and you know the Way.

> Intimate God-experience births God-obedience. Know the Way, and you know the Way.

It's true: We almost lose the farm. God weds us to hope. Again and again, we keep losing and finding each other, keep learning and knowing and *yada*-knowing each other, mapping more of each other's inner landscape and finding more to love, choosing to love more. To know someone is to stand a thousand times over the grave of who they once were, and then walk with them on the way to further knowing the inner terrain of who they are becoming.

When I'm terrified of the next cavernous valley, plunging farm markets, and then skyrocketing debt, plummeting crop yields and then steep, dizzying pig losses, mountain and valley, wave after wave after wave, Darryl leans his forehead against mine and whispers it.

"What's the worst thing that can happen, Ann?"

And I would nod and *yada*-know, know it over all the waves of a lifetime. Turns out you can be about bankrupted, shamed, walked out on, labeled, ghosted, slandered, diagnosed, abandoned, cut off, humiliated, guilty, fired, vilified, charged, destroyed, ruined, devastated, grieved, wrecked, and left for dead in a million ways, and this is the ocean floor, this is at its base: When you know you are fully known and still fully loved, nothing can still scare you.

There is a reason that God is Love and He is with us: Because this is all we need.

When you're lost in a mess of difficulty, you find you're found when you simply know your identity: *beloved*. God is Love, and love is at rock bottom, love is underneath everything, when everything falls away, and God is with us, and Love marries us.

I am known and begin to know how to say it out loud: "The worst-case scenario is that all the very worst things happen, and I am still loved."

When you know you are fully known and still fully loved, nothing can still scare you.

When he finds me in the middle of the night under thin cotton sheets, we know how to read each other in the dark: Love looks you straight in the eye and says, "I know where you are most ashamed, most afraid, most alone, and nothing could ever make me walk away."

Ocean kisses land, the moon completes the stars, God seeks to know the whole soul, two everywhere becoming the one love of a consummate love.

chapter five

THERE'S NO PLACE LIKE HOME

Fully to enjoy God, is infinitely better than . . .
fathers and mothers, husbands, wives or children . . . or . . . earthly friends. These are but
shadows; but God is the substance . . . These
are but streams; but God is the fountain.
These are but drops; but God is the ocean.
—JONATHAN EDWARDS

xamining the face facing yours can, in ways you never
imagined, feel like a coming home. I first saw pixels of
her heart-shaped face on a night in early February while I was
standing in a garden under strings of lights and a blanket of stars
in a Texas sky.

Darryl and I had just celebrated more than twenty years of keeping the vows. Married and melded more years than we had even lived when we had bound our lives with the vows, exchanged rings, and become a metaphor for something more.

He had this receding hairline that seemed like a vulnerable revelation, and I only loved all of him even more. And I had this growing waistline that left me softer, less sharp and angular around the edges, and nothing about either of us had been a straight line, but the long, winding way can bind souls strong. Strange how our ways only make sense when we look back, but we can only take the next step, if we keep looking forward. Turns out you only find the way through when you look both back and forward—and believe that no matter what direction you're looking, nobody gets to bypass the hard roads, that this handful of five tried-and-true ancient words are your most honest compass: "And it came to pass." The hard roads will pass, and the easy roads will pass, and the only way through keeps holding this as the true compass. Never let go of this.

JUST A GIRL, LOOKING AT HER PHONE, FALLING IN LOVE

And so it came to pass that I'm standing about midroad, in the middle of my life, Edens and Gethsemanes both behind and ahead, Darryl and I parents to half a dozen glorious kids, wandering this circuitous maze of a way of life, when I find myself under an expansive spring sky, at a gathering of women who are world-changers and Jesus-brave and visionaries running nonprofits, all telling their stories of fighting the dark and injustice and oppression and never giving up.

But I'm not looking up at the stars, or even at the women mingling about with their sparkling waters. I'm looking down at pixels on a phone, looking into the face of a blanket-wrapped baby in this wee white hat with these knitted lamb ears. Maybe a babe of three to four months old? Somewhere overhead, Aries is this cluster of stars that the Hebrews call *Teli*—"lamb of the world."

I've just been introduced to an organization that cares for pediatric cardiac patients around the world, and apparently this one wee babe, in a deeply loving foster home in China, has hypoplastic left heart syndrome—literally living with only half a functioning heart. Her parents, without resources to provide her desperate care, placed their baby where they hoped she'd be found, adopted, and given a fighting chance at life. I'm looking into the face of a dream. Her mama's dreams, and her dreams, and she's lost her mama and her mama's lost her, and there isn't a dream that hasn't been shaped by desperation and disappointment and the dark. A notification had run for weeks and weeks in a paper in China, with the hopes of finding her mama, of a reunification and medical support to preserve the family, this attachment, their hearts. The notice had echoed unanswered.

Looking at this picture of one little baby, I want to rage-howl at the moon, the stars, their Maker, to orchestrate a way for this one wee babe to find her way back to her birth mama, whose heart beat steady for nine months over this child like a sonar of love. Can't anyone connect their dots, a constellation of mother and child who belong to each other? Lose connection to your loved ones, your dreams, your community, your Maker, and what you will always find is trauma. Lose connection, find trauma. I can't turn my eyes from the piercing baby-brown eyes in pixels. We're all WayFarers who need to be connected to our North Star. The planet's a small marble—how can we bear losing the people we need?

Someday, this curl of a babe will need more than heart surgery. She will eventually need a complete heart transplant under the lattice of her ribcage. To survive hypoplastic left heart syndrome that's what has to happen: You need a new heart. For any of us to survive, we need a new connected heart, woven to Beloved and all His body.

> Lose connection,
> find trauma.

I let my thumb reach out and touch the screen, like I can softly caress her cheek. Every broken heart just wants to be rocked calm in the knowing they are never too much and are always more than enough to be loved. I can't stop looking at the screen and into her eyes telling this story that I never want to end, and there are moments when the trajectory of your one life turns and you don't even feel the ways you've shifted.

Her Chinese caregivers, her *ayis*, have named her Yu Xin, but the English name she's so lovingly been given in her foster home—is Shalom.

"Shalom?" I feel like a star has streaked like a prophecy across the dark. Like I'm holding the wholeness of glory.

Shalom means more than complete peace—it's peaceful completeness. Wholeness. And shalom isn't a completeness that we arrive at like a destination; shalom is a completeness that we experience along the way, like an orientation.

I can hardly whisper: "The only other Shalom I've ever known is . . . our daughter Shalom."

It's like even the stars are reverberating with one divine line I can feel pounding in the space between my own tender arteries.

Maybe this Shalom—is meant to be with your Shalom.

My interior orbit tilts.

For this wee Shalom—to be with our Shalom—would mean . . . adoption? Adoption is this heartbreaking, holy, bewildering hallelujah and yet still, it feels like the whole night sky above flashes with epiphany: The Great God Dance keeps making a way to expand the promised land of His love.

Under a flung canopy of stars, I'm feeling what C. S. Lewis called a "longing to be reunited with something in the universe from which we now feel cut off, to be on the inside of some door which we have always only seen from the outside."[1]

How can I feel cut off from a child whom I've barely laid eyes on, how can I be falling in love all over again, and is this wrong? Yet isn't this how God loves uniting with us? Hadn't the completeness of Jesus, shalom Himself, left the shalom of the Trinity, to be our only way back into the triune Great God Dance of shalom? Hadn't Jesus signed up for a costly love that He knew would be the price of admission for intimate union? Wasn't this union the very meaning of all being, the apex of the very best news: "For this is the design of the gospel, that Christ may become ours, and that we may be engrafted into his body."[2]

I'm looking into her eyes in this photo that's been handed to me, and my soul is longing for her to find the way to the safety of home, for her to know the perfect fit of arms curling around her, for her not to bear the wounds of this broken world. Could we enter into the heartbreak of loss and brokenness with her,

> You never know the way
> of love without knowing
> the way of suffering.

trusting that love always finds a way in, right through the heartbreak?

Every mother, every child, every human being who breathes feels it: You never know the way of love without knowing the way of suffering. The only way to avoid heartbreak is to grow so hard you become unbreakable.* The only way that's completely pain-free is a way completely free of love. The way of love is always the hard, heartbreaking way; real love never takes the easy way that ends up being far more heartbreaking in the end. And maybe when we most desperately wish there was a way out of the heartbreak for someone is exactly when we need to enter into their heartbreak, to be a witness, giving withness, in it. The cosmic truth is:

1. Suffering is part of any road that any heart's ever known, and trying to avoid suffering at all costs is what causes all kinds of unnecessary suffering.
2. Whatever the story or form of suffering, it can be transformed into a restoration story.
3. Suffering always happens on the way, and there is always a way through and out of the suffering

---

* "To love at all is to be vulnerable. Love anything, and your heart will certainly be wrung and possibly be broken. If you want to make sure of keeping it intact, you must give your heart to no one, not even to an animal. Wrap it carefully round with hobbies and little luxuries; avoid all entanglements; lock it up safe in the casket or coffin of your selfishness. But in that casket—safe, dark, motionless, airless—it will change. It will not be broken; it will become unbreakable, impenetrable, irredeemable. The alternative to tragedy, or at least to the risk of tragedy, is damnation. The only place outside Heaven where you can be perfectly safe from all the dangers and perturbations of love is Hell." C. S. Lewis, *The Four Loves* (1960; repr., New York: HarperOne, 2017), 155–56.

because the Way Himself is with you, hand in yours, guiding you.

The WayMaker cups her face, mine, all our faces:

> "Don't be afraid, I've redeemed you.
>> I've called your name. You're mine.
> When you're in over your head, I'll be there
>> with you.
>> When you're in rough waters, you will not
>>> go down.
> When you're between a rock and a hard place,
>> it won't be a dead end—
> Because I am GOD, your personal God . . .
> I paid a huge price for you . . .
> *That's* how much you mean to me!
>> *That's* how much I love you!
> I'd sell off the whole world to get you back,
>> trade the creation just for you.

> "So don't be afraid: I'm with you."
>> (Isaiah 43:1–5 MSG)

I ache with all the loss and broken dreams and hearts in this broken world: Life is hard, not because you've taken a wrong turn. Life is hard because this is the way of love—and Love Himself will be with you every step of the way. Is that stirring I feel—yes, that's it—like my soul made a marriage covenant to be a home for one man's soul—is it now feeling moved to make an *adoption covenant* to be a forever home for her? Every covenant to each other is ultimately a covenant to suffer *with* each other. Is my stirring to humbly enter into the heartbreak of her story and be forever with her in it—is this the way God Himself feels about entering into our heartbreak, so we are never alone in it? God's love *for* us is ultimately a covenant to suffer *with* us.

I can hardly bear how her searching eyes in that one photo fill me with ache for her loss and love for her always. I look up. Spiritual adoption is never to be wrongly conflated with the profound trauma of societal adoption, and in that moment, I'm only focusing on the spiritual reality, that before the triune God created even one of the stars dangling like a benediction over me, before there ever was even one breath of history, the triune God "long before he laid down earth's foundations, he had us in mind, had settled on us as the focus of his love, to be made whole and holy by his love. Long, long ago he decided to adopt us into his family through Jesus Christ. (What pleasure he took in planning this!) He wanted us to enter into the celebration of his lavish gift-giving by the hand of his beloved Son" (Ephesians 1:4–6 MSG). *What pleasure Abba Father took in planning to make you His! Spin stars!*

Adoption predates creation. Before God even made the world, God planned a way to *hesed*-attach His heart to our traumatized, broken ones. Attachment to God is older, greater, grander, surer than all the galaxies and the Milky Way, and *hesed*-love is the way older than stars and waves and the tried-and-

> Marriage and adoption—the most intimate of relationships—are signposts, waymarkers, pointing to the reality of God's certain way of attachment, communion, and union with us through every suffering way.

tested way through, the way of love that comes to enter into our suffering.

It doesn't matter where I turn; there it is because it's true: Marriage and adoption—the most intimate of relationships—are signposts, waymarkers, pointing to the reality of God's certain way of attachment, communion, and union with us through every suffering way.

I look back down at the phone, memorize her wide brown eyes, all her *imago Dei* glory, and just like time felt gloriously suspended in that moment when Darryl grinned in that high school hallway—this moment hangs achingly full, pregnant with the possibility of holding her and falling in *hesed*-love forever. There are these times when time slows, heavy with love. "When the fullness of time had come, God sent forth his Son, born of woman, born under the law, to redeem those who were under the law, so that we might receive adoption as sons" (Galatians 4:4–5 ESV).

Twirl and spiral, galaxies, and it's my own soul that is small and lost in the universe and in the fullness of this moment, my own Father's eyes hold mine, and He gathers close, and we are all spiritually found: Redemption is never the end but a means to the ultimate end: Adoption. *Attachment.*

Salvation *by* God is ultimately for attachment *to* God.

Everything on the way, or in the way, is making a way to be soul-attached to the One who is the Way, who can do nothing less than carry you through every heartache to home.

All the hard and inexplicable ways of the cosmos, the bruised relationships, the roadblocks to our dreams, all the bewildering ways of God, have this redeeming purpose of attaching us, like marriage, like adoption, to the enfolding heart of God.

The whole purpose of redemption is to make way for

spiritual adoption; the whole purpose of atonement is to make a way for attachment, literal at-one-ment, God one with us in our sufferings.

He came for more than cleaning us up and making us right; He came to adopt us and make us *His*. God's about far more than the optics of us looking right; He's about being our actual birthright. Chosen by God, for God, to inherit nothing less than God (Ephesians 1:14), exhale, universe and soul. The goal is God, and Christ cannot fail, and the way home is guaranteed.

Someone's tapping me on the shoulder.

My ride is apparently leaving the garden. The constellations, all of heaven, are drawing nearer, waiting. There's nothing in me that wants to leave; all I want is to—somehow find the hand of this little WayFarer who seems as far away as Oz and tether my own broken heart to hers so she knows she's not alone in a world of loss and trauma and profound brokenness, and we'll hold on to each other to find our way together, expecting the way to hold heartbreak, which is the tender beauty of what happens if we let our hearts hold love. Isn't this the passion of God's *hesed*-love for all He chooses, adopts, engrafts safely as His very own?

WHEN YOU KNOW, YOU KNOW

How am I seriously even entertaining the possibility of—adoption? There. I'm naming it, owning it. But why go ahead and consider societal adoption that can be fraught with self-centering, instead of adoptee-centering, that has cultural, racial, and traumatic implications for every child who loses their birth family? Wouldn't a better way, to make this a better world, be to focus on preservation of vulnerable families instead of any uninformed creation of new ones? Yes. And yet, it's painfully complicated and difficult. While we do the direly needed societal work of vulnerable family preservation with one willing, faithful hand, how do we still enter into the heartbreak of children who already find themselves traumatized and vulnerable and offer them our other, tender hand? And in the beginning was the Word, the Logos, the literal logic of God, and in the logic of God, the mystery of manna can sustain us all on hard journeys, and five fish will feed five thousand bellies, and the only One who literally loves you to death will rise and raise you with Him too. In the logic of God, life embraces suffering, and they travel as one, and there is nothing to fear on the way because you are in the Way Himself and He is fail-safe.

So let all the pounding waves crack and crash; the cross points the way for us all to climb up into the safe chambers of His heart. God's not some huckster selling cheap tickets to some promised land of our own puny imagining, but He's the aching, nursing mother who will "never forget you—never" and proves it by flinging up wrinkled-veined hands with you, you, right there: "Look, I've written your names on the backs of my hands" (Isaiah 49:16 MSG), then makes good on the promise to adopt all of us, and rock us, and our losses, forever in the arms of the Great God Dance. God's ways are always to make a way to rest in His strong arms and trace His kind face, especially in the pitch-black dark.

A friend nudges me again out of the garden, out toward the street with our idling ride, but my mind's carrying that look in the child's searching eyes, not letting go of her waiting, fractured heart. Love is wild and redirects everything, her and me and God.

I try to maneuver through the mingling mass. But all the people, the crowd, everything literally starts to spin—slide. I reach for the back of a metal chair to steady myself. It's like the topography of my life is shifting right under me. The whole patio feels like it's heaving, waving. I slip down into the empty chair. *Steady, steady. Look the right way, always look the right way.* Let the compass hands turn; let God reorient all your ways. The meaning of life is not about finding your way to some good life—but about being found in His great love. *Here and now.*

The best way of life to adopt is to never stop being aware that you are soul-adopted by God. *Here and now.*

A friend kneels down by my chair, asks if I need water. Someone fans my face with a menu. A friend asks, winking, "You been drinking too much, Ann?"

"Definitely," I mumble, closing my eyes, head bowed under the Austin sky, "Only water—and her, I drank her all in."

All can shift and quake, but God is the chin-lifter, the chin-turner, the chin-holder, and whatever is in the way can be the way that causes us to lay our heads on the shoulder of the One who cannot let us go and walks on waves, adopts, weds, unites, attaches us to Himself.

"Wait. What? You drank who in?" My friend leans in.

I look up and words spill before I can even think: "I think—I just saw a picture of my daughter."

Where on a humid Texas night did those words just come from? They say the tongue's the tail of the heart, and my tongue's betraying what's pounding loud within, and the moment the words are out of my mouth, I want to yank them back, hide them, keep them close, holy and sacred in inner chambers. The audacity of the words I've just given oxygen to, all splayed and looking presumptuously foolish out in the world, seem embarrassingly preposterous—*impossible.*

No. Way.

But let go and embrace the next impossible wave, and it can carry you to shore.

"Your . . . what? Did you just say *daughter*?"

The stars and the night sky stop spinning and still. The tilting settles, like everything finding its place, finding its new place.

I find my feet, tuck the chair back into the table, smile thinly to a ring of concerned friends. Hush now. There are no more words. There are things too holy for words. There is a time to hold close the mysterious way of the heart and simply trust the way love doesn't make sense but always has the best sense of direction. Ask God.

I nod, turn, walk toward the street and toward the skyline all lit in this brazen bright hope.

ONE STEP

After I wing my way back home on a stream of prayers, I find this t-shirt that's been stuffed into the bottom of my splitting-at-the-seams tote bag. Swag from some conference vendor, it's a worn blue cotton with tattered edges, emblazoned in rust red across the front: *#myONEstep*. The thing looks worn into comfortable velveteen, like it's real and old and full of stories.

It's what I pull on that first morning home. It may be a brand-new t-shirt, but it's frayed and faded to look like it's weathered a thousand hard miles, all uphill through hurricane-force winds. I wryly grin. Appropriate.

Something's burning in the kitchen. Burnt toast? Something ignored until it's too late.

I run a comb through my hair, but what I can't stop running through my head is, *If the holy covenants of marriage and adoption are about covenanting to suffer with each other, and marriage and adoption are the metaphors for our relationship with God, then doesn't that mean that the way forward always is to enter into a covenant of suffering with God?* That. That is how everything is reorienting.

All roads don't lead to Rome; all roads lead through suffering to seeing Him as our only home. All roads with the Way Himself are the Via Dolorosa, the Way of Suffering, the way that Jesus carried His Cross through Old Jerusalem toward Calvary. Only the way of suffering will lead us Home. Everything else is mirage.

If marriage and adoption are sacred metaphors of how Love Himself chooses to suffer with us, then it's not a cliché, but the most revolutionary truth in the universe: God is love. He is not frown or disgusted sigh or flattened cardboard caricature of judge and jury with gavel and shackles, but He is holy, right-making, kindest Love Himself. Isn't that He is the embodiment of kindest love what we most question, what we are most suspicious of, what we keep doubting all along the way? When—not if—the shock, drop-dead phone call comes on a napping Thursday morning, when the doctor shakes her head and can't look you straight in the eye, when your road takes a sharp turn to the south and all you can see are No U-turn signs, does God really *hesed*-love me? We may say God is kind love, but we live like God is kind of untrustworthy. We may say God is our Father, the vigilant Dad who stands between the world and His kid like a protective old bear, teeth bared, but too often we live like He's the lumbering slow Dad who's likely hibernating. We may say we have safe oneness with God, but we live like He is the one who is unreliable.

If any authentic attachment—in marriage or in adoption—is ultimately about one's reliability, dependability, trustworthiness in our pain, is this why we most often are so poorly attached to God? If we don't genuinely experience Him as trustworthy, we can't ever be genuinely attached to God. If we don't trust the lines of our story to God, have we truly put our faith and trust in God? Do we live more like God is a master merely interested in obedience from us, instead of trusting that God is a lover whose ways are all about forming deep attachment with us, covenanting to always suffer with us?

If marriage and adoption are the two holy-ground metaphors God uses to draw a picture of the way life with Him looks like, I can feel the whole meaning of life shifting: The only place we ever need to arrive at is where we fall in love with God, who suffers with us. The only place we ever need to be is the place where we know how much He enjoys being

> The only place we ever need to arrive at is where we fall in love with God, who suffers with us.

with us always: God's curled round us, especially when we are curled in a fetal ball, God's holding us behind the bathroom door, God's wrapped round us in the middle of the sleepless night, and where we ache, He's not ashamed to be with us, and there is no other place He'd rather be than with us. We've arrived when we've come to the place that keeps tracing our own name engraved on the back of His hand.

I finger the frayed edge of the t-shirt. There it is in the mirror: #myONEstep. I had taken one step toward Darryl, and then eventually walked all the way down an aisle and into a covenant to suffer with each other. Our journey after the vows had valleys and vistas and our babies took their first steps and we had our painful missteps and yet, always the turning to stay in step with the Spirit. And now I can feel my heart unexpectedly taking this step toward a little heartbroken baby. This is the breathtaking trip into falling in love, and then covenanting to enter into each other's sufferings.

A blue jay calls from somewhere outside the window, somewhere out in the cedar hedge, and I turn, but miss its flash of wings. Sometimes I weary of trying to peer and see the right way through. I think—I think I just need to go for a walk. I just need to go grab my old red parka hanging on a tangled pegboard of draping winter coats and scarves in the mudroom, lace up my snow boots, and I need to take one step, one trusting breath, at a time. I can feel this sense of something tender, new coming to find me and I feel—apprehensive? Or—full of anticipation? Who knew that fearful trepidation stands so near to hopeful anticipation? Take one step, one trusting breath, and your whole world can turn. Darryl finds me in the mudroom lacing up my boots.

"I just have to get some air—I just have to . . ." I'm muttering as I tie them in double knots, like I know the only way to breathe without angst is being securely tied to the only One who knows and has weighed all the options and can be trusted to make the best way.

"You want company?" He's reaching for his coat but it's like he's reaching for me. And yet it's only a few hairs past one p.m. in the middle of the day? He's just finished up lunch, grilled burger with thick slices of tomato and cheese, and he's got old mama sows and their rooting litters of grunting piglets suckling down lunch in the barn, all waiting for him to return. In all our twenty years of marriage, he's never gone for a walk in the middle of the day with me. But sometimes you don't know how to take the next trust-breath until you just take the next step, until you walk it out. "Yeah, it'd be kind if you came for a walk with me. To figure this out with you." My eyes come home to his.

He smiles easy, nods, and I can read his mind after all these faithful years: If you stay in Christ, everything can be figured out.

The air outside the back door jars, cold Canadian winter air frigid in nostrils. Our red lab, Boaz, runs ahead, down toward our galvanized and tilting mailbox with the red flag still up like a beckoning to come. The snow crunches under our every step like a witness. "You kinda seem—like you're wrestling?" He reaches for my hand as we turn at the end of our laneway, head toward the waiting woods. Do I tell him about the moment I heard her name? *Shalom.* Or that I actually whispered out loud that I thought I saw a picture of our daughter? I dive bold, straight into the deep end.

"I think—the greatest thing that's ever happened to us is our literal adoption, which is God covenanting to be with us in our suffering."

He raises his eyebrow and sure, maybe I'm thrashing and flailing and maybe I shouldn't have quite started here—but I'm trying to explain and why does getting this right matter so much? Because *she* does.

"God doesn't have any naturally born children. We're all adopted. Our deep identity is that we are all chosen adoptees." In Christ this is true. And this is true too: The Scriptural metaphor of adoption does not translate into any societal mandate to legally adopt* and the way of Christ is always to first try to find a way to preserve families, His will that every child will know and stay in the loving arms of father and mother. Honestly, how can we be about entering into the sufferings of both vulnerable families who need preserving, and vulnerable children who need a family?

"This is the thing—you're wrestling through?" I can hear it, the way he's slowly and carefully—tentatively—stringing his sentences together.

I breathe February frost deeply into lungs.

Let the beats in the heart slowly form into words.

"What—would you think of—adopting a daughter with a literal broken heart, who needs a life-saving heart surgery?"

So what if you look like some sputtering, mad fool, embracing the crashing waves? Isn't the whole notion of adoption like a wild ocean of beauty and suffering to wholly immerse ourselves in, and no matter the way, the God of the cosmos is making a way through all of life's waves, for us to be more fully consumed in Him?

J. I. Packer called our spiritual adoption "the highest privilege that the gospel offers: higher even than justification."[3] The waves in the deep end of love are higher than you dreamed, carrying you further than you imagined.

Being made *right* with God may be of first importance as

---

* "While I believe modern adoption can be affirmed by Scripture, the wrongful use of Scripture to spiritualize the modern adoption experience can be harmful to adoptees in various ways; contributing to feelings of shame when we think about our birth parents or ethnic background, making it difficult to verbalize the painful aspects of our experience," wrote adult adoptee Tiffany Henness in "Adoption in the Bible Is a Metaphor, Not a Mandate," The Art of Taleh, November 12, 2019, http://www.theartoftaleh.com/adoption-bible-metaphor-not-mandate/.

we navigate our way through life—but what is of *greatest* importance is that we are adopted as *God's very own* children, as a *way*
of life. You were made for this ocean, for this baptism of passion
over skin.

We aren't merely a ragtag, limping bunch of followers, flailing
behind God; we aren't merely a motley tribe of wounded drifters,
rallying around God; and we aren't merely a straggling remnant
of wanderers, leaning on God to split a way through everything
to make an easier way to some oasis in our imagination. In Christ:
We are more than mere followers of God; we are kin to God. *Kin
to God!* We are the clan of Christ, the house of the holy, of the
tribe of the Trinity, family of the Father, sibling of the Savior,
and we are bone of God's bone, wed to Him, adopted by Him,
sutured, fastened, and bound as one to Him, and He has made a
way for us to be seen and saved, secure and safe,[4] and there isn't
a loss or failure in the world that can change how this reality is
forever sealed. Let the waves of relief come.

"I guess what I'm saying is"—I lean toward him—"I can't
stop thinking about what it means that we are actually adopted,
and in the middle of her loss and trauma and heartbreak, can
this little girl's heart be sutured too?" And then I say her name.

"Shalom. The little girl's English name is Shalom."
Wholeness. Completeness. Peace.

The whispered words are so quiet, so tentative, they almost
blow away in the wind.

"Is—that where you're thinking—our road goes here?"
He looks down our snowy country road, winding through the
woods. "Toward—a baby girl with a broken heart?" Now the
wind carries his steady voice and his courage rests on me, right
there on the curve of the cochlear.

"Look—I don't know." Heart trauma. Heart transplant. Heart attachment. This road leads us into heartache, to sit and lament with a little girl in her trauma and lostness, and covenant withness and witness for always and forever. But the hellish roads aren't the ones of suffering. The hellish roads are the ones that suffer from lovelessness.*

"I don't know what this road holds."

But what I do know is *whatever our road holds, Jesus is our road*.

Jesus is our road.

And He holds.

WE JUST KEEP FALLING IN LOVE

A blast of cold air blows up through the woods, up the road, and I tuck my bare cheek into my shoulder, burrow my hands deeper into my pockets.

"Yeah, who knows where this way leads, but, after everything we've been through, I think we both know that the way that saves is a love that's open to suffering." When we bear each other's suffering, life itself becomes more bearable. Open your hand to embrace the wave, accept the wave.

I search Darryl's face.

"I guess . . . why wouldn't our road go this way, toward her?" I'm daring to be the wild fool who believes that a road marked

---

* "Fathers and teachers, I ponder 'What is hell?' I maintain that it is the suffering of being unable to love." Fyodor Dostoevsky, *The Brothers Karamazov*, trans. Constance Garnett (New York: Modern Library, 1996), 360.

with suffering leads the way into a richer way of life; a road to shalom.

I turn to face the wind, face him, face the sea and the spray and the swelling tumult, and you don't have to wait till you're not afraid to kiss risk as she rises to meet you. The best way forward is to keep falling in love with life as it comes to you, falling in love with God, who is with you in the moment.

"Yes, entering into someone's suffering is a risk, but do you want to risk not wholly loving?" I remember to breathe, brave a smile. (Exercising a smile can be this brave exercising of our faith.) "I mean, I know it doesn't make much sense?" But life doesn't have to make sense to make good, to make joy, to make love, to make waves, to make light of everything. The logic of God turns wind into water.

Not to confuse spiritual and societal adoption, yet the logic of God is: Adoption into God's family isn't God's afterthought—it's always been His first thought (Ephesians 1:4–6). How could anything sweep in with more hope than our adoption by God? "The Spirit himself testifies with our spirit that we are God's children. Now if we are children, then we are heirs—heirs of God and co-heirs with Christ, if indeed we share in his sufferings in order that we may also share in his glory" (Romans 8:16–17).

Large flakes of snow start to drift down. The logic of God turns even air into manna.

And I keep circling it, or it keeps circling me, and all fears are being sucked into this vortex of truth: We are more than heirs to the promises of God, we are heirs who actually inherit *God*. Name anything in the universe, in the way, in the Bible, that could be greater than this dream come true.

Adoption into the family of God gives us more than the

dream of some promised land; we get to inherit more than the *land*. We get to inherit the *Lover of our soul. When we get that we get God, what else do we need to get?* If our adoption already gives us God, can anything really be in our way? Lacy flakes catch in the fur ringing my hood, and I brush them free. Free! *Free!* Darryl catches my hand.

"I wasn't expecting the conversation to go quite like this—and she may be small but . . ."—he winks—"adoption is no small thing."

Yes, it's a thing of deep trauma and painful lament and *maybe it's the everything of a brokenhearted hallelujah.*

"Just honestly, Ann, you know what's always been the most important to me—to make sure I'm being the kind of father who is just . . . present, dependable, loving." He squeezes my hand. "Let me pray about it? Ask God, listen to Him—follow God, whatever way He chooses to lead?"

Yes, yes—that's always the way that makes sense.

"And maybe sometimes"—I exhale, still smiling, hopeful—"maybe the way forward isn't about making sense, as much as it is about having a right sense of direction."

He tightens his grip on my hand, smiles gently, and calls for the red fox lab, bounding down through deep snow in the ditch, to turn and come back.

Whatever is up ahead, whatever happens, there are going to be ditches and wrong turns and the overwhelm of being in way over our heads, and the King of the Cosmos doesn't get disgusted, doesn't shame, doesn't intimidate, but through Christ, He embraces us in the Spirit of full acceptance, "the Spirit of adoption as sons, by whom we cry, 'Abba! Father!'" . . . "God's Spirit touches our spirits and confirms who we really are. We know who he is, and we know who we are: Father and children" (Romans 8:15 esv; Romans 8:16 msg).

I turn in the direction of the winter wind coming with a whirl of snowflakes that were once traces of ocean waves, and the very Maker of this whole wide world incomprehensibly makes Himself our very own Father, and it's truest true: Who knows what the road ahead holds, but Jesus is our road and He holds, and if God were only our King of kings, we'd give Him regard— but the King of kings adopts us and becomes our actual Abba Father and gives us His *heart*. When the heartbeat of the King of kings beats with the love of the Father within your own heart, how does that not beat away all your fears? I try to memorize Darryl's face, this father of already half a dozen children who just committed to pray about adopting the seventh, and that's warming me in a February wind, in the middle of a country road, in the middle of trying to find a way through, that "everything that Christ taught, everything that makes the New Testament new, and better than the Old, everything that is distinctively Christian as opposed to merely Jewish, is summed up in the knowledge of the Fatherhood of God. 'Father' is the Christian name for God . . . Our understanding of Christianity cannot be better than our grasp of adoption."[5]

"Hey?" It's more of a caress than a whisper. But Darryl hears, turns toward me, as the dog turns, lunges up through the snow toward home.

"You know—when a woman commits her life to a man, she has no way of really knowing how she is covenanting to suffer with him, how he will commit his life to their children's lives? And when I gave you my hand for forever—I had no idea how you'd take our children's. You don't just take care of us—you *take* us. You're the kind of father who takes after the kindness of Abba Father."

It's not the cold of the wind that's making my eyes sting.

"You've always chosen your children's hearts above your heart, so your children could trust that, even when your ways were above their understanding, they know your ways are always, always, always for them . . . that you're always standing with them."

A shaft of sun breaks through the snow clouds and all these falling flakes catch with light. He smiles. "C'mon, Ann, I've got to get you home."

chapter six

YOUR KINGDOM COME

When we no longer know which way to go we
have begun our real journey. . . . The impeded
stream is the one that sings.
—WENDELL BERRY

oxology can rise like a dream come true, and raise you,
too, cutting a long cold night short.

The depths of snow all around the farm start to give way to
waiting soil and spring, and, like snow, time is melting away at
the edges of things. Some kid lost a red glove that's a soggy sigh
in a skiff of snow out past the cedars. Looks like the dog nicely
stress-chewed a comforting hole right through the left thumb.

The spruce trees towering behind the house glitter with
snowflakes made into waterdrops, a jeweled string of willing

surrender. Ice water drips . . . drips . . . off the edge of the eave, like there's a song in this quiet letting go, a song I don't know at all how to sing. Strange, how all this snow was so obvious and certain only a few days ago.

When I brave asking Darryl again about adopting, his quiet grin pleads the Fifth.

"Hey, you." I smile. "I know you, and I know what you're up to. When you grow old with someone, you start to know how things go, you know?"

"Yeah, you think so, do you?" His eyes flirt gently, egging me on.

"Yeah—I actually do." I poke his chest with my index finger, softly laughing. "It's always me asking what you're thinking, asking if you're leaning yes, or leaning no—and you always smiling really cute like, like you think you can distract me with that twinkle in your eye, but not *reeeallly* ever answering my question."

"Really, eh?" He grins, grabs my hand to pull me in close. "Is it working? Good strategy?"

I guffaw laugh.

"Well, it's almost working cause you're so dang cute . . ." I'm chuckling, shaking my head, playacting like I'm peeved, but maybe what I'm really playacting is that I'm just playacting. "But really, we've got to figure this out. Are we adopting or not?" I'm laughing, hoping he can read my eyes kinda pleading with him. I could be an open book and he could mark this page.

"Do we have to figure this out?" His voice lowers, trying to soothe whatever line it is he reads in my eyes. "Or is God figuring it out and we just have to wait—be attentive, receptive?"

Or I could be cupped open hands and he could be a waymarker pointing to God.

Wait. Be attentive. Be receptive.

It is deceptively easy to think life is simply about knowing and going the right way. That isn't the whole of reality, nor is it particularly wise. Life is not only about *activity*, but also about *receptivity.* Simply let God lead you on, let God love you now, let God make the way, let God's mind be your mind, let God's Word be your heart, let God's Way be your way. *Life is letting. Come let Me love you.*

> Life is not only about *activity*, but also about *receptivity.* Simply let God lead you on, let God love you now, let God make the way.

I think about that all day. How it's a strange and stealthy way to live, pretending, especially to yourself, that you're openhanded and receptive—*surrendered*—to whatever comes your way, when in actuality maybe you're trying to subtly manipulate everything in your way, to forge your own way. What if I'm really the snapped-shut book, the closefisted hand in need of being marked by His marks of surrender?

"Just—can you tell me?" I ask him late that night, after he turns out our bedroom light, turns back the old quilt.

"Are you still praying about adoption or not?" I ask it gently, genuinely.

"Honestly, Ann, I am—" He turns his pillow over to the cooler side, his words soft, trying to warm my own coolness. "I really am sincerely trying to listen and hear God."

Why do we have to wait for the Word to give us a word, and why doesn't God speak with cosmic-sized bullhorns or mega-banners flapping clearly behind planes, or angels singing, or a giant neon marquee flashing it out:

DON'T MISS IT, TODAY AND TODAY ONLY:
THIS IS THE RIGHT WAY, RIGHT HERE.

Why doesn't He cup His hand to our heart, lean close, and breathe the warmth of His whisper into the cavernous and reverberating chambers, filling us up with Him and the Word and the clear way forward and home?

"Any idea when you, uh, will know you've heard Him?" I ask after he's turned the pillows and is settled and still, the question hanging quiet in the dark like my own banner.

"I guess . . ." His bare foot finds mine under the sheets. "I guess I just keep praying the way He told us to—Our Father who art in heaven, hallowed be Your name, Your kingdom come, Your will be done."

THE AGONY OF WAITING

Darryl's not wrong. Prayer isn't about moving heaven to do things our way but about moving us to do things God's way on earth. It's being prayed at all times, even in this very moment, a chorus rising from this spinning earth: *Our Father who art in heaven, Your kingdom come.* Wasn't it N. T. Wright who said that "'Thy kingdom come, on earth as it is in heaven' . . . remains one of the most powerful and revolutionary sentences we can ever say"?[1] It's revolutionary to pray "Thy kingdom come" because it's turning the soul from the clutches of our kingdom to the totality of God's kingdom. Pray and turn the pages open, turn the palm up, turn and surrender to the King who is kin. The truly wise want more than their dreams to come true; they want God's kingdom to truly come. There's no praying "Thy kingdom come" until you're living out "my kingdom's *done*."

Are the roads I want to go down ultimately about where I want to get to—or about wanting God's kingdom to come down?

I loosen my grip on Darryl's hand—*receptive*—murmur it quietly in the dark of our bedroom, that one revolutionary line, like the Way Himself had taught us to pray, to turn my one heart around because all of life turns on the turn: "Our Father who art in heaven, Your kingdom come. Your will be done on earth as it is in heaven . . ." Is that muddied glove out there in the dark, in the melting snow? Is it lying palm up?

Our Father, Abba, who art in heaven, who is always here, right here,* heaven being as near as the next breath—how is it that our lips can murmur the same tender Abba cry that fell from Jesus' lips more than 170 times? Jesus was once the sure twelve-year-old boy whose first-ever recorded thought, though He knew His earthly father, Joseph, was searching for Him, was that He knew He had to be in His true Abba's house (Luke 2:49), and I could be the tenant, the squatter, the heart-dweller, who moves back home with her Father and lets His kind smile be the roof that opens her up to trust. Jesus, too, was once the God-man hanging on the cross, and again one of His very last earthly thoughts was His heart turning to Abba: "Father, into your hands I commit my spirit" (Luke 23:46). Commit, commit: Open hands into His hands, commit everything your hands hold

---

* "[The] meaning of the plural *heavens*, which is erroneously omitted in most translations, sees God present as far 'out' as imaginable but also right down to the atmosphere around our heads, which is the first of 'the heavens.' The omission of the plural robs the wording in the model prayer of the sense Jesus intended. That sense is, 'Our Father always near us.'" Dallas Willard, *The Divine Conspiracy: Rediscovering Our Hidden Life in God* (San Francisco: HarperSanFrancisco, 1997), 257.

into His because no One is committed to you like He is, and this is the way to wed peace. I roll over onto my worn side of the bed. "In peace I will lie down and sleep, / for you alone, Lord, / make me dwell in safety" (Psalm 4:8). Might as well roll all the things to Abba's feet because God the Son stretched out His arms on that cross in no small part to make His own Abba, our Abba (John 20:17) so that all our prayers now are through God the Son, who binds us in a covenant of grace to the heart of God the Father. None of this is just theology—this is reality; this is what's in the lungs in the WayFarer in Christ. Genuine prayer is having a genuine conversation with our Father; pull up a chair, lay your head, your heart, in His big, ole faithful hands. Prayer isn't giving God information to act upon but God giving us intimacy to rest in. What undergirds every single prayer is the reality that we are held by our Father.

Abba? Father? Just me again, pounding hard on Papa's chest, so open Your ears, let me in the back door of Your heart because You know about here and the near and dear and impossible things. And if there's no way, is there any way You can slip me a Word, drop me a text, chapter and verse, so I can just know now and get the waiting out of the way, sooner than later? Because, look, I have only one life to live, only so much time to write a sturdy story that will stand and walk sure into eternity, so whichever way this is going to go, can You just let me know? God, You tell me, how can the emptiness of waiting feel like such heaviness? You tell me, how long . . . how long? God. Because the longer You or Darryl take Your sweet time and wait, her little heart gets sicker, and You've got to know it; she's the one who can't wait. I'm just telling You how I see it—and, yeah, I realize, You have a heaven's-eye view—so I'm not ever here to forecast Your answers to prayers but to cast all my cares on You. So—here You go.

I'm fool enough to believe: The best place to let your broken heart spill is always at the feet of Abba Father. I can hear a sled of snow give way and slide off the edge of the house roof. I pull the covers up over my shoulder. The eave keeps drip . . . drip . . . dripping.

Waiting for the right time can feel like everything is going wrong. The lookouts and the lovers will both testify: The sacrament of waiting can feel the hardest of all.

And yet—in all this waiting, this, too, is what comes: Waiting is a letting go to let something grow. The waiting need not destroy the soul but *grow* the soul. Waiting is a kind of expecting—expecting to have the capacity for hope and pain and love and life to expand. Farmers

> Prayer isn't giving God information to act upon but God giving us intimacy to rest in.

know what the mothers do: Waiting isn't loss; it's enlarging. The longer the heart waits, the larger the heart expands to hold the largeness of a different way of life.

Waiting does not diminish us, any more than waiting diminishes a pregnant mother. We are enlarged in the waiting. We, of course, don't see what is enlarging us. But the longer we wait, the larger we become, and the more joyful our expectancy.

Meanwhile, the moment we get tired in the waiting,

God's Spirit is right alongside helping us along. If we don't know how or what to pray, it doesn't matter. He does our praying in and for us, making prayer out of our wordless sighs, our aching groans. (Romans 8:24–26 MSG)

Nursed by the tender Spirit, that always attentive medic, tending and groaning with the aching waiting, I lie awake on a bed of His soothing comfort and preach truth back to my anxiousness:

NOTHING IS LOST IN THE WAITING PROCESS BECAUSE ALL WAITING IS A GROWTH PROCESS. WAITING IS GESTATING A GREATER GRACE.

Maybe life has no waiting rooms—life only has labor and delivery rooms. All our waiting rooms are actually birthing rooms, and what feels like the contraction of our plans can be the birthing of greater purposes. Waiting is the sacrament of the tender surrender, and this is the art of a soul growing large. Every waiting moment is heavy with the weight of glory, and this waiting midwifes a fuller life. Lying there on my back, staring at the ceiling in the dark, I can feel this expansion within. They may say waiting is the drumming of impatient fingers, the unbearably slow watching of the face of the clock, the long sitting in front of indifferent calendars and hoping so wide your heart cracks. But the brave and battle-weary will flat-out tell you, if you're waiting for a dream to stir, or a turn at any hospital bed, or for the word you need to finally turn onto the road you've been forever dreaming of going down, you know waiting isn't an uninvolved twiddling of thumbs because you have felt it: Waiting is a herculean widening of everything within you into a canyon—that can fill with a rising ocean of hope. Hope is never passive or stagnant, but always rising. Like the poet said, hope "is a fighter and a screamer,"[2] a fierce buoyancy, the life preserver that wars the currents and the waves to haul you up on shore.

> Waiting isn't loss; it's enlarging. The longer the heart waits, the larger the heart expands to hold the largeness of a different way of life.

"Hey?" I turn to him in the dark. "Don't ever doubt, okay? Your kids couldn't have dreamed of a better dad." I find his hand. "You'd be a dream dad for her too."

His large, leathery fingers lace mine and hope preservers can hold through the dark.

"Hey?" He murmurs it softly. "Don't ever doubt, okay? He is a good and kind Abba Father—and He is for you too."

Your kingdom come, Your kind will be done.

DODGING DOUBT

Before my eyes even open come morning, she's already there in my mind, Baby Shalom, big brown eyes looking for someone looking for her. Was she held and rocked today on the other side of the world, did she cry alone, is her heart still beating strong, how blue are her pursed little lips, how much oxygen can fill those lungs of hers, and did someone brush her forehead today with a kiss? Will she ever know how desperately I wish I could find her first mama and work in any way possible toward the preservation of her family and that to honor her and her first mama, somehow, expresses my searing grief over our part in horrifically broken systems, in a traumatically broken world, that as a family, we've provided for four heart surgeries, for four Chinese children, to preserve four Chinese families as we sorely wish we could have done for her and her mama. Why does love sometimes feel so much like ache, if that in and of itself doesn't prove that the meaning of love is the suffering of sacrifice?

Waiting is never passive—waiting is passion: Loving long enough to suffer.

I lean over to the chair beside my bed and grope around for my smudged glasses on a stack of books.

"You're beautiful, you know that?" He interrupts my internal hail of questions and conflicted grief. He's sitting on his side of the bed, turned, pulling on his socks, watching me run fingers through my mess of wild bedhead.

"Uh-huh." It's too early and I haven't had coffee, and he just wants the surrender of a smile and I half acquiesce.

"Yeah." He grins. "You know how I love when your hair's wild and crazy like that?"

"Uh-huh," I'm pulling up my side of the cream quilt, nodding toward his side.

He tucks in the sheets, and I feel like we're skirting around the edges of the dozing elephant in the room that sprawls between us.

"So—" He straightens the white pillowcases on his side of the bed. "What does today look like for you?"

"Well . . ." I'm trying to find my other running shoe under my side of the bed. "It mainly looks like being haunted by a baby I can't get out my head, begging God to finally speak loud and clear about what to do in a busted world with broken systems and medically fragile babies.

"It looks like me only looking like I'm surrendered to God and accepting His ways while I dodge doubt-grenades hissing by with the lie that God is clearly inept at being God where babies and families and life hurts like this, and any Tom, Dick, or Harry could write the story infinitely better than the Word Himself, thank you very much"—not one word of which I say in the least because sometimes wisdom is the finest filter.

What I say instead is just as true: "Today looks like . . ." I struggle to find the right words. "I think today just looks like one step in front of the other, walking forward—and waiting still, waiting to hear God still?" There. That still feels honest.

Since I was a little girl standing in a shaft of sunlight under a stand of spruce trees back in the farm woods, I have believed this: "The great and universal end of God's creating the world was to communicate himself. God is a communicative being,"[3] wrote the tried-and-true theologian Jonathan Edwards. God's deepest desire is also ours: to be known. *Yada, yada, yada.* Because God wants to be known by us, He communicates with us, and He communicates through creation around us, through our conscience in us, through Christ with us even now. All the world's a seashell, and if you lift it up and really listen, you can hear the ocean of God.

Darryl's reading my eyes like he knows they translate the soul. Can he read the language of my wrestling, my waiting, my craned listening?

"You know, I know you too." He steps closer, smiling slowly. "Sometimes I can hear all the things you aren't saying." He gently kisses my forehead, like I'm a shell he's pressed up against and he can hear my rushing waves. "I'm waiting to hear a word from Him too."

I close my eyes, drop my head upon his chest. "Waiting in prayer is a disciplined refusal to act before God acts" is what a faithful preacher man used to say.[4]

I tell myself this, though every fiber in my being is worn with this waiting and hungry to taste and see that my own way is good. I tell myself that *life is letting*. Letting go of my plan, my dream, my map, my vision.

Abba Father, Your kingdom . . . Your will, Your way.

THE LOADED QUESTION

The dog thumps his tail at the back door like he's a drummer boy marching the sun up the dawning sky, first daylight streaming in shy through the windows and across the old pine floor planks. The house is still, kids still sleeping. Darryl puts the kettle on, the water slowly heating then breaking into a rumbling boil, like it's applauding the coming sun. Listen, listen, press closer, hear it, even now: All of creation communicates the closeness of God.

I reach for a match there at my bench by the window, light the candlewick into its diminutive, dancing flame, open a worn copy of the Word, pen in hand, and I find it scrawled across a note stuck in my Bible:

If you want to hear His will, the ways God will always communicate are through
1. Communion
2. Circumstances

3. Counsel

4. Conviction

Because God doesn't prop floppy sandwich-board signs up outside your window (*marry the guy!*) or have the archangel Michael waving a placard out on your front porch (*take the job!*)—not customarily, anyway, though He is God and there was a pillar of cloud on fire, and the stone-words carved with a finger, and a whole host of prophets and honestly, after how it went with Balaam's donkey, there is arguably precedent set that He can use any old ass to speak His will and His love.

Donkeys and asses notwithstanding, this has been the circuitous process, this is the circuitous process, this will always be the circuitous process: *Communion* with God is the landline for divine *communication* with God. Firstly, lastly, always, literally: God speaks in Son. The Father's mother tongue is always the Son. And whatever He communicates, it is never different from how "he has spoken to us by his Son" (Hebrews 1:2).

And it comes, communion through sitting with His Word open, pen still in hand, ready to take dictation, communion in flat-out awkward and honest prayer while staring at the ceiling at midnight, communion with His Spirit while pulling up the bedsheets and straightening the pillows and putting one foot in front of the other, communion though fasting from the world's noise and comforts and distraction to hold fast to Him. These are no small things, but real seashell pressings, to hear the coming tide of God. Listen, listen, He comes in:

> I am the LORD your God
>> who takes hold of your right hand

> and says to you, Do not fear;
>> I will help you. (Isaiah 41:13)

The LORD himself goes before you and will be with you; he will never leave you nor forsake you. Do not be afraid; do not be discouraged. (Deuteronomy 31:8)

Let nothing get in the way of your communion with God, if you want to hear God communicate the way He loves you. Hearing comes from drawing nearer. Hold the seashell close.

I've thought of it only a thousand times: That Sunday, when the kids were little, and we were standing just outside our little country Bible chapel, after a Sunday morning service. Cornfields rolled out to the south of the chapel. Maple woods stood quiet just behind the chapel to the west, behind the gravel yard where all the farmers parked their pickups. And on the far side of the chapel, just to the north, Leary's Pond.

Our Hope, she was just three, and every Sunday after the sermon, when we all streamed out of the chapel, she was wide-eyed scared of that pond, scared to go play on the side lawn with the other kids. The girl wanted a fence and rules and the way she should go made clear. The kid got it—pylons and flags and fences and formulas are far easier: This is the best life and that is the less life, this is the way and that is the wrong way.

But Darryl, he scooped up his little girl and said it in his gently spoken way.

"Look, I'll keep a close eye out for you. But you listen for me, okay?" He had held Hope's chin close in his field-worn hands, so he could hold her eyes. "If you can hear my voice when I'm talking, you are safe. You are where you're meant to be. But when you can't hear my voice anymore? You're not where you are meant to be—so then come back to me."

You have to stay close enough to the Word to hear your Father's voice.

Is this the way? All the searching world reverberates, echoes.

> Let me hear in the morning of your steadfast
> > [*hesed*-attachment] love,
> > for in you I trust.
> Make me know the way I should go,
> > for to you I lift up my soul. (Psalm 143:8 ESV)

Lift your soul up to Him, listen, listen.

And yet there's this resonance that rushes through the arteries of my own heart: We want clarity and God wants communion. We want a road map and God wants a relationship. We want answers and God wants our hand. God didn't give Abraham a map; He gave Abraham a relationship. Why would God give a map when He can give Himself? We need the person of God more than we need the plan for our lives. The heart of faith is the ear. And God's will is something we will have to keep listening for, waiting for, turning for.

"The LORD says, 'I will guide you along the best pathway for your life. / I will advise you and watch

> We want clarity and God wants communion. We want a road map and God wants a relationship. We want answers and God wants our hand.

over you'" (Psalm 32:8 NLT). The closer you are to God, the closer you are to seeing more than the way through, the closer you are to seeing the way He is for you. "Return to your rest, my soul, / for the LORD has been good to you" (Psalm 116:7). Tilt the seashell, the head, shift on the bathroom floor, turn the eyes, the heart, there's still a holy way to hear and see.

I let my fingers touch the page, underline and trace the open vein of love on the page. The only way we know we're going the right way is if our hearts, our thoughts, our minds, our ways are aligned with the mind of Christ and the Word of God, not the god of our own minds and making. My pen slowly underlines:

> Because he holds fast to me in love, I will
>   deliver him;
>   I will protect him, because he knows
>   my name.
> When he calls to me, I will answer him;
>   I will be with him in trouble;
>   I will rescue him and honor him.
> With long life I will satisfy him
>   and show him my salvation.
>   (Psalm 91:14– 16 ESV)

This is the way God speaks: God makes vows. Even when the claw of death stalks and the chemo scorches, when our story sickens and we kneel on the bathroom floor, heaving with a wretched story we can hardly swallow, God weds Himself to the WayFarers and God commits: I will answer, I will deliver, I will rescue, I will satisfy, I will be with you—in ways you didn't dream, with answers you never prayed for. Whatever I know about God's will, I know He is the God who covenants Himself to me with His "I wills" that always will come in ways beyond imagining. And if God vows to protect me and keep me, in sickness and in suffering, save me and hold me, so we are not even parted by death, isn't His way enough?

I sit with pen and God's "I wills" ringing in my ears like He's slipped a covenantal ring on my hand and His wills make me soul-safe. This is why I read the Word: I don't read the Word to merely know how to obey God's will for me—I read the Word to know God and how He's for me. Am I close enough to hear my Abba Father's voice?

He is more than good; He is love, He is kind, He is *hesed*-lovingkindness, and He wrote His will and all His "I wills" down on pages, so I lay my cochlea against the Word and the world, and that's all you can hear, on every holy page, in every hard place, these same four lines, like a wave of love always coming for us, like God's oceanic love song:

> *Never fear.*
> *Always with you.*
> *Always love you.*
> *Turn, turn, and I'll always carry you.*

Darryl drinks his coffee at the window. The island of snow out by the cedar has nearly melted away, gone. His Bible's open on his desk, his every page pulsing with that passionate beat:

> *Never fear.*
> *Always with you.*

Always love you.
Turn, turn, and I'll always carry you.

He and I, we're on the same page. If you want to read His Word, you can hear as much of God as you want.

"She could die, Ann."

Did—did I hear that right? I put my pen down. Is that the note that's been unfolding in his heart, that he now hands me to read?

"You mean—because of her heart? Yeah—you're right, she could . . . she could die. I mean, she is going to die if she doesn't find a home and heart surgery. And even then—yes, she could die. But there's exactly zero percent chance that any of us get out of here alive. We're all guaranteed that: *to die.*"

He turns from the window, sets his mug down by his Bible, like he's punctuating what he's about to say next.

"You know—how your sister's death destroyed your parents' marriage?" His eyes find mine, but it's like they aren't satisfied, like his gaze is trying to find a way deeper in.

"Are you ready for the way this could all really go?"

Is he asking me, or is he telling me that he's—actually scared about us?

"You're asking if I am ready?" I'm buying time because I know he's dead right. God takes us into Gethsemanes, literally, the place of the oil press, where the weight of the world presses down on us and our crushed soul becomes an oil that anoints the feet of Jesus with a love that says even if He doesn't give our dreams, even if not, being with Him is enough. Just because God vows His "I wills" doesn't mean that I will love the way things will go.

If she dies—if any of us dies—will I doubt that a good God can exist? Unless you commit ahead of time to what you will believe about God, circumstances will dictate what you should believe about God's heart. I believe this: As for me and my house, as the waves come, we will unwaveringly trust the Lord. And I believe I may claw-howl to the heavens, but God knows that wrestling with some doubts is what vaccinates the soul to a pandemic of pain.

I mean, the question that really has to be decided once and for all, no matter the way: Can I still believe in a good God when our way may hold pain and suffering? Can I believe that the suffering itself holds evidence that God Himself is actually with us?

I decide to believe in the strange truth of it: You can say there is suffering only if you believe there is a God.[5] If there is no God, there can't be suffering, only life and the harsh reality of survival of the fittest. To believe there is suffering implies there is injustice. But if you believe there is no God, there can't be any injustice; there can only be pain and the natural outcome of natural selection. But if you believe there truly is unjust suffering, if you believe that babies shouldn't die and diagnoses shouldn't devour dreams and violence shouldn't violate hopes, your very conscience is appealing to a higher moral law. How else do you explain the indignation over the wrongness of suffering, except that the indignation itself seems to explain that you *know* there is *rightly* supposed to be more?

Only after my sister was killed, after my parents' marriage imploded and blew away, papery ash in the wind, after we stood over freshly dug graves of babies we'd held and loved, did I let the mystery of God touch me, hold me, comfort me, song in the wind. If there is a Maker who exists as a far greater being, then it's actually right and fully expected that His ways are far beyond understanding. The meaning of God means exactly that: He is beyond the ways of this world.

If your prayers always happened, then you would happen to be God. If God thought it best to hand out the answer key to all the haunting questions, He would. He swears on the Bible He would. But, instead, He slips His hand through ours because the key to all the questions is being with Him, the answers found in laying our head close enough to hear the thrumming loving-kindness of His heart. He is God, and I am not. He is the Word; let Him write whatever story He deems best and right.

Theologian C. S. Lewis pondered the power behind the cosmos, positing:

> If there was a controlling power outside the universe, it could not show itself to us as one of the facts inside the universe—no more than the architect of a house could actually be a wall or staircase or fireplace in that house. The only way in which we could expect it to show itself would be inside ourselves as an influence or a command.[6]

This is the soul stir that we all know, the murmur of the Maker Himself inside of us saying this world isn't what it was supposed to be, that there is suffering exactly because of violations of His higher moral law.

And yet what exactly is Abba Father saying when you blink and your beloved dies, what word from God do you expect to hear when a doctor says sorry, or a door clicks closed for the last time, or when the absence of that one voice is so loud it deafens hope? How is the triune God speaking His will when life sucker-punches you straight in the gut and you have to keep willing yourself just to breathe? Do I know the way to interpret the language of God when His ways don't unfold as I expect?

> "Can you get Venus to look your way . . .
> Do you know the first thing about the sky's
> constellations? . . ."

> "Can you take charge of the lightning bolts
> and have them report to you for orders?"

> "Are you going to haul me, the Mighty One,
> into court and press charges?"

> "Do you presume to tell me what I'm doing
> wrong?" (Job 38:32–35; 40:2, 8 MSG)

If I cannot make a way for stars to spin across velvet night skies, or make a way for wind to whisper through willows under full moons, how can I fully understand the mysterious ways of God? Why does God have to answer to me, and why do I have to know the answers unless I make myself a kind of god? "We never really know enough until we recognize that God alone knows it all" (1 Corinthians 8:3 MSG).

Through every crashing wave, God is still writing an oceanic love story.

I think that's my answer to Darryl, that right there. We don't need answers from God like we need attachment *with God*. And when the waves crash, again and again, we will fall into God, again and again. I gently set my Bible down on the bench there

131

at the windowsill. I've read God's Word and looked God right in the eye, and now I stand to look Darryl in the eye, steadied by what I've seen.

"Are you worried about how we will get through if we lose her?" I touch his arm. "Or if we lose us? Or both?"

"No . . . not worried." His eyes are still waters. "Just—I want you to be sure about what your expectations are—about the way this could go." He's right: There is no way that doesn't hold trauma, and there may be the disorientation of post-traumatic stress disorder, and still there can be the post-traumatic growth pathway.[7] "In some way, suffering ceases to be suffering at the moment it finds a meaning."[8]

Maybe my expectation is that only math gives us answers, but life gives mystery, and embracing the mysteries, letting them lead us to deepen our relationships, heighten our gratitude, strengthen our God-attachment, and grow our soul resilience, this is the way we find meaning and keep standing. All is meant to grow the soul toward the goal of God. The waves may pound: But how would understanding the reason for suffering matter more than knowing God Himself stands with us in it? How would it help to have a God who's small enough for us to understand standing with us, when only a God standing *with us* who's great enough to be *beyond* all understanding can help us at all?

If we had a God small enough to understand, how could He be a great enough God to stand with us against all that we face? I don't understand why the waves crash, but I know I'm buoyed by His oceanic love.

This is all I expect, a post-traumatic growth pathway, right through waves because this I've experienced: Great suffering is bearable when you know a great God bears you in His great arms.

"I—don't expect that this will be easy. But I know God's been good at being God for a long time, through hard times, so you can't go wrong trusting Him *all the time*."

Can I live by my own words? Ultimately the triune God of Christianity doesn't scratch down a note with solutions to the problem of suffering for us but lifts our chin and points to the cross, the ultimate signpost, and says, *There is no way so dark—not even this—that I won't restory and restore into a resurrecting way.*

Life is wild waves, and the rising will always come again. I drop my head down on Darryl's chest. And it comes again, my steadying prayer:

> *We don't know what the road holds, but Jesus is our road. Our pathway of growth is Him. He is the way through waves. He will hold. His hesed carries. The Gethsemanes will press and grow us into more.*
>
> *Into Your hands, we commit our hopes.* Your will be done.

SIGNS AND WONDERS

When Darryl goes out to check the mail midmorning, I expect him to bring in a stack of bills, glossy flyers from Home Hardware, coupons from Zehrs Grocery Store, maybe a faithful card from Mrs. Shupe, but not a word from God Almighty up on High.

So I don't think anything of it when he pulls it out from between the electricity bill and a 50-percent-off sale on seedless grapes, today through Thursday only, and watch him read the outside of what seems like some random envelope. It's only when

I see something—*recognition?*—flicker across his face that I put down the cream I'm pouring into coffee.

"Who's that one from?" I wait over a cup steaming with this tendril of hope.

"The Lord." He drops the envelope down on the counter.

"Oh, really?" Apparently God has our home address?

I don't read the postmark because it's what's written in bold text along the bottom of the envelope that's grabbing our faces with both hands and pulling us close: "Religion that is pure and undefiled before God the Father is this: to visit orphans and widows in their affliction" (James 1:27 ESV).

Oh, really. No need to open the envelope. What matters is reading Darryl's face.

"God always speaks. He is the Word, not the silent treatment."

The man who's been praying about adoption picks up the envelope to read the Word right there again: "Visit the orphans in their affliction."

I close my eyes, warm cup of coffee in hand. The Word made the world, and He has not fallen mute. The world may pound God's door, demanding answers, and God answers the door by being the Door, and He speaks in Son, and "God is not silent."[9] Sunlight ignites the bottom spruce boughs outside the window. God signs His inconspicuous signature everywhere; everything is a signpost that points to His love.

"Apparently, sometimes God speaks through His Word in the pages of Scripture, and sometimes He sends His Word in the mail on the outside of envelopes." Darryl smiles.

"Yeah. Circumstances." My smile meets his.

God speaks the Way (1) through *communion*, (2) through *circumstances*, (3) through *counsel*, (4) through *conviction*. And not one of the ways He communicates can ever contradict what His Holy Word's already communicated.

"Did—did I tell you what God already spoke this morning?" Darryl's reaching for his Bible lying open on his desk, atop a sprawl of bills and receipts and unopened mail.

I wait for him to find the place on the page, his index finger scrolling like a cursor looking for the epiphany.

"There it is—what I read early first thing."

Blue smudged ink underlines words throughout the worn and curled pages. I love him and the unassuming way of life he's making: The wise don't read Scripture to get a word from God but to know the God of the Word. *Yada, yada, yada.* He knows: The point's not to read Scripture to grow into someone better but to grow deeper into God, not to be good but to be with goodness Himself. You don't read Scripture out of rote duty but because of God's irresistible beauty, not to get God to love you but to fall in love with God.

"It's not like what I read are new words or anything, but just that I heard them differently." He runs his finger along the wobbly, inky line:

> He began to be deeply distressed and troubled. "My soul is overwhelmed with sorrow to the point of death," he said to them . . . Going a little farther, he fell to the ground and prayed . . . "*Abba*, Father," he said, "everything is possible for you. Take this cup from me. Yet not what I will, but what you will." (Mark 14:33–36)

Darryl stops. Looks up at me. He's just read it, how the God-man is distressed, troubled, overwhelmed, to the point of death—the very definition of trauma.[10] Gethsemane, literally, that place of the oil press, presses Him down, great drops of blood falling from His brow, but He doesn't take the way out of Gethsemane but takes the cup and drinks it down, down, goes down under the waves, and this Gethsemane pressing down forges the way that yields to the way of God: *not my way be done, but Your way.*

"Not what I will—but what you will." His voice is steady, sure.

"What do you mean, *not what I will—but what you will?*" I'm trying to keep my voice from sounding . . . concerned. "You—don't want to adopt?"

"I didn't say that for one minute—I'm saying that God speaks His will, and His will is always that we turn and say, 'Not my way . . . but His way.'" His hand's resting on the page, like he's at rest, yielded and pressed.

"But what I'm hearing is . . ." I whisper it gently, slowly . . .

Before the words are out of my mouth, his phone chimes. His eyes are still resting in mine as he reaches for his phone in his back pocket. He's saying "hello," but I'm ringing with chimes of my own . . . chimes like church bells. *Abba Father, not my will, but Your will be done, on earth as it is in heaven.* God in heaven speaks on earth through communion, through circumstances, through counsel.

When you say, "Not my way, but Your way be done," you're saying, "Not my own way, but I'm one with *His* way." You're detaching from love of self—because your love is attached to Love Himself.

Watching Darryl on the phone with the seed guy, it's like he's growing into someone different right in front of me. Growing into love. That . . . that is what the greatest love says: "I have my will, and God has His will, and when those two don't meet, I let go of mine to take up God's." This is a movement of the divine exchange: He takes my brokenness and gives me His wholeness— and I give up my way and take up His.

We are bound in this *hesed*-lovingkindness of salvation, and the sacred vow is more than an exchange of my sinfulness for His righteousness. It is an exchange of *my will and way for His*. "I will . . . I will . . . Not my will, but Your will." It's the covenantal, *hesed*-love faithfulness of Christ alone that saves us—and we respond to His *hesed*-saving faithfulness, by covenanting *our will* to be faithful to *His will alone*. It is by grace that you've been saved by Christ's *hesed*-faithful fidelity; and the saved respond with a faithful fidelity of their way to Christ's way alone.[11]

Darryl's still talking on the phone, but he turns at the window to look at me, and I'm nodding, seeing him, seeing the greatness of one life that yields to Love Himself, and my chin's quaking with the reality of it: The greatest act of faith is to pledge allegiance to God's way and surrender your own. The only way to fulfill God's will is to fully let go of your own will. *Until there's a release and a turning from your way, there is no going God's way.*

Press the ear to the seashell, and hear it: If the way you're walking doesn't have crosses, afflictions, persecutions, and self-denial, you're not on Christ's way. His ways are waves, and ours the shore, always resisting. Our way is self-formed, God's way is cruciform; our way is wide and self-comforting, His way is narrow and

> The greatest act of faith is to pledge allegiance to God's way and surrender your own. The only way to fulfill God's will is to fully let go of your own will.

self-denying; and our way rarely crosses His, as His way always means a carrying of a cross. Let the shore give way to the kiss of waves and their caressing, sculpting ways.

I can tell he's trying to get off the phone. I step closer, lay my hand on his and wait, knowing. When you surrender and vow fidelity to Jesus as the way, the truth, the life, you take Him to be your way, your truth, your life, and you are one: one mutual heart, one mutual mind, one mutual will, one mutual way—you in Him, and Him in you.

When Darryl clicks off the call, he turns to me.

He's still.

Whatever the questions, attachment is the answer, all the Word and world singing the refrain:

> *Never fear.*
> *Always with you.*
> *Always love you.*
> *Turn, turn, and I'll always carry you.*

I wait.

He breaks into this smile. That breaks me into this kind of smile that heals and another wave breaks.

"Yes."

"Yes?"

"*Yes.*"

A fresh wind blows the red glove, palm up, across the lawn.

chapter seven

RED SEA ROAD

Christianity is more than a theory about the universe, more than teachings written down on paper; it is a path along which we journey—in the deepest and richest sense, the way of life.

—KALLISTOS WARE

On our way to that first appointment with our social worker, our next step in the adoption journey, Darryl slowly turns left onto Monkton Line. Out front of the Three Sisters Antique Shop on the corner is this trio of vintage wooden spindle beds on the sidewalk, all with no mattresses, like the three sisters had up and absconded in a blast of wind from the west, tattered quilts and all, their own flight out in the middle of the night.

Can I be the fourth sister who flies away through blue skies? Because I'd had enough heart-halting parenting moments with our tribe of a half dozen over the last month that I'm now seriously second-guessing the wisdom of being anybody's competent mama. All my initial eagerness has turned more than a bit skittish . . . flightish.

"Look . . ." I turn to Darryl sitting there in his threadbare Wranglers behind the worn steering wheel of his white Ford pickup truck, his grease-etched hands gently cupping the wheel's surrendered curve. I can hear the wide-open road beneath us, wheels whistling with the defiant promise of possibility, always possibility.

"There's just absolutely no way right now we can think about adopting because, if you haven't noticed, we are already facing our own kind of impossibles, and I'm not winning in any way, anywhere." Just the night before I'd stumbled onto how one of our brave kids was dangerously careening off the rails, and the train wreckage of the crash was still smoking, stinging the eyes, the twisted ache of everything making me feel more than a tad nauseated.

If I grabbed Grandma's old double wedding ring quilt, threw it around my shoulders, waited for a strong nor'western blast, maybe I could be caught up to the Three Sisters?

"I mean, we've got a mess of crisis and grief and loss and kids and farm and fields and this whole shebang of a life, and— frankly? We are in way over our heads."

Just past Three Sisters, I turn and am flat-out honest with him: "I just think there's no way that I'm in any place to find the way right now to be a mama to one little girl, right across an ocean, with an actual broken heart . . ." It seems—absolutely impossible, and I want to cry and laugh, and maybe the way you don't turn away from God is to be brutally frank with Him that nothing's turning out as dreamed.

In Jesus' Gethsemane moment, He marks the way to be pressed into more: In prayer, He first marks out His feelings, then marks out His wants, then is marked by surrendered trust.* Gethsemane prayers mark the way to resurrection.

> *God. Why is this hard, and why in the world do You speak one way with signs and wonders, then throw up what reads like No Way signs everywhere I turn? Maybe You care more about the turn toward You, so we care less about the way we want and more about wanting You.*

Maybe I am thinking more about how anything could make a highway through this sudden life-tsunami and a way around the curvature of the planet to China, and that slight curve of one little girl's waiting, reaching hand, more than I am thinking about the One who has my name carved right into the palm of His hands and walks on waves. I reach for my husband's hand, like the only way forward is to find a hand to hold on to.

Mine. Hold on to My hand, the only One who has ever loved you to death and back the realest and forever life.

The Farmer squeezes mine, like he's trying to loan me courage to believe that there is a way through a Mariana Trench of impossible—if you keep your eye on the One who makes even

---

* John Mark Comer noted similar thoughts in his sermon, "Gospel of Matthew: Gethsemane Prayer," Bridgetown Church, May 30, 2021, https://bridgetown.church /teaching/gospel-of-matthew/gethsemane-prayer-2/.

waves into highways. But I can't help myself from saying it again, this time asking it as a question instead of stating it like a fact:

"Honestly—how do we find a way—when there really seems like there is no way?"

The words aren't even out of my mouth, when the phone beside me on the truck seat rings, like God Himself is calling to say in baritone, *Excuse Me?* God speaks in the mundane and miracle, the holy message, and in ways easily missed by the hustling.

THE MESSAGE

I just let the call go to messages, as one does when it could be God. When I hold up the phone recording there on my message app, what I hear is: "Hey there, you."

Not God, not today, though God speaks in Son and glory stars and a thousand accents and dialects of grace. Is it Ellie— Ellie Holcomb? Haven't heard from Ellie in maybe the better part of six months, a year?

"Hey!" She's all this light. "I just wanted to reach out to say—I read some words last week that really struck, words that you wrote, Ann."

Words I wrote?

Turns out I had written an article with this sentence: "Hope makes a Red Sea Road where there is no way."*

---

* From "How to Keep Hoping for Things That Seem Impossible," Ann Voskamp (blog), May 28, 2014, annvoskamp.com.

My head whips toward the Farmer. Umm . . . me, the lady here with chronic soul amnesia, wrote that—*last week*?

I hold the phone tight against my ear so I don't miss what comes next. And Ellie tells me that she's turned that line into a brand-new song. I can hear Ellie start plucking on her guitar.

"So we took that line of yours, Ann, and we wrote it into a song right now—and you're the first person that we wanted to sing it to."

I choke it to Darryl: "She's—going to sing to us a brand-new song—right now?"

And there is Ellie's gravelly voice, right there with Christa's and Nicole's, and the plucked strings of the guitar, and the guitar bears witness: In the right hands, every emptiness can sing. And Ellie's voice aches with a song she calls "Red Sea Road":

> *How, can we trust*
> *When You say You will deliver us from*
> *All, of this pain, that threatens to take over us*
> *Well, this desert's dry*
> *But the ocean may consume*
> *And we're scared, to follow You.*
>
> *When we can't see the way*
> *He will part the waves*
> *And we'll never walk alone*
> *Down a red sea road.*

What in the actual world? It's like the Shekinah glory has come down. How had I just finished saying out loud that there is absolutely no way, just as my phone beside me rings and now there's a woman singing live to me about how there *is a way* in this newly birthed song, just minutes old, with words I had forgotten I even wrote?

I turn to my husband, slack-jawed and God-awed:

"I guess"—I blink it back as the highway blurs—"sometimes God does call you in real time, and He may even sound like the voice of a friend—but don't miss that it's His voice." There's a rustle, Ellie murmurs her love to us, whispers bye in that glorious raspy voice of hers—and then *click*.

BEYOND IMAGINATION

"Did a song just fall out of heaven—because that wasn't the radio—" I want to take my shoes off. Dried up bushes of faith can kindle into an inferno of presence.

"What just happened here?"

I think I see a sliver I had never imagined: Jesus knows turns you never heard of, makes roads you wouldn't have dreamed of, makes miracles happen exactly where you never would have imagined. There is a reason He is called the Way. There is more beyond what we can see, feel, imagine, and there is always dry land ahead. There is always a Red Sea Road coming to meet you. In unlikely ways. Waves may heave, but you have to believe: Love always finds His way to you.

That's what had happened: I had had no imagination for the ways of God. In my mind, there had been no island of new possibilities, no dry land of change, no way through to something other than what I'd already known. It's when, as far as we can see, behind us and ahead of us, we only envision endless waves of pain, that despair tempts us to end it, to toss in the towel, to give up. Hopelessness rises when the pain of the past floods all of the future. And when it feels like all hope is lost, that's exactly when it's time to ask: "Where is my hope?" Hope in plans, in expectations, in dreams, in outcomes, in jobs, in bank accounts, in medicine, in people, in timelines, and any of those things can wander

> Jesus knows turns you never heard of, makes roads you wouldn't have dreamed of, makes miracles happen exactly where you never would have imagined. There is a reason He is called the Way.

off, fall through, disappear, taking your hope with them. We're not meant to find hope in anything in this world; we are meant to lose hope in all the things here.

Ask "Where is my hope?" and you can feel the relief of the answer: Hope is never lost—because Hope Himself never loses track of you. God is the One who keeps asking that Edenic query, "*Ayekah?* Where are you?" Hope is always the one constant you can count on because you can count on Jesus constantly with you.

Hineni. Here I am.

I catch my reflection in the rearview mirror, and I'm smiling. The way not to lose hope is not to lose a holy imagination in the ways of God. It's a poverty of imagination that bankrupts hope. Even when you can't imagine how He's working, He's working His way to you, working all things together for good, working out a good story because He is the Word, and He only ultimately writes good stories.

> "Pay attention . . .
> Listen to me, nations.

> Revelation flows from me.
>> My decisions light up the world.
> My deliverance arrives on the run,
>> my salvation right on time.
>> I'll bring justice to the peoples.
> Even faraway islands will look to me
>> and take hope in my saving power."
>> (Isaiah 51:4–5 MSG)

The God who creates *ex nihilo*, something out of nothing, can create exoduses through anything. The God who raises the dead can raise any dead dreams, and while God is not by any means bound to write the plotlines that we imagine, we who are bound to Him can ignite with a holy imagination for the ways He can move by any means. Hope isn't insisting on the way it's imagined but has an imagination that whatever comes our way will be worked out *for our good*. I want God to engrave it with His finger up my bare arms so I don't forget what's just happened here: *It's a poverty of imagination that bankrupts hope.*

Surrender to ways beyond ours. Surrender not knowing everything. Surrender to possibility. Surrender to unknown vistas and all kinds of ways opening up in unimaginable ways. Surrender to miracle. Lift up life's curled rug corners, sweep the dust bunnies out of crannies and shift the teetering stacks; miracles and manna and mercy are waiting for all the willing to see. I wonder if, *What we most often fear is that we won't get the miracle of God with us.* I wonder if, *What we fear most is that we will end up somewhere that God can't get to us, somewhere beyond the grip of God.* But I don't wonder, I know it: Even, especially, in the pitch-black dark, when you can't see your own hand in front of your face, if

you close your eyes and are still long
enough, you can remember it, see
it, memories on your mind's screen,
taste it even, the sweet mercy manna
and goodness and withness of God.*
Wait for this, savor this. The one
miracle you can always count on, like
forty years of manna, is the sustaining withness of God. Without
fail. With God, hope is always justifiable. God will slice an ocean
of waves in half to find a way to be with you.

> With God, hope is always justifiable. God will slice an ocean of waves in half to find a way to be with you.

Where there seems to be no way—is exactly the way to
miracles.

I look over, and Darryl is just smiling, a mile wide, like an
open road.

STILL, STILL, STILL

When we walk through the back door after that first social worker's
appointment, with this daunting stack of adoption forms that
require us to just go ahead and splice a vein and leak our whole
messy life story across the pages, I drop the binder on my desk
and instead turn the pages of my worn book to Exodus. Did I just
imagine this whole Red Sea Road? Or did I just need an *imagination* for a Red Sea Road? I'm desperate to unfold whatever miracle
happened in the pickup. I reach for a chair to pull up while I'm
already reading:

---

* "Open your mouth and taste, open your eyes and see— / how good GOD is. /
Blessed are you who run to him" (Psalm 34:8 MSG).

The Israelites looked up, and there were the Egyptians, marching after them. They were terrified and cried out to the LORD. They said to Moses, "Was it because there were no graves in Egypt that you brought us to the desert to die? What have you have done to us by bringing us out of Egypt?"

Moses answered the people, "Do not be afraid. Stand firm and you will see the deliverance the LORD will bring you today. The Egyptians you see today you will never see again. The LORD will fight for you; you need only to be still." (Exodus 14:10–11, 13–14)

I stop reading. Sit back. I can see a starling sitting at the top of the Manitoba maple off the back step, his wings iridescent in afternoon light. He's still in a crosshatch of branches, still before a gilded field of wheat rolling out to the east.

Your battle is to keep still—while God does the battle. Your battle is to still—and, no matter what, to trust God still.

"I dare say you will think it a very easy thing to stand still, but it is one of the postures which a Christian soldier learns not without years of teaching," said the prince of preachers, Charles Spurgeon. "[Stillness] is one of the most difficult to learn under the Captain of our salvation. The Apostle seems to hint at this difficulty when he says, 'Stand fast and having done all, still stand.'"[1] Stillness may be the most difficult to learn, and to still stand.

I wonder if that starling atop the Manitoba maple can see its reflection in those stilled puddles down the lane in the wake of last night's storm that flattened the wheat, that likely blew the Three Sisters up and away.

When everything stills, you can see your reflection, see into the depths of your own soul, see the contours of things. To fully see a situation, to see the lay of the land, to see the way forward, necessitates stillness. But you actually see more than your own reflection when you look into stilled waters; you see the heavens. Still hearts still see God. When there's no agitation of soul there can be a revelation of God. That's the beginning of all knowing: Be still—and know that He is God. The only way

> When there's no agitation of soul there can be a revelation of God.

to know what you're about, the only way to know the way you're about, is to so intimately know God that you see yourself as God sees you.

Something in me settles.

Stillness is knowness.

If it's true that our deepest desire is to be seen and known, then we are only seen and known as much as we are still. There is no seeing when nothing is stilled. When waters know agitation, no revelation is known. Stirred waters, blurred sight.

I need to grab a pen, sketch this Red Sea Road, write it down:

STILLNESS TO KNOW GOD

I don't think I had noticed that before, that *God* is all the verbs in the story of the way through the sea. In my stillness, *God moves*. Maybe if I'd actually be still and not struggle to be God, I wouldn't struggle to *trust* God. It's only endless trust in God that can end fear. The starling perched still, perfectly still, outside the back window catches light, flashes.

Your strength is your stillness—because your stillness says you're trusting Him still.

Strange paradox—how stillness is the first step of a Red Sea Road.

ATTENTION = DEVOTION

My finger tracks across the page, tracks how the next line of the holy writ reads: "Then the LORD said to Moses, 'Why are you crying out to me?'" (Exodus 14:15).

My heart's pounding loud—it's like the wind's stopped dead in its tracks. Like the starling's eye turned, is watching me, waiting for me. Between the sounds, stillness slips in. I am all ear. And all I can hear is: In the stillness, there can be attentiveness beyond our own questioning *of* God, to the questions *God is asking us*.

Like therapist Curt Thompson asks in *The Soul of Shame*, isn't God asking questions of us all the time?[2]

"Where are you?" God called in the garden, the One always looking for the way to us (Genesis 3:9).

"Who do you say I am?" Jesus questioned Peter (Luke 9:20).

"What do you want?" Jesus asked His disciples (John 1:38).

"Where have you come from and where are you going?" the angel of the Lord asked a fleeing Hagar (Genesis 16:8 ESV).

Maybe if I begin to attend to, to answer, God's questions, I'd be less likely to question God's ways? Maybe asking yourself the questions God asks you starts to give you answers? Maybe if I could locate the answer to God's questions, I'd locate who I was, where I was headed, where my head was in relation to my soul—maybe I wouldn't feel so lost.

I am paying attention.

This is my location.

Life is about location, location, location—and attention, attention, attention.

Is that starling up in the maple attentive to this Spirit wind in stillness? Does it know that its ancestors were brought across the waters from Europe by some guy named Schieffelin who'd hauled sixty European starlings into Central Park and released them to take flight? Something about that rather oddly obsessed Mr. Schieffelin wanting every single bird Shakespeare had ever mentioned in his writings to nest somewhere on this side of the pond. Sometimes a starling, a moment, speaks without words. I sit with the Word in hand, sit with the starling that soundlessly speaks, and the text talks, God guides, and time fills with this Great Dance of the Trinity. I'm stilled before an exodus I can feel beginning within: Still to the Spirit.

Attentiveness to the Word-wind. Do more than listen to your life—listen to your Lord. The sheen of starling's purplish-greenish ruffling wings, and a gust of wind sounds like water rushing near, and it is everywhere, and you can feel it, in the stillness and attentiveness: "The LORD is compassionate and merciful, / slow to get angry and filled with unfailing [*hesed*] love" (Psalm 103:8 NLT). His love like a rising river of kindness, breaching banks, flooding into everything. Attentiveness to what is happening around us is a way of being attentive to God *with* us.

Attentiveness leads to receptiveness. And the more attentive we are to what is happening in our lives, the more receptive we are to God's way, and my attentiveness to God's questions, God's asking, might ground me, reroute me, return me. My pen finds the page again, writes down His words, His questions right there in the Word, like the questions He asks of His people at the exodus:

1. Who do you say that I am? (Mark 8:29)
2. Where are you coming from and where are you going? (Genesis 16:8)
3. What do you want? (Mark 10:36)

Attend to God's questions to tend your own soul. Attending to where you are tends to change the *way* you are.

Hadn't the Israelites proven it on the brink of finding their way through: The way you answer *God's* questions of you is the answer to your quest to know the way.

Was the way through an actual way of life, a way of *thinking*, emerging right there at the exodus as my own Red Sea Road?

STILLNESS TO KNOW GOD

ATTENTIVENESS TO HEAR GOD

THE SIGN OF THE CROSS

I turn back to the Word—turn, always the turn—and read what God said to Moses: "Raise your staff and stretch out your hand over the sea to divide the water so that the Israelites can go through the sea on dry ground" (Exodus 14:16). I read the lines again—and see it there on my wrist, a cross inked in black. If Moses was a type of Christ—if Jesus is the new and better Moses—then didn't both of their exoduses down Red Sea Roads begin with hands raised, arms stretched out, in cruciform surrender to the will and way of God?

We only cross through our waters when we surrender to living like the cross.

Your seas split when you see the way to be cruciform like
      Christ.
True life transformation happens wherever a life chooses
      cruciformation.

If "the life of Jesus is an exodus, hidden in plain sight"[3]—
then maybe the only way to my exodus is to *live* the life of Christ
in plain sight—cruciform in all things.

"Indeed it is the exodus that provided the primary model of
God's idea of redemption . . . one of the keys to understanding
the meaning of the cross of Christ."[4] If the exodus is not only the
primary model of God's idea of redemption but is one of the keys to
the very meaning of the cross, why wouldn't the exodus become the
primary model of my life, the key to my exodus found in forming
everything cruciform? *"Exodus-shaped redemption demands exodus-
shaped mission."*[5] A cross-shaped life is an exodus-shaped life: always
a way through. By growing a new way, thinking a new way, being
a new way, by embracing a cruciform way of life.

Could I practically figure out what it means to live a cross-
shaped life to know an exodus-shaped way through my life?

I scratch it down on the next line on the page:

STILLNESS TO KNOW GOD

ATTENTIVENESS TO HEAR GOD

CRUCIFORMITY TO SURRENDER TO GOD

I stand up, step to the window, step into these streams of
light. What exactly is happening here? True, in a thousand different ways, I'm standing in front of my own impossible Red Seas
everywhere I turn—seeing no clear way from where I am as a

limping mother to where I want to be for my kids for whom I'd cut out part of my heart and give to them if it would make even one breath of theirs any easier, and for one little girl on the other side of the world with a failing heart. Seeing no earthly way to change wrongs I've splattered throughout my story, no way to turn around the coming diagnoses that would fly off with what we hoped would be our future, no non-horrifying way through the violent valley of death that I'd no idea would one day come, the shadow of death proving to have arms and the evil will to lock you in a death-choke of its own. But where is my holy imagination for the otherworldly ways of God? What if: The way through opens up where we kneel down into another way of being?

THE REVELATORY DARK

That starling up there at the end of the tree limb looks like it has one eye on me, waiting, anticipating. That starling, they say, is now one of millions of starlings in North America, descended and ascending from the mere sixty that were brought across the ocean and released in Central Park by that odd Eugene Schieffelin. Who in the world would have ever imagined that?

I pick up the text again and read:

> Then the angel of God who was going before the host of Israel moved and went behind them, and the pillar of cloud moved from before them and stood behind them, coming between the host of Egypt and the host of Israel. And there was the cloud and the darkness. And it lit up the night without one coming near the other all night. (Exodus 14:19–20 ESV)

The cloud—lit up the night . . . a cloud that's fire in the night? Who would've ever imagined that?

A shroud of cloud with a flaming blaze at its center, "to give them light on the way they were to take" (Nehemiah 9:12). I turn to the window again, like I'm seeing what I've never seen before: What's clouded in mystery is a flame to light the way.

The cloud over you is also the light before you.

Clouds can be light.

There will be days when I think this is a mocking joke, any of these dark clouds lighting the way, and I will weep, but there will be days when I know it and am not afraid: Terrible clouds can be torches. Even the dark is not truly dark—everything can be a lighting thing.* Within the clouds is a light to lead the way. Mystery holds revelation. Trust how the mystery cloud leads to the mystery of manna, still, and taste grace here. If you ever needed a sign, this was it: a cloud on fire.

> What's clouded in mystery is a flame to light the way.

But isn't the Word, this Spirit-book that I'm holding in my hands, the Spirit Himself, a sign for all time now, a certain revelation of God? Like the pillar of cloud-fire once led, the presence of the Spirit-fire leads now. Like God gave the children of Israel a cloud-fire guide, He gives His children now the Holy Spirit as a Guide. First, the "LORD went before them by day in a pillar of cloud to lead them along the way" (Exodus 13:21 ESV), and now it is said of His children: "For all who are led by the Spirit of God

---

* "Even the darkness will not be dark to you; / the night will shine like the day, / for darkness is as light to you" (Psalm 139:12).

are sons of God" (Romans 8:14 ESV), which means there is a light that isn't just at the end of the tunnel, but there is Light Himself with us now who leads the whole way through.

The Mystery of His Spirit leads through every mystery.

I reach again for the chair in front of the open Word, lay my hand down on the lines, on my lineage, on the history of my people, and there it is: You have your own cloud aflame, and it is the comfort of the Holy Spirit. You have your own Holy Ghost to lead you through the thick dark. You have a Mystery to lead you through your mysteries. *Mystery holds revelation.*

I grab my pen again, map out this Red Sea Road and these emerging markers of every exodus:

STILLNESS **TO KNOW GOD**

ATTENTIVENESS **TO HEAR GOD**

CRUCIFORMITY **TO SURRENDER TO GOD**

REVELATION **TO SEE GOD**

I don't know what is happening here, but the Word under my hand, the Word under all my wounds, it's moving, it's speaking, it's rising like a Red Sea Road of its own. The Spirit-book speaks to the soul caught between a rock and a hard place, and its every word is a revelatory story of an exodus out, through the Father, Son, and Holy Ghost.

Deep speaks to deep.

SOUL EXAMINATION

It reads, right there:

Thus the LORD saved Israel that day from the hand of the
Egyptians, and Israel saw the Egyptians dead on the seashore.
Israel saw the great power that the LORD used against the
Egyptians, so the people feared the LORD, and they believed
in the LORD and in his servant Moses. (Exodus 14:30–31 ESV)

I underline it in ink: *Israel saw what God did that day.* Israel
saw the great power of God; Israel reflected on what God had
done; Israel examined how the hand of God had forged an
impossible way. At the end of the day, Israel examined God's
hand—and it changed their hearts.

Maybe when we relive the day, we see more reasons to believe
in the Lord.

Maybe part of the way out of the hard is to examine our
hearts. Maybe there's no exodus without an examine.

Hadn't John Wesley, George Whitefield, Ignatius all made it
a daily practice to examine their hearts, scout out the topography
of their souls, locate themselves in relation to God, to nurture
their relationship with God? Hadn't David said, "I have con-
sidered my ways / and have turned my steps to your statutes"
(Psalm 119:59)—because God Himself said, "Consider your
ways" (Haggai 1:5 ESV)? Hadn't Paul implored: "Each one must
examine his own work" (Galatians 6:4 NASB)? But I didn't. Was I
too often feeling lost, like there was no way because I hadn't made
a habit of examining the way I was on? Maybe it was more than
high time for my heart to murmur it with all of God's people:
"Let us examine and probe our ways, / and let us return to the
LORD" (Lamentations 3:40 NASB1995).

Daily experiences may teach us, but daily examining our
hearts is used by God to change us. Unless we make time

for daily reflection, we can be making a road in the wrong direction.

I write it down like I'm writing down directions, sketching out a map, like the Word is forging an exodus:

STILLNESS TO KNOW GOD
ATTENTIVENESS TO HEAR GOD
CRUCIFORMITY TO SURRENDER TO GOD
REVELATION TO SEE GOD
EXAMINE TO RETURN TO GOD

The words on the page look like they are unfolding something—like they are unfolding into a Red Sea Road, into more than finding a way through but a new way of being. I can imagine how, any moment, the black starling would fly.

I can hear that black starling's ascending whistles, its ratcheting clicks, its warbling song, coming across the waving ocean of wheat like hope. That starling, it's listened to the world—and it's heard and mentally mapped other bird songs, expanded its repertoire, and it never stops imitating, folding new sounds into song. They say a starling has one of the longest and most complex songs of all, that a starling can even learn how to talk, can imitate human words.

I read once that the eighteenth-century clergyman Laurence Sterne had said he heard a starling crying from a cage in a stairwell in a Paris backstreet. Sterne had stopped, turned to what he thought was the cry of a child, only to hear what was a starling begging the words it had learned somewhere along the line: "I can't get out; I can't get out." Stunned, Sterne had reached for the cage: "God help thee, but I'll get thee out!" But the cage was so hopelessly twisted with wire, Sterne's attempts failed miserably, and the preacher said he had to concede to the starling: "I fear, poor creature, I cannot set thee at liberty."

The starling, breast pressed desperately up against the cage, kept begging: "I can't get out; I can't get out."[6]

When the starling at the end of the branch turns and warbles into the evening wind, I want to tell him how I am listening. How I am hearing the Word speak, tell him I am learning exodus words—"There is a way, a way through, a way forward!" There is a Red Sea Road.

My own hope repertoire can change.

I can surrender to imagination and miracles.

I can be in Christ, imitate Christ, live the way of Christ, and I can learn the language of exodus, and I can find the Way. I want to tell him that and witness him carrying that song to the world.

DOXOLOGY OR DARK

And what comes after the exodus?

Then Moses and the people of Israel sang this song to the LORD, saying,

"I will sing to the LORD, for he has triumphed
gloriously;
the horse and his rider he has thrown into
the sea.
The LORD is my strength and my song,
and he has become my salvation;

> this is my God, and I will praise him,
>> my father's God, and I will exalt him."
>> (Exodus 15:1–2 esv)

I smile slowly. Of course. Doxology. Thanksgiving. Praise. That was a road I'd known: I had once been dared by a friend to record one hundred—*hey, how about one thousand*—gifts from the Giver, and I had been fool enough to do it.[7] I'd seized a pen and wielded it like a weapon against the dark and jotted down gifts, moments of grace, throughout the day, and for years I'd fought for joy because any life worth living demands that you refuse to let anything steal your joy because what steals your joy, steals your strength. And I'd radically discovered: If Jesus chose to give thanks for the cup of suffering since, out of a cosmos of possibilities, thanksgiving was the preferred weapon to face and fight the dark, do I have any better way? And if Jesus can give thanks even on the night He was betrayed, then I can give thanks in the midst of anything, and there is always something to be thankful for and thanksgiving always precedes the miracle of more God.

I hadn't lost the habit of giving Him thanks; I was still writing down my gifts, my thanks, every day. When I'd been holding on by a thread, what was holding me together was this looking for a thread of grace still running through everything. And this—this was the going higher up and deeper down into God, the next holy step. A habit of thankfulness is always our exodus out of bitterness. Christ-exaltation always leads to some kind of exodus.

Any way of life that finds a way through has always had the cadence of doxology.

There. I laid down my pen:

STILLNESS TO KNOW GOD
ATTENTIVENESS TO HEAR GOD
CRUCIFORMITY TO SURRENDER TO GOD
REVELATION TO SEE GOD
EXAMINE TO RETURN TO GOD
DOXOLOGY TO THANK GOD

A Red Sea Road! An exodus emerging—directly from Exodus!

A map, a way to a meaningful life. That was it: Finding a way *through* was really about finding a *way of life*, a rule of life.

A new way of thinking.

A new way of being.

What if the question is never "What's the way out of this?" but "What way can I be in this?" The way through happens wherever we stop focusing on how to get out of something and focus on what we can get out of this to become Christlike. Freedom isn't about looking for a way out, but the Way deeper down, the Way to grow into more, to be pressed into the narrow pathway through.

> Finding a way *through* was really about finding a *way of life*, a rule of life.

And in a flash, I witness the small starling finally take wing, a WayFarer through blue skies.

SELAH

I can feel this unfolding into wing and the wind of the Spirit lifting, lifting.

From this vantage point, I see everything differently, the whole of the story, always making a way into the promised land of union, the WayMaker parting everything to set us apart for deeper intimacy with Him.

I look down and see what I hadn't seen before:

(S) TILLNESS TO KNOW GOD

(A) TTENTIVENESS TO HEAR GOD

(C) RUCIFORMITY TO SURRENDER TO GOD

(R) EVELATION TO SEE GOD

(E) XAMINE TO RETURN TO GOD

(D) OXOLOGY TO THANK GOD

Sacred! Set apart! The Red Sea Road—a SACRED way of life! Every step of the way through that Red Sea Road—*stillness, attentiveness, cruciformity, revelation, examine, doxology*—leading out of bondage to bonding with God is a sacred way of life that the WayMaker is working to set me apart for Him!

I flip back through my journal, look back through the story, and there it is, right from the beginning, chapter by chapter, line by line, how the WayMaker, even, especially, when I was oblivious, has been at work, always making sacred dreams of connection and communion come true:

 till, it's hard to confess: We were married only four short days when we cut our honeymoon three days short.

 ttentive to the road stretching straight ahead of us, we leave all we dreamed behind, and he turns right, off Bluewater Highway, and onto Gore Road, making our winding way toward home.

 ross that hearth of ours, he carried me like a timeworn choreography. But I hadn't known that this cleaving of souls could feel more like an axe severing you off from hope.

 evelations like "you can't figure out the way to consummate your marriage" can very well land you in therapy.

 xamining the face facing yours can, in ways you never imagined, feel like a coming home.

 oxology can rise like a dream come true, and raise you, too, cutting a long cold night short.

I lay my hand down on the page. What was a mystery can someday hold revelation. What's clouded in mystery is a flame to light a sacred way into a holy communion. He is the Word, and He is always at work, especially when I'm unaware, always writing all things into a good story. The story may seem to make no sense, but the WayMaker's working all the lines into a way through it all, to be in sacred union with you. Even when you can't see that He's doing *SACRED* work, He's working to part waters to set you apart for a deeper communion with Himself. The WayMaker never, ever, ever, ever stops making a way to be closer to you.

When I look up, I can see out the window how the starling that had taken flight turns and soars, swoops and rises. Like a wind I can't see has split the skies and swept it up into a great dance.

Part Two

chapter eight

INTO THE STORM

> Shalom I leave with you. My shalom I give to you; not as the world gives, give I to you. Don't let your heart be troubled, neither let it be fearful.
>
> —JOHN 14:27 HNV

> Now may the Lord of shalom himself give you shalom at all times in all ways. The Lord be with you all.
>
> —2 THESSALONIANS 3:16 HNV

When a friend unexpectedly invites me, in the middle of our adoption journey toward China, to join her in the Holy Land for a week, Darryl kisses me tender and whispers,

"Go." As I board the metal bird bound for Israel, the flight attendant greets me and every passenger at the plane door, welcoming with a nod: "Shalom, shalom."

I stop short, my carry-on heavy in hand, stifle a ridiculous laugh. Are you serious?

Shalom, shalom?

Is she making some airline prophecy over me for a two-Shalom-daughter kind of life?

"Shalom, shalom" may be a common Jewish greeting, but it's like she's a flying prophetess speaking some divine will over me, about a baby in China named Shalom and a girl at home on the farm named Shalom, and some double-fold measure of peace. A restless, searching people, the seeking beat of the human heart is ultimately only for that: Shalom, shalom.

I haul my carry-on down the narrow aisle, and it's the greeting bandied back and forth—*shalom, shalom*—all down the cabin by flight attendants, and, for me, it's hilarious and holy and I am all cochlear, pressed to this seashell world, attentive to the rush of God in the moment.

HAM SANDWICH PRAYERS

When I'd stepped behind the Farmer into the social worker's foyer for that first home study interview, the social worker had reached out his weathered hand and said, "Call me Ted! Nice to meet you! Come on in, folks, come on in!" Ted's already leading us toward the kitchen like he's dropping God crumbs and I'm hungry and, it's true, manna is everywhere because so is He. I'd smiled thinly in Ted's kitchen, the late afternoon light sliding in gold—but, honest, I kinda wanted a brown paper bag to hurl in, like when you're about to take some high school math exam and you can't remember a thing about the Pythagorean theorem. Except this isn't a test of math. This is a test of the fitness of our parenthood, of my motherhood. Indiscretions in youth? Mental health issues? Marital strife? Dysfunction in your family of origin? And then, step right up: private interviews—(interrogations?)—with each of our children. Grinning Ted's about to slice, splice, and dissect, to detect our dysfunction and then execute his report to decide if our dream of little Shalom can even begin to come true. Can I just nicely hurl in your welcoming plant over here in the corner, Mr. Ted?

Or can I set my mind apart for a moment, and reorient to the way, the way through, the Way Himself?

Stillness: Be still . . . live into a tender surrender because the Lord fights His way to you, fights for you in ways you don't even know you need.

Attentiveness: Attend to who you say God is, to where you are in relation to Him, and what you really want.

Cruciformity: Surrender, arms wide-open, let yourself be formed cruciform, reaching out to God and people.

Revelation: How is the Word revealing Himself to you in this moment?

Examine: What are you afraid of?

Doxology: What can you give thanks for right here and now?

I swear, there's a SACRED way of being that reroutes into a new way of being. Shalom, shalom.

"So, folks." Ted's bringing mustard and pickles to his kitchen table. "Mind if I just pray and we grab a light dinner here, before our first interview together? I also teach adoption classes Tuesday evenings, so sorta just eating on the fly here."

What happens next, we will repeat over and over again. Ted does not bow his head to murmur, "Lord, bless this food . . ." Ted does not sit in a moment of silent prayer. Instead, Ted opens his mouth to sing a hymn sung from old church pews, and the first four words about make my heart stop: "Shalom, my friend, shalom."[1]

Wait. Shalom? Why is our social worker, who has never even heard yet the name of our longed-for Chinese daughter, the man who will ultimately determine if we are fit enough parents to adopt, now singing a prayer that has *Shalom* as its very first word? Like—*Shalom, our youngest daughter, and Shalom, our longed-for daughter-to-be? Shalom, shalom?*

Why does the mystery of manna sometimes taste like a long, heavenly surprise?

The Farmer is kicking my shins underneath the table, like he is an alarm shaking me awake to whatever divine sign is flashing here. As the Farmer is bruising my shin with shock, Ted is belting the second verse a cappella, about God giving you shalom, giving you shalom.

Darryl is kicking me relentlessly under the table now, and I want to holler, "I know, I *know*!"

But that's the miracle I'm just beginning to know: Christ brings us shalom regardless of whatever else life brings.

That's the actual revelation. This isn't some revelation that we'd be approved to adopt, not a revelation that our Shalom would become a big sister to baby Shalom, nor a foreshadowing of how the story, or our road, would go. That's ultimately the prophetic moment, the answer to our every prayer, our every dream: Even when we can't see it, the WayMaker is working and making the way, not to a place but to a Person, the only One who brings us shalom. Peace isn't a place; peace is always a Person.

SHALOM IS THE DREAM, AND
JESUS IS THE ONLY WAY.

While my heart's burning with the closeness of His warm shadow, I am stilled, attentive: He is not a small, far-off distant God but a God who comes near to carry you the distance, to whisper secret hopes in your ear and cut the fears down small, the God who talks through time. The Word spoke in ways that moved the world and is still speaking in ways that move through the world.

THIS IS THE SACRED WAY: GOD MAKES A WAY
TO GIVE YOU SHALOM, TO GIVE YOU SHALOM.

"Shalom, shalom." An airline stewardess, echoing good old Ted, smiles and steps out of the aisle, and I nod and want to sing her Ted's ham sandwich prayer, and does she know that in the Hebrew stories of old, the colloquial question to greet a newcomer was *hashalom*? Which was one's way of asking, "Is everything all right?" (2 Kings 9:11). Everything is all right *not* when we have seized the dream, fought off all suffering, attained our own promised land; everything is all right when we still and rest in the shalom of wholeness and oneness, *attachment*, with *God* who is our everything.

THE WAY THINGS OUGHT TO BE

When I was hopeful-round with our sixth babe, already the parents of four sons and one daughter, our little six-year-old girl with a posse of brothers crawled into bed every night, folded her hands, and white-knuckle begged God for a baby sister. I winced every time. What if you beg God for a fish and He gives you a stone? Does that mean God has a stone heart, or does that mean He knows that you have a fish allergy, and He knows you'll need a stone to start a fire, grind some wheat, and make some bread? What if God doesn't hand you what you want, but hands you what you didn't know you needed, and that's when the tenderness of His spellbinding, bonding hand brushes yours?

Our lone daughter had traipsed about announcing to anyone who'd listen that she was going to have a baby sister, and I'd touched my swollen belly heavy with life and wondered if I was going to birth a boy and crush her faith in God.

The night I finally swayed into labor, we drove to meet the midwife with only one boy's name ready for this child: Job. I'd told Darryl late one night on the front porch swing under a bespattering of silvery stars pinning up night's blanket that I couldn't dream up a better namesake for a son than Job, the same Job who stood over the gaping graves of every single one of his children, whose wealth and security had been whipped away in the blink of any eye, the same gutted Job who still dared to stand defiantly against a hurricane of dark and surrender to God like a holy fool: "The LORD gave and the LORD has taken away; / may the name of the LORD be praised" (Job 1:21). This is always the compass that orients all who arrive. I'd laid my hand on my growing mountain of hope and this curl of child within, whispered it to Darryl, that every time we said the name Job, we'd be saying what we know, what we'd wrestled relentlessly to live: "Though he slay me, yet will I hope in him" (13:15), yet will I turn to Him and trace His face slow, till I find the contours of His kindness. At least that was the plan on paper.

But when I'd bent into that work of a mother that never ends—the labor and delivery and always having to remember how to breathe—the wailing furled babe that about slid out onto the floor was only saved in a cotton sheet by a midwife who dived in like a football player determined not to miss the play.

"Well, go ahead and look, then tell us." The midwife placed the hardly wrapped babe on the bed. Darryl had grinned, winked. And I'd slowly unswaddled this holy ball of being. And? Babe was a girl. Second daughter. Sixth child. There she was in all her vernix-washed, squalling glory. The daughter whom the first daughter had begged the God of the heavens for.

She was not Job, but we would name her something akin to Job.

I'd slowly fingertip-outlined her lips, then gathered her up close, and that's the only word, the only name, I'd wanted, everything in one word: "*Shalom*. I think that's your name, child: Shalom."

It's more than a greeting, more than a saccharine, nebulous feeling. Shalom is an identity, a way of being, a way of stilling and deeply trusting. And it means more than peace. While peace may mean no distance between hearts, shalom means no distance between one's heart and God's. Shalom means a heart that is one with God's.

Shalom "is the way things ought to be," is what theologian Cornelius Plantinga wrote.[2] Shalom, and its related word *shalem,* refers not only to the whole, uncut stones of an altar (Deuteronomy 27:6; Joshua 8:31)—but also to the wellness of a whole, undivided heart (2 Kings 20:3). I'd touched the thin pages of the Word and the epiphany of it is a thin place of its own: The only way a heart can ever be unafraid and untroubled is for it to be undivided. Why beg God to divide seas for me if my heart for Him is divided? Why expect that God will split waters for me if I'm just giving Him my split attention? Why do I expect God to make a way if I'm often going my own way?

> The only way a heart can ever be unafraid and untroubled is for it to be undivided. Why beg God to divide seas for me if my heart for Him is divided?

I would think of this when I would rock Shalom to sleep in my arms, her heart beating next to mine, the child whose name means whole.

The night we named our prayed-for girl Shalom, I'd claimed it as her life verse:

> You will keep in perfect peace
> those whose minds are steadfast,
> because they trust in you. (Isaiah 26:3)

I hadn't known then that "perfect peace" in the Hebrew of that verse is literally "shalom, shalom." But my life is leaning and stumbling and tripping and learning it again: Where the mind stays, the trust is. Lean your mind and its weight of worries on God's sure shoulder, and your mind curls around Peace Himself. Stay, mind. Don't wander off. Stay and bind your mind to Him, exhale into God. Shalom, shalom.

I slide my beat-up carry-on up into the overhead compartment and turn to settle myself into the window seat. The sun's low and warm, like it's swollen with all the grace it's gathered from a wild ride across the sky. Soon that ball of light will set on our horizon, and a whole plane of us, graced with the benediction of "shalom, shalom" will fly a red-eye through the night toward the Holy Land, pungent with the lingering scent of God.

MEMORIZE THIS

"You can give me another name," is what our Shalom had announced one night at dinner over a plate of heaping homemade hash browns and peas. "I mean—if we adopt little Shalom from China, we can't both be Shalom."

"No, no, you're not losing your name." I passed her down the salt. "We'll find another name—that means something similar, to honor that her first English name was Shalom, too, because you know what happened the day you were born, right?"

The kid had rolled her eyes because she knew how I would launch into the story of how she'd been born at 12:15 a.m. mid-June—and by two that afternoon, with a babe just a bit more than twelve hours old curled on my shoulder, I'd watched the sky from the kitchen window turn a monstrous shade of green and the terrifying underbelly of a storm scrape across our fields, devouring whole trees. Quaking like the leaves, I'd grabbed the hand of our toddler and retreated with only-hours-old Shalom to the basement, as a twister tore through our county, spewing out roofs, shredding up barns.

Darryl had called from the fields, hollering over the lioness roar of the wind, the connection snapping and crackling between us, "You in the basement? Trees coming down everywhere, Ann. You've got Josh and Shalom? You okay?" With rain rattling the basement windows like a pummeling of gravel, and Shalom's sleeping baby breath right there at my neck, I'd whispered, "Yes—I've got Shalom in the storm."

Peace is a Person, not a place. Peace isn't found in a place on a map, or in a place in our imagination or dreams, or in arriving at any place in the cosmos—it's only found in a deep attachment to the Person of Christ. *Peace isn't found in any present, peaceful circumstances but in the presence of Christ.* Peace isn't getting *somewhere* but in giving your life to *Someone.*

In the stunned and eerie wake of the twister, Darryl had to pick his way home through splintered trees splayed across roads like strewn stilts the giant storm had left in its wake as it thundered across the countryside. By the time the man made it back to me, the storm was churning dark to the east, the sun bathing everything battered and dripping wet in this tender golden light. We stood out on the back step watching the storming beast move on. Darryl had scooped up a barefoot toddler, another one pressing against his leg. Feeling that singular fragility from giving birth not twenty-four hours prior, I'd leaned against Darryl, stayed on him, his arm steadying me and half-day-old Shalom swaddled close and in perfect peace sleep.

And over the flattened fields of wheat, this defiant rainbow bridged across the sky as the covenant that is always there but that you see only through the refraction of rain.

"Shalom in the storm." He whispered it into my hair like a caress. I stood stilled, attentive.

I would end up telling Shalom the story of the day of her

birth dozens of times. Sometimes the kid would roll her eyes, and sometimes she'd reach over to hug me, lay her head on my shoulder all over again, like neither time nor change could ever alter the truth of shalom in a storm.

That whole scene's replaying like a clicking reel of old family movies in the old head, when the pilot's voice comes over the intercom, welcoming us to this nonstop flight to Tel Aviv, while the airline attendants make their way through the cabin checking the overhead compartments. Next stop: the Holy Land. I didn't know then what walls our home study file would slam into on the way, I didn't know then if one little Shalom would ever come home to another Shalom who is getting ready for bed back home on our farm, but somewhere today Ted has sung his prayer for Christ to bring us all shalom, and I'm going to believe that is the dream come true, no matter what. I twist the plain band on my ring finger. I didn't know then.

Buckle up.

chapter nine

PILGRIMAGE

～

"Give your entire attention to what God is doing right now, and don't get worked up about what may or may not happen tomorrow. God will help you deal with whatever hard things come up."

—JESUS, MATTHEW 6:34 MSG

Stepping off the plane, I take this deep breath, a kinda wide-eyed kid feeling. Ignatius of old, who called himself "the pilgrim," upon arriving in the Holy Land "felt great consolation; and as the others testified, this was common to them all, with a joy that did not seem natural."[1] It does feel like a supernatural joy: I'm on Holy Land soil now, walking now where my father Abraham walked without a map, where Jacob laid on earth and wrestled until the hand of heaven touched his hip socket and he forever led with a limp. Moses walked through the no-way of waves to get to this place here, and here is where Jesus walked right across waves. I am walking into the geography of God. God's people wed their future to God right here. But do I know what I'm walking into?

When I get to the slow choreography of the carousel at baggage claim, I run my finger along the days and times of the itinerary, locations and Scripture readings, Tuesday to Tuesday. A one-week pilgrimage of literally walking the way, through John 2 to John 21, following the way of Jesus. And that sacred way of Jesus is not merely a path, route, meandering line on a map:

> The Way that is Jesus is not only the roads that Jesus walked in Galilee and to Jerusalem but also the way Jesus walked on those roads, the way he acted, felt, talked, gestured, prayed, healed, taught, and died. And the way of his resurrection. The Way that is Jesus cannot be reduced to information or instruction. The Way is a person whom we believe and follow as God-with-us.[2]

Glancing up at the conveyor belt, I keep looking for my battered gray bag that I wished I'd tied some singularly garish ribbon to, to finally come sauntering around the carousel, and I've got this one thought going around and around in my mind: *This is the Way of Jesus: More than information or instruction but intimacy. The knowing of* yada, yada, yada.

There! My bag appears at the top of the conveyor belt. Now

embark, Pilgrim! Begin again, WayFarer! Lean into the way—wherever it leads. My mad attempt to awkwardly snatch my bag blithely rolling on leaves my laminated itinerary slipping to the floor. When I bend over to pick it up, I catch it—what I hadn't noticed before.

Thursday: 11:30–13:00, Shiloh, Hannah, and Peninnah (1 Samuel 1–2:10)

Shiloh?

Shiloh's in the Old Testament. Not the Gospel of John. Shiloh's in the West Bank. Palestinian Territory. Sometimes tours don't take risks to even head into Palestinian Territories because of strained tensions. Sure, for hundreds of years, Shiloh may have been the epicenter of the entire nation of Israel, the home of the ark of the covenant, the destination of pilgrimage, but this is a New Testament tour. Why is the WayMaker working things toward a pilgrimage to Shiloh?

I know exactly where I was standing, in front of stacks of books in the cabin back on the farm, when I read what I knew we'd name that little baby in China if the ocean miraculously split and she found herself in our arms. I knew. Or had I actually heard her name like a rush of wind coming across the fields?

Shiloh.

An echo of shalom, meaning: Peaceful. Tranquil.

Shiloh, noted thirty-three times in the Old Testament that all but once references a place, the exception being the first time it appears in Genesis, a blessing given to Judah by his father, Jacob: "The scepter shall not depart from Judah . . . until Shiloh comes" (Genesis 49:10 NKJV).

Until Shiloh comes.
If Shiloh comes.

HOW TO WEAR A HABIT

When early morning streams of light fall across my bed the next morning at the kibbutz just outside of Jerusalem, I'm reaching for my worn journal and the sacred book because pilgrimaging isn't just walking where Jesus walked but walking the way Jesus walked wherever we are, and the spiritual practice of SACRED is the soul's very real and directing compass to keeping company with God. Habits (or lack thereof) change where we arrive. Rhythms build roads; lack of rhythms leaves us lost. Small daily turns decide destination, and we only have one life.

I'd read, and think often, how originally a habit meant a piece of clothing that we inhabit, pull on, live in. As nuns dress in habits to express their devotion to God, so habits, like clothing, reveal our own kinds of devotion. More than something we do, habits make us who we are. Habits are uniforms that reveal identity; change your habits and you change who you are. All pilgrims wear their habits, every WayFarer wears a way of life, and by our habits, we wear our hearts on our sleeves.

Habits are the way we dress in our deepest desires, and our daily rhythms reveal our truest romances. A habit of turning to Facebook before opening the Word and facing His face, of being more consumed by the news than the Good News, of turning to Hollywood's stories to understand our own holy story, instead of staying in His Story—and we're wearing our real love on our

> Our way of life is forming the way we are. Our daily way of life is the way we put on Christ—or not.

sleeves. Our loves become our liturgies, and we know what we love by our liturgies.[*] Our habits build what kind of life we inhabit. Our way of life is forming the way we are. Our daily way of life is the way we put on Christ—or not.

Slipping my journal out from bottom of tote, I press open the battered linen-covered notebook on the humble kibbutz desk, along with my curled leather Bible and, with pen, locate my soul in relation to the WayMaker, every relationship always about location in relation, about distance and orientation. SACRED journaling into Christ's sacred heart takes a handful of moments every morning that you can't afford to lose, but who can afford for their soul to lose its very way?

If you don't take time to find your soul, how do you ever find yourself?

The liturgy, a love liturgy with God, begins with the pen scratching it down, line upon lifeline:

Stillness

What always comes first is being still, to know that He is still God. Stillness defiantly trusts: Because He is always with us, we are always soul-safe. There is only one way to be a pilgrimaging WayFarer on the way: You have to keep on letting go of where you are. The very act of being a follower of Jesus is to be a surrenderer—you can't

---

[*] "If you think of love-shaping practices as 'liturgies,' this means you could be worshiping other gods without even knowing it." James K.A. Smith, *You Are What You Love: The Spiritual Power of Habit* (Grand Rapids, MI: Brazos Press, 2016), 37.

keep following Him if you don't let go of where you are right now.

The only way through is to let go of the way you've come. *Surrender.*

Attentiveness

Who do you say that I am? I say that You are Abba. Father. Chin-lifter, Wound Binder, *yada*-Knower, *hesed*-Holder, Safe King of the universe who binds Your heart to mine, Way-Maker. Your way be done, not my way.

Where am I? Honestly, I'm just in this place of wondering why You're making a way for me to stand at Shiloh when I have no idea if there's ever going to be a way to little Shiloh herself.

Sometimes we live into a tender surrender, and sometimes we live into a terrified surrender, and sometimes simultaneously both, and yet His *hesed*-lovingkindness lets you surrender the part of you that says fear or drama or stress is helpful—when in reality they help you gain nothing—and lets you surrender to a love that lets you see you always gain the most by being happy in God.

What do I want? Do I want to be distressed, anxious, bothered—what do they help me gain? Stress will always try to convince you that it has a reason to stalk you if you let it. There is always something to be worked up about if you want. But the reality is that God is always at work, and there is always something to be thankful for, which is what makes you joyful if you want.

Of all the wanting of all the ways, doesn't it come down to wanting just this along the way: More interior stillness, more trust, more thankfulness, more expansive joyfulness, more genuine *shalom, shalom.* Today is going to happen, one way or another. Why not want most to be happy in God? If you want shalom the most, you will want for nothing.

Cruciformity

To form your life into the shape of a cross is to live with your arms stretched wide open, to let go of all forms of control, to live with your vulnerable heart exposed, to love vulnerable enough to be hurt, but this is what love is. This truth is at the core of the universe. I open myself wide-open, stretch myself out, cross-formed, surrendering, living given, reaching out to God and people, and relentlessly talk back to every worry with the cruciform prayer: *Into Your hands, Lord, I commit this.* Commit this fear, this person, this worry, this situation. *I surrender to You my sins, my people, my dreams, my tomorrows. Surrendering all of me, reaching out to people, reaching out to You.*

Revelation

A word from His Word, as His revelation to this stumbling WayFarer today, from my chronological reading in the Word:

> "Behold, I am doing a new thing;
>> now it springs forth, do you not perceive it?
> I will make a way in the wilderness
>> and rivers in the desert." (Isaiah 43:19 ESV)

It's true for all the pilgrimaging: Deserts are places of

dependence on God. Deserts are not places where God deserts you but a place deserted of noise so you can hear a word from God. Every wilderness holds God's tenderness, and the driest of deserts can be the holy of holies. Deserts aren't places to fear: Deserts are trust greenhouses. Rest in today's pasture, and fret not about tomorrow's provision. The WayMaker always leads into deserts, not to desert His own people but to lead to an appetite for more of God alone. The desert that seems in the way . . . it's making a way to lean on the Way Himself. Always: What is in the way . . . is making a way. Maybe wildernesses are not out of the way but are making the way—*to hear Him more clearly. If I choose to be still and attentively listen to the ways He is working, moving, wooing.*

Examine

What are you afraid of today? Today, I think, if I examine my heart and am flat-out honest? I think—I think I'm afraid of going to the place of Shiloh and baby Shiloh never actually coming to us. Shame dies when our story is shared in safe places, and what place is safer than on the page, before the Word, to share our fears without shame? Sharing our fears with our Father regulates our fears. If Abba Father is not a knot of worry, then why not trust? Let everything loosen into trust, binding my being to His. One. Union.

Doxology

Thanks be to God that I know in my bones: God withholds no good way from us,* so there is a way God is making

---

* Psalm 84:11.

across the sea of my soul, and if He ceases the hard winds and the storm, I will miss the miracles of many Red Sea Roads in my dreams, in my spirit, in my way of being. Thanks be to God: Deserts are not places of despair—deserts are sacred spaces of divine dialogue. Thanks be to God: Every wilderness, every desert—is not where God deserts—is where God woos with a whispered word. Thanks be to God to dare to believe even this. Unless I give thanks for the hard gifts, I've miscounted the gifts.

There. I let my heart leak honest on a page, poured it out, and now God has my heart. I gave my heart to Him not just once, at the point of conversion, but right here this morning again. God is not way off, that you have to scream for His attention; He is right here in the way between heartbeat and next breath, sitting already with your most sacred thoughts, choosing to *yada*-know you. Handing those secret, sacred thoughts to God is to brush the kindness of the divine and feel His warm resurrection breath across the flickering chambers of your embered heart. It's when you give your whole self to the Way Himself that you know there's going to be a way through. Trust. You're going to make it.

ALL ROADS LEAD TO SHILOH

Thursday morning, our Messianic Jewish guide, Arie Bar David, leads us into the West Bank, drives us down winding roads into the stony hill country of Palestinian Territory, and I read it there on the sign as he slows to make the turn: Ancient Shiloh.

"So—this is where the very first capital of the nation of Israel once stood." The guide walks up the stony path. "Where the tabernacle once stood with the ark of the covenant for 369 years in the holy of holies, where the people of God once came from all over the nation to stand here and directly connect with God. Generations of the entire nation of Israel pilgrimaged to Shiloh, the sacred heart of the nation."

On the other side of the planet, Shiloh Shalom Yu Xin is sitting on her foster mother's lap in a Chinese hospital with her half a heart, a broken heart, heaving hard with pneumonia. And I'm in Israel, walking up to Shiloh—regardless of if she ever comes to me. Is this real time? In a pair of cork-cracked sandals, I'm walking back three thousand years in time, walking up to where the actual tent of meeting stood, and laying my own messy heart bare before God, telling Him how my heart longs for baby Shiloh Shalom, telling Him right here at Shiloh, where, for more than three centuries, Holy God Himself tabernacled.

"After the Israelites came across the Red Sea, wandered forty years in the wilderness, and finally entered the promised land, the entire nation of Israel made its way here to Shiloh to make their sacrifices to God." Our guide, Arie, is now pointing toward this rocky outcropping, to where holes were found carved into the rocks, perhaps the very postholes that once supported the tabernacle itself.

"All sacrifices to a Holy God happened here. The burnt offering, the flour offering, the peace offering, the sin offering, the guilt offering. Sheep, goat, grain, bull, dove—all of the sacrifices of God's people for all their heart wanderings, all their sins—happened right here."

I've got nothing. No flapping dove in the backpack. No bull at the ready, no bag of wheat slung over the shoulder.

"Now, when the tabernacle was right here," the guide says, holding up two fingers, "you could have come here with two different kinds of sacrifices—the *olah* sacrifice, a sacrifice that is completely consumed in flame before God, or you could come here to Shiloh with the *shelamim* sacrifice, which comes from the word *shalom*—the peace offering."

Shalom? A shalom sacrifice? Here at Shiloh? Did the WayMaker lead this mother of one girl named Shalom, desperately trying to adopt another girl we've fallen in love with and would name Shiloh Shalom, into this wilderness to speak a holy word—to sacrifice and lay down every one of her dreams? I step in closer, try to memorize the guide's words that come next.

"And this peace sacrifice, it is actually eaten by those who sacrifice it, almost like a shared meal, almost like a feast between man and God, almost like a communion—an expression of connection."

Sacrifice—is an expression of connection?

Sacrifice—is a way of communion?

"Wait—" I interrupt the guide, touch his shoulder before he moves on. "Sacrifice—doesn't mean give up or lay down or go without or let go of?"

"No, no, no. . . . Sacrifice doesn't mean that at all. Sacrifice in Hebrew is *korban*." Arie flips the pages of his worn Bible to show me. "See. Sacrifice, *korban*, comes from the Hebrew root, K-R-V, which literally means to come near, an approach, a moving closer, to move into a closer relationship."

Sacrifice is not losing something but moving closer to Someone. Sacrifice isn't about loss—sacrifice is about love. Surrender to love. Sacrifice is about detaching from one thing—to attach to a greater thing. How do I take off my shoes, give up shoes, give all of me to Him?

"Before I leave you with some time alone here for your own prayer and communion with God"—our guide is closing his Bible—"I want to leave you with Hannah. See her in your mind's eye, how Hannah came

> Sacrifice is not losing something but moving closer to Someone.

right here to Shiloh, ate her sacrificial meal, her peace offering of communion, then bowed down and poured out her heart to God tabernacled here—that if it pleased the Lord, that He somehow would make a way for her to hold the child she dreamed of."

I can hardly swallow for the burning ember in my throat.

"Like Hannah"—our guide nods as he begins to withdraw to leave us alone in this sacred place—"you're here at Shiloh, where the Lord Himself dwelled for more than three centuries. Like Hannah, pour your whole heart out, all your hopes, before your God here, right here."

Dropping to my knees, I press my forehead into the heat of the holy place. Even when I don't see how He's working, He's making a way for *all roads to lead to Shiloh because all roads lead to a sacrifice to draw us closer. Come to Shiloh with your* korban *sacrifice, come to Gethsemane and be pressed out, come, the WayMaker's making everything into a way to become one.* It's like my inner ear's been turned by truth and I can fully hear; I can come near. Stretching out arms, palms turned wide-open to the heavens, my heart leaks honest:

> *Here. Here are my paper-thin dreams.*
> *Here are my bruised and broken hopes.*
> *Here is my tattered map*
> *of the way I thought things would be.*
> *Here, take all my ways as my sacrifice*

189

> *laid down at Your feet,*
> *laid now out of the way between*
> *my heart and Yours.*
> *So now, please,*
> *just take me.*
> *That we can be close,*
> *near,*
> *here, right here.*

This is the wilderness prayer of a Hannah heart. This is a *korban* prayer. This is all I have.

Where I'm kneeled here at Shiloh, Hannah prayed for a child with such dire desperation to God that she seemed lush drunk—only to vow-pray that if God gave her that wildly longed-for child, she would give the child back to God. Hannah made good on the vow: When Samuel was but a little child, she gathered up her dream child God had made a way for and made her way all the way back to Shiloh and let her dream go, gave her dream child back to God, to serve with the priests in the temple of God, all the days of his life (1 Samuel 1).

Why ask God to make a way—and then give back to the WayMaker the very dream that He made a way to? Who does that?

I blink it back.

Someone who doesn't want anything to get in the way between her and God.

chapter ten

THE FEAR OF BEING FOUND

> Seeing that a pilot steers the ship in which we
> sail, who will never allow us to perish even in
> the midst of shipwrecks, there is no reason
> why our minds should be overwhelmed with
> fear and overcome with weariness.
> —JOHN CALVIN

> You rule the raging of the sea;
> When its waves rise, You still them.
> —PSALM 89:9 NKJV

A fter a week in the Holy Land, finally waking up next to him in our bed feels a bit like waking up in a promised land. How does his bare shoulder smell earthy and salty and like home to me? How does Darryl taste like sweet relief?

"Hey, you." He rolls over, kisses my forehead, pulls me close. "You been gone long, up there on a mountaintop with God. You okay coming back to just us here?"

"Always happy coming back to you . . ." I smile slow. "And you know: After every mountaintop comes the valley," I tease.

"Is that what I am now, huh?" He's laughing gently at my ear, like home.

WHAT ARE YOU AFRAID OF?

After the table's cleared that evening, after the kids have descended to the basement for a few rousing rounds of Ping-Pong, and the dishwasher's humming its little working song, he and I sit down to begin what we didn't know would be a descent into the adoption paperwork. My hand has already started to cramp when I get to this line: *Have you ever had therapy or been in counseling?* Am I about to be assessed poorly for once assessing that I needed to get well? Getting help isn't a sign something's wrong with you—it's a sign that you are doing things right.

"Filling in this blank space with just these words." I'm chuckling, pen at the ready. "Therapy is gym for the mind. Not ashamed to have a membership."

"You're really going to write that, eh?" Darryl catches my connection turn reaching for him and turns from his forms.

"Yep." I'm having fun now.

Instead, I write three honest letters: *yes*.

It was 1993. I was eighteen years old when I walked into my first therapy appointment in a stifling hot upstairs office with one window, no air conditioner, to see a counselor with teased bangs and a frizzy bleached perm. Mama had just signed herself into a psychiatric ward for the fourth extended treatment, each months long at a time. Dad had fallen into a vortex of depression, and I was trying to remember that the WayMaker makes His way to meet us in the dirt when we are at our lowest and kisses us to life with His breath when we don't even know how to breathe. I tell myself this, try to believe this: No past can earmark you when you've heard the divine whisper of who you can still become. Souls are a kind of story that can turn pages. And when those pages are soiled and torn, grace can turn them again.

"What are you actually afraid of?" Darryl's looking over at me, looking for what's happening underneath what's happening.

He knows how I'm making SACRED the rhythm, the way of my life, the spiritual discipline of my thoughts, which is to say I'm daily answering the question Jesus asked His disciples: "Why are you so afraid?" (Mark 4:40). Darryl lays his black-inked pen down on the stack of papers, prying a bit too close to the bone for my liking.

"You mean, what am I actually not afraid of?" I laugh awkwardly, too loud.

"Well, yeah—that too." He laughs gently but waits. He knows: A life unexamined ends up unfulfilling. Passing your days with no soul examination is how you fail your only life. And this woman with chronic soul amnesia exhales and remembers: Unpack why you're afraid and you send the devil packing.

"I think it's . . ." I'm just waiting for the words to come slow, rise, break the dam . . . then to come in a torrent. "I think I'm just kinda terrified that I am blithely walking into every mother's worst nightmare and am about to be officially labeled by this social worker with my own blazing scarlet letter *F*—Failed

Mother—even though I'm already a mother. That the actual powers that be will collectively determine I am not good enough to mother—not subjectively, but objectively, maternally unfit to adopt any child, and I'll have to somehow live politely through the shame of that and come home to look directly into the eyes of the six kids we already have and somehow, someway, have to find a way to go on—as their mother. And that's just what I am afraid of in this particular moment." I smile thinly.

Are all of us afraid to be found out, and then have to find a way to go on? Is there a way forward if the way you are isn't enough? Can I be compassionate with my fears, gather them close and soothe them again with truth: *When you know you are fully known and still fully loved, nothing can still scare you.*

"Ann—" Darryl is quiet, looking out across the fields to the east. Then he turns and connects. "Do you remember the night you became a mother?"

Yes. I hadn't been married eleven months, twenty-one years old, the eve of Mother's Day. Listening to the sleep breaths of our swaddled newborn son and couldn't sleep for the fear: How in the world was I going to raise a tiny fetal curl of a babe into a future man? Sometimes mothering feels like you've only been given broken tools to sculpt a soul.

"And what did you do that eve of Mother's Day?" Darryl asks quietly.

I'd held him bundled in one arm, held a Bible open on my lap, my hand running over and over that page and that one verse in Isaiah, like I'd wanted the words to get under my skin:

> He tends his flock like a shepherd:
>> He gathers the lambs in his arms

and carries them close to his heart;
    he gently leads those that have young.
       (Isaiah 40:11)

I had stroked that page of holy script like a begging, and He had hushed all that night long like the refrain of a sacred song.

"And what was the way through, when you didn't know what to do?" Darryl leans in.

It's simple, and it's not because it means you will have to trust: The way through is to simply let the WayMaker hold you close and let Him lead the way. *Into Your hands I commit this.* Trust is only hard if you don't trust Love Himself holding you.

Two weeks later the home study social worker emails, and it crashes like a wall of water.

"We will need to see your full counseling files before going any further."

What do you call that feeling when you might laugh-hurl and your arms tingle with flushing shame down to your fingers? Yeah, that. I can actually see the scenes written in those counseling sessions from twenty-plus years ago: The cutting to relieve rising tension through my teen years. Anxiety attacks to flee fears at university. Mama's psych hospital stays when I was a child. Dad's workaholism after my sister was killed. It's the paradox of a soul, wanting to be seen and known—*yada*-known—but wanting no one to truly see and know the way we've come and the way we are.

A cursory Internet search for the intake therapist pulls up nothing. Looks like she's long since been freed from that overheating upstairs office where she and I first met twenty summers ago to do the work of walking my own Red Seas through trauma when all my cool friends spent their Friday afternoons heading up to the lakeshore to play Frisbee on the beach.

Why be afraid of waves that are making the way through the sea that you can't yet see? You may only see waves, but that doesn't mean waves won't be your actual way through the sea to see more of God. Exhale into trust.

Email the adoption social worker:

> My apologies, the intake therapist is no longer practicing with the
> agency and that file was closed more than twenty years ago. We're
> working on completing our medical physicals with our physician.
> Hope to have that mailed by week's end. Have a great day, friend!

Press Send.
Interior waves calm a bit.

WHY WE EXAMINE AND
NAME OUR FEARS

In the beginning, "no shrub had yet appeared on the earth and no plant had yet sprung up, for the LORD God had not sent rain" (Genesis 2:5)—not until He sent water up from the ground, which is *ad* in Hebrew. And out of the dust of the ground, which is *adama* in Hebrew, God made humanity, Adam. In the beginning, there was the water coming up from the ground, *ad*, and out of the dust of the ground, *adama*, God formed the first human being, Adam. Humanity lives between the ways of water and high ground. Facing waves, and finding a pathway through, has been part of the human experience from our very first breath.

There is a wall of water in front of you not because you did something wrong or because you took a wrong turn; there has been a wall of water in front of us right from the beginning because this *is* the human experience.

Life is waves. Grief comes in waves. Suffering comes in waves. Losses come in waves. There is no controlling life's storms; there is only learning to live with waves. The real work of being human is mastering how to process losses while being in the process of moving forward. The real work of being human is trusting the way is the waves, right through the valleys and crests. Across the waves, even now, right now, the Spirit hovers.

Late afternoon, just as I'm shaking the oregano over a simmering pot of chicken soup, my sister calls, her voice kind at the end of the line.

"Hey, you know a social worker named Ted? He called here this afternoon, had a whole slew of questions about you, about Darryl and the kids. Asked about any counseling in the past."

I set the oregano down on the counter, gently put a lid on the pot of soup.

Life is waves.

"Ah, you met my friend Ted!" I'm laughing quietly, uncover the pot, stir the soup, but I'm the one stirred, churning, turning a bit green. "Ted's doing his job, and he's doing it well. Every single child absolutely deserves and needs to be fiercely well protected." I just hadn't realized that maybe my own doing the hard work of growing well might not be enough to be the kind of mom they think should hold a child.

"You hanging in over there? For real?" My sister doesn't want to just slip a lid over whatever I'm feeling.

"You know, I think what's happening—" And what surprises

me are these words that surface from the deeps: "My own SACRED way, these rhythms of stillness, attentiveness, cruciformity, revelation, examine, and doxology are literally holding back the waves, or rather making a way through waves." The SACRED way of life, my rule of life, my way of life, is literally making the way through my life! The spiritual discipline of SACRED is discipling the internal waves of worry and making a way to lean back and trust the wraparound presence of God holding me safe.

That's what is happening: You can withstand life's rhythms of waves as long as you have your own interior sacred rhythms with God who rocks you safe. The daily habit of a SACRED way of life holds back a storm of worries, a tsunami of fears, by setting the soul apart, through stillness, attentiveness, cruciformity, revelation, examine, and doxology, to let the Spirit soothe the heart with gospel truth. It's the soul's daily habitual turns that become the soul's eventual destination, and it's the SACRED spiritual disciplines that keep turning the heart to see, to arrive, in the arms of the WayMaker who keeps making the way, His way, to *yada*-know and be one with Him, soul-safe.

As James K. A. Smith wrote: "Learning to love (God) takes practice."[1] That's what I tell my sister: The spiritual discipline of SACRED is literally making a Red Sea Road through a whole sea of worries, straight to God, and that feels like nothing less than a coming out of Egypt into freedom. And I tell her that, frankly, the possibility that our file could even be matched specifically with little Shiloh Shalom Yu Xin's file is like standing at the farm kitchen sink with a red strand of thread and trying to thread the eye of a sliver of a needle being held ten thousand kilometers away across an ocean, a needle held outside a foster home on a backstreet in Beijing, China. Translated: Snowball's chance in hades. I know that. And yet: Unlikely stories can still become love stories, and impossible plotlines can turn on one fierce line of hope, and biblical hope is not about good odds but about trusting the ways of a good God.

Ted's email pops up like a friendly hello wave that evening:

Please email the Family Health and Services Agency at your earliest convenience & request a search of their files for the counseling files!

    Thank you!

Yes, sir! Red Sea Road, wherever it goes, leading me to *yada*-know the contours of His *hesed*-lovingkindness. I do this: One line at a time, I compose that email request, per Ted's request, but what I really want is for little Shiloh Shalom Yu Xin to know a story of healthy attachment, deep connection, safe security, no matter what, here or not. How could any parent want any other way for their child? How could our Father want any other way for any of us? He withholds no way from us that can make a way—or Gethsemane-press us—into the way we've always dreamed. Not my way but His.

"You hear back from anyone yet?" Darryl turns back the quilt on our bed that night, bends over to pull off his socks still carrying dirt from the fields.

"Nope. Not a file, not a letter, nada from Ted." I crawl in under sheets, emotionally exhausted from the long gestating of waiting, the long way through this valley. It's true, I know: The most wanted destinations are always the most delayed. But the long waiting and long valleys have always been the way: Abraham faced his own no-way, no-win situation; Hagar wept in the desert for her no-way future; Jonah tried to run from his no-way-out predicament; Job ached with his no-way-forward life; and Elijah saw no hope, no relief, no way forward and begged to lie down and die. And before Noah could even see dry land, he let his hope take wing. Hope is the sacrament of waiting when there are waves as far as you can see.

Hope takes wing over waves, trusting there is land out there when you only see waves from here.

Darryl turns on his side of the bed, carefully cups me close in our own love liturgy, whispers it there at my ear about what to make of the storms and harsh headwinds: "Strong winds blow the miracle of Red Sea Roads everywhere." Everywhere: What is in the way is making the way.*

And I lie there, hand on his wrapped around me, us all held by *hesed*-lovingkindness, and let my mind take its SACRED way, and end the day examining my own soul because if you end your day without a soul examination, you can end up soul sick, which is to say: If you get into bed at night without cutting your fears down to size, you get into bed with the devil. So I keep returning to it every night, to what Jesus asked His disciples to examine in their own hearts, out in the middle of a storm: "Why are you so afraid?" (Mark 4:40).

> "Strong winds blow the miracle of Red Sea Roads everywhere."
> Everywhere: What is in the way is making the way.

No question may matter more. Because if we let fears surge

---

* "The impediment to action advances action. What stands in the way becomes the way." Marcus Aurelius, *Meditations*, Book 5.20.

in the mind, they'll turn the needles of the heart, if our lips never speak those fears out loud—the fears remain slippery, morph large in the dark, turning our hearts away from Love Himself.

Only what you actually name can you regulate. Only when you open up, name, express your fears, can the fears begin to ebb, which is why the Word asks us to calm our fears by putting words to them, by bringing them to the Word: "Do not be anxious about anything, but in every situation, by prayer and petition, with thanksgiving, present your requests to God. And the peace of God, which transcends all understanding, will guard your hearts and your minds in Christ Jesus" (Philippians 4:6–7). "Cast all your anxiety on him because he cares for you" (1 Peter 5:7). Jesus asks us to examine why we are so afraid because He knows: Fears can turn and burn our hearts so they ignite fight-or-flight responses, making our fears masquerade like anger, like control, like perfectionism, like procrastination, like self-harm, like a thousand other masked faces.

God knows no question may matter more than asking ourselves why we are so afraid, which is exactly why God commands us, more than any other command in Scripture, "Do not fear." Because God knows, and I've been slow to know and slower to admit: Fear is about losing what we love. As Augustine wrote: "Fear startles at things . . . which endangers things beloved."[2]

Wherever one is afraid, one is afraid of losing what one loves.

As Augustine also pointed out, "We fear nothing save to lose what we love."[3] Our deepest loves drive our deepest fears.

"The evil in our desire typically does not lie in what we want, but that we want it too much" is what Calvin himself said.[4] When we want what we want too much, when our love for what we want outsizes our love for God, our fears outsize our living.

In my tsunami of questions and doubts over the adoption file, colliding with whatever was in those counseling files, my fears have been startled at things that endangered things beloved—fears of losing what I loved: my hopes, my dreams, my relationships, my reputation, my future, my sense of self. All the fears are me-centered.

But in practicing the SACRED way, and the daily habit of asking my soul what Jesus asks—"Why are you so afraid?"—I think, examining under all the layers, that maybe at the core: Fear is love of self. Jesus asks us to explore what we are so afraid of so we can see what we love more than Him.

Come morning, while my coffee steeps there on the edge of the counter, I notice an email that came in late. From a Betty—at the Family Health and Services Agency:

> Forgive us, due to an illness and subsequent staffing changes, we have just read your email and per your request, please find attached a copy of your counseling files.
>
> Best,
> Betty

Interior waves roil. Do I dare click the attachment open? Sometimes you don't find skeletons in closets, just bits of your petrified heart.

Click.

The smudged facsimiles of looping handwriting are faint, hard to read, but there she is, my flailing and trying nineteen-year-old self: There are my panic attacks, the cutting with glass, the years of disorienting agoraphobia. There's poor Mama staggering with grief over her wee Aimee killed, and Dad working all his pain to death, and I'm transported back to another hurting lifetime. Do—do I feel shame over the labels scrawled in the therapist's messy penmanship, labels slapped on the wounds of a family grieving an accident that killed their baby girl, small and crushed out in the farm laneway? Or do I feel shame that Ted will read all of this and decide who we are? Or do I want to enfold all these hurting people on the pages and gather them up with *hesed*-lovingkindness of God? What people label, God loves, and who gets written off, God writes their names on the palms of His hands, and when we fall way too far short of being enough, God makes the way to move into us and be our home. God knows all of us are but dust, but look what God does with dirt, and He makes a way for dust to resurrect and breathe for all time and eternity. No, there is no shame: All you can feel is tender toward all the brave who refuse to surrender to the dark but keep rising until their lungs' last rising.

Screen's blurring. Whatever Ted decides: If this is the end of our dream of becoming family, little Shiloh Shalom Yu Xin, I'm so sorry for this broken world, with broken systems and structures—I tried with all the bits of my broken heart. In all our hearts, you're a love story that will never end.

I'm just about to close the file out when my eye accidentally catches it in everything swimming a bit on the screen.

"Client is considering marriage to boyfriend of several years, and I expect that this marriage will be a very difficult one . . ."

I stop. Wave-slapped.

Move the cursor back. Draw myself up. Blink hard. I wasn't expecting that.

Read the line again. Therapist expects that the marriage will be . . . difficult?

However I interpret the rest of the file, in that moment something hisses in my heart: *Difficult?*

chapter eleven

KIN

I cried out to God for help;
    I cried out to God to hear me.
When I was in distress, I sought the Lord . . .
Your path led through the sea,
    your way through the mighty waters,
    though your footprints were not seen.
        —PSALM 77:1–2, 19

There isn't a day that doesn't beg for exodus after exodus, a way out, but there's no exodus without an entering.

One year to the day when I first saw Shiloh Shalom Yu Xin's wee photo in that handknit lamb's hat at that gathering in Texas, I find myself back at the very same annual gathering in the same great state of Texas when my phone unexpectedly rings. The director of our adoption agency? Today? Right here?

Turns out she's gotten word from our good friend, Ted: "Police background checks, medical files and physicals, reference letters, financial records, and home inspection all passed! Strong interviews with each of your kids! Supervisor Gwyneth said no need of counseling files more than twenty years old! Great news: all was submitted!!"

Drop my head with relief. Happiness leaks. Thanks be to God. But the reason for the call: Yu Xin's file has been expedited because of her precarious heart condition and decreasing oxygen levels. Her lips and fingertips are bluing, she's struggling to breathe, her half heart's wrestling to pound on, and she's been hospitalized a total now of thirteen times for pneumonia.

"I have to tell you: Your adoption dossier's been matched in China with Yu Xin. I'll email you all the confirmations, but get ready to travel."

When you live *in via*, on the way, you live always ready to surrender and move forward. When waves crest, peak, it can be hard to breathe too. Breathe: "The most incredible thing about miracles is that they happen," wrote the pithy G. K. Chesterton.[1]

"Ah . . . uh . . . okay . . . yes, yes . . ." My mind's spinning. For more than several dozen reasons, none of this should even be possible. How is it one year to the day that I was standing back here in Texas, in this very same place, holding a baby picture in hand, and I'd turned and foolishly murmured to my friend Jennie, "I think—I just saw a picture of my daughter," and now she actually is?

Fingers trembling, I call Darryl, twenty-five hundred kilometers away, standing at home in the farm kitchen, just in from the mailbox with the red flag at the end of our lane.

"Darryl? D! You're not going to believe this."

"Neither are you."

"Wait—what?" Had the director of the adoption agency called him first?

"You should see what just came in here with the mail. What I've got here in my hands right now. Check your texts." I can feel the warmth of the smile in his voice.

When I click open my texts, there's a photo of a card in his hands, a pencil-sketched card, with this graphite sketched sea splitting in two walls of waves, and Moses upholding a staff, and the pillar of cloud making a way where there seems to be no way.

The image he's holding in hand is a Red Sea Road.

Hesed-lovingkindness always holds us.

"But—I—where? How?" A heart can split wide-open and the cloud on fire can walk right in and make Himself at home.

"It just came in the mail right now, drawn by a child sponsored through Compassion International. A handwritten thank-you card, grateful for the ways there's been a reaching out to meet children's needs—and on the front of the card, there's this drawing of all the children of God standing before a split Red Sea. I guess because—God makes a way for the real needs of His children."

"Darryl?" I can hardly speak, hardly whisper. "The adoption agency just called right now. Our dossier's been matched—with little Shiloh Shalom Yu Xin."

Long pause, heavy with awe.

Even when you don't see how He's working, He's working all things to move nearer to you, move into you.

"Strong, hard winds blow Red Sea Roads," Darryl's voice chokes.

Does he hear it in his head, too, Ellie singing Red Sea Road words of mine back to me, just as I'd said there's no way:

> *When we can't see the way*
> *He will part the waves*
> *And we'll never walk alone*
> *Down a red sea road*

And here we are, as our hearts are tied forever to our daughter, Darryl's opening a card from the mail with this sketch of the waves of the Red Sea splitting into a road of hope leading straight to the pillar of Him.

"All real Red Sea Roads never go to a place—*but to* a Person."

This is the way it always goes:

> Your road led through the sea,
> your pathway through the mighty waters—
> a pathway no one knew was there!
> (Psalm 77:19 NLT)

The WayMaker works all the waves you see into the way you can't yet see.

And all the Red Sea Roads are exoduses to more than some promised land but to the promised arms that will hold you safe, come any hell or high water.

Darryl sets the Red Sea Road card right there by the kitchen sink.

I start looking for a way to fly over half a world of water.

> The WayMaker works all the waves you see into the way you can't yet see.

CHINA

The moment I first see her around a corner, she seems like a flicker of light from the upper heavens, like a bit of silvery ocean starlight riding in on a wave. Her *ayi*'s carrying her high in her arms right into this room heavy with the scent of fried rice and dumplings, floor lit with these planks of the rising China sun. She is all I can see, she's a prism of light, broken and fracturing light into a kaleidoscope of color everywhere for me. *My word, child.* Your story of trauma and loss will always have a witness, and all my withness, and I promise you, you will never, ever have to walk this road alone.* You are deeply safe to ache with me, you are fully free to grieve with me, you are wholly seen and known, as you truly are, by me, and together we will hold space to hold deep pain in one hand, and the real grace in the other, because this is what it means to be wholeheartedly human. And in the middle of the trauma of this brokenhearted hallelujah, know too: You are a constellation we were always looking for. You are a shore we had to find. You are a wonder, an unexpected answer to how many years of lost echoes. Her *ayi*, gently leaning forehead in to touch her bowed one, points to me, calls to me: "Mama! Mama!"

Daughter.

Daughter.
My heart for yours,

---

* "Trauma is not what happens to us, but what we hold inside in the absence of an empathetic witness." Gabor Maté, foreword, in Peter Levine, *In an Unspoken Voice: How the Body Releases Trauma and Restores Goodness* (Berkeley, CA: North Atlantic Books, 2012), xii.

my walk with yours,
my life bound to yours,
till my last breath, then always and forever.

Tiny hands clinging to her *ayi*'s shirt, Shiloh Shalom Yu Xin, not yet two, is in less than the bottom third percentile for weight, her single ventricle, broken heart breaking her into the million crystals of light of a breaking wave, and my hands are wide-open to catch all this light. Maybe a broken heart makes you break into your own kind of light? She is tiny, but for me, for us, she has gravity and means a whole world to a bunch of us a world away. I can only wish Darryl, our children, were all here, hushed by the holy luminance that is her.

But a mere forty-eight hours after our dossier had logged into the agency in China, we'd landed in the ER with Malakai, our fifth-born son, gaunt, pale, and startlingly weak, only to get slammed with the shock that our boy had a blood glucose reading of 34 mmol/L (612 mg/dL), a dying pancreas, and a diagnosis of Type 1 diabetes. The only way he'd survive is if we figured out how to become a 24/7 manual organ for him, be his pancreas, and inject him with the correct dosage of insulin every time he opened his mouth to eat—or he'd die. Our little old world wobbled on its axle. "There's no way we can both leave Malakai right now, as his pancreas is dying and his blood sugars and insulin levels are erratic, and we're just trying to figure out how to navigate this." Darryl's eyes read steady, surrendered. "God made a Red Sea Road. Go—bring Shiloh Shalom Yu Xin home."

We likely should have figured out another way.

We should have had a holy imagination for some way for our

own newly diagnosed diabetic son to still be safe, then found a way for Darryl to fly to China, too, a way for our hearts to be grafted with Shiloh Shalom's together, instead of me flying alone. He thought I was more than capable of flying to the other side of the world and bringing home a baby on my own. I thought he was more than kind to cover and juggle a million other things at home. As we tried to navigate how to travel to China, a healthier way would have been for me to say, "I need you," and for him to say, "I need to be with you," and for us both to realize how one little girl would need us both. We didn't know it then: What we all need most is to need. Need, dependence, reliance is what cultivates trust and deepens attachments that make us secure. This is the way of faith.

We only know it now: Sometimes you don't know you've turned the wrong way till you're down that road a long way. And yet, especially then, *don't doubt that the WayMaker makes wrong ways right*. This is the work of a good and kind God.

> What we all need most is to need. Need, dependence, reliance is what cultivates trust and deepens attachments that make us secure. This is the way of faith.

Shiloh's already cradled and rocked to sleep in the arms of her *ayi*, when one of the civil affairs government officials motions that it's time for me to reach out and take Shiloh in arm, as they need us to stand right over here for a photo of mother and daughter together for the legal paperwork.

"Yes, yes." I tentatively turn, reach out arms aching with the weight of the moment, and her *ayi* nods, too, and stretches out her arms and sleeping Shiloh Shalom Yu Xin's entrusted from one heart of love to another in her brave line of mothers.

Shiloh stirs. Looks up at me, terrified, sees where she is—and where she isn't.

Sweet baby wails.

Ayekah? Hineni.

Mama is here, right here.

I just keep whispering that, as the officials snap the picture, as they motion for me to come sign papers. And with a few inky lines, she becomes mine and I become hers.

> *If you're ever lost—I'll make your way through.*
> *If your heart ever breaks in two—I'll give you*
>   *my own.*
> *If you're ever alone—I'll make a way to hold you.*
> *Because as long as there's a way for our hearts to*
>   *stay close,*
> *everything's going to be okay.*

What all our brokenness needs is withness and witness, and He is here, right here, God whose very name is "God is with us."*

I kiss her fingertips.

SCHOOLED

One day I'd meet a professor, a theologian, whose desk I would sit across from, and ask, "Why do we end up living more lost, far, distant from God, than in communion, deeply attached to Him?"

---

* "The virgin will conceive and give birth to a son, and they will call him Immanuel" (which means "God with us") (Matthew 1:23).

"Well, I wonder if it's because we've got the metaphors of our reality turned around. Seems to me that the main metaphor that's become our map for understanding who and where we are in relation to God is legal, judiciary, God primarily as judge," which is to rightly say: Relational wrongs have been done, heartbreaking sins have been committed, and a Holy God rightly requires justice.

> When you were dead in your sins and in the uncircumcision of your flesh, God made you alive with Christ. He forgave us all our sins, having canceled the charge of our legal indebtedness, which stood against us and condemned us; he has taken it away, nailing it to the cross. (Colossians 2:13–14)

It is true: The triune God then comes in the perfect person of Christ and pays the debt we could not pay because He lived the life we could not live. The triune God judges the perfect sacrifice of the Son of God on the cross, in our stead, as payment in full, and we, who have been bought with a price, the precious blood of Christ, are released from the bondage of sin and set free.

> All are justified freely by his grace through the redemption that came by Christ Jesus. God presented Christ as a sacrifice of atonement, through the shedding of his blood—to be received by faith . . . He did it to demonstrate his righteousness at the present time, so as to be just and the one who justifies those who have faith in Jesus. (Romans 3:24–26)

This is real and good and right and the story of our rescue and redemption and our only literal hope.

And I'd nod and remember how some would say that the whole of the gospel itself can be summed in these four words: "Jesus in my place." Jesus on the cross, paying the price for my sin, the great exchange, Him taking all my brokenness, and me taking His place of wholeness. This is no small thing but everything. "For our sake he made him to be sin who knew no sin, so that in him we might become the righteousness of God" (2 Corinthians 5:21 ESV).

The professor of theology would roll his chair behind his desk.

"This is truth—and, yet, there is truly more to the story. If your only biblical metaphor for the reality of the gospel is that your wrongs have brought you into court before a Holy God, who pays the price and makes things right when you exit that court of law? You may not know that the way forward, the way of Jesus, is to live in intimate communion *with* God."

"So how do we then wake to a lived attachment with God, moment by moment withness, a life of transformative daily communion with God, actually living the way of Jesus, *in* Christ, *with* the Way Himself?" My Bible is sitting there open in my lap.

"That's easy. We need to see our relationship with God the way God sees it." The theology professor would smile. "Like the marriage and adoption that it actually is."

It's like lightning right electrifies me. I'm right spun round the right way.

Marriage and adoption have legal implications, but they are more than only a legal reality. Marriage and adoption are meant to be a *lived reality*, a *lived attachment*, a *communion reality—a love story!*

God is Lawgiver, *and God is Lover*! God's heart is bound to ours *contractually* and His heart's bound to us *covenantally*.

It's the *covenantal* faithfulness of Christ alone that saves us, and we respond to His saving faithfulness, by *covenanting our own faithfulness back to Him.* It's the Gospel truth: We are saved by God's covenantal *hesed,* for covenantal *hesed* back to God. Saved by the faithful fidelity of Christ alone means those who are saved respond with a faithful fidelity to Christ alone.[2]

Legal *and filial,* contractual *and convenantal,* His heart *for* ours, *with* ours, *in* ours.

If we chain our image of God up in only a courtroom, we'll never experience how He courts us with lovingkindness, frees us from aloneness for oneness, drops all the sentences against us to write us into a saving love story, line after tender line. If we only know God as the holy Judge and right-making King who sacrificed and saved us, we may give Him love *for* all of that. But if we intimately know Him as the ultimate Lover, Father, Husband, Brother, who is the King and Judge who sacrificed and saved us, we may love Him *with all that we are.* If there's a deep disconnect in the church between what we believe and how we actually live, is it because we've forgotten the way to live actually and intimately connected to God? Our walk will only match our talk when we live attached to His heart.

The whole of the New Testament could be explained in these three words: "Adoption through propitiation," claimed the esteemed J. I. Packer.[3] Theologian R. Michael Allen offered a road map for the way of understanding our kinship with God: "The marriage precedes the married life, while the adoptive declaration founded the familial ties. But the marriage is for the sake of a life together, and the adoption proceedings" *for a life together.*[4]

And it's true too: From the moment I first held her photograph and looked into Shiloh's eyes under that starry Texas sky,

I knew she was mine and I'd die for her. She was sealed in my heart as mine long before my hand signed on any dotted line.

> Our walk will only match our talk when we live attached to His heart.

Love's *covenant* to you moved Him to sign the *contract* with His blood at the cross to make you His own because what He ultimately came for was intimate *communion* with you.

What the WayMaker is always making a way to is a way of life *with Him. What our brokenness ultimately needs are withness and witness.* No way is wrong if it's *with Him* and every way is good if it's *in Him.*

I'd looked down at that inked cross on my wrist: While it's a true story, that the gospel is "Jesus in my place," maybe the whole gospel story is then these four words: "Jesus is my person." This is actually *everything.*

Jesus is *my person.* Jesus is my person on the cross, Jesus is my person in the valleys, Jesus is my person through the storms, Jesus is my person on the waves. Jesus is my salvation, my destination, my direction, my orientation, my shelter, my home, my way, my Lord, my Lover, my King, *my Life.*

The triune God who is King of the universe also calls Himself our Father, Husband, Lover, Brother because our greatest fear is abandonment, and our greatest need is attachment, and God enfolds our every breath:

I am your King, and I am your kin, and I am your Father, and what is there ever to really fear when the King of the universe is your very Father? I am your Father, and you are made in My image, and because we are kin, we are of the same kind, so you can completely trust that I will always be kind to a named one of Mine. Once your Father, always your Father, once your Husband, always your Husband, once the way, the truth, the life, always your way, your truth, your life. Your WayMaker is the covenant maker who moves in to be your safe home anywhere, to carry you home through everything. Trust. And let Me take you and take you the whole way.

This is no small miracle: The atonement that happened at the cross is for more than righting things; it's for attaching us to God—our at-one-ment with God. "For Christ also suffered once for sins, the righteous for the unrighteous, *to bring you to God*" (1 Peter 3:18, emphasis mine). *Atonement is for attachment.* The very reason God forgives us is to give us kinship. Salvation doesn't *just* save us *from* our life of sin; salvation is saving us *for* life *with* God. *Kin.* He sheds His blood to share His life with us. Saved *from* sin, saved *for* communion. *Kin.* The cry of Jesus on the cross was a cry for communion. It's seen in the stretching arms of Jesus on the cross, seen in the cry of every cross worn and clung to down through the ages: The gospel is more than just escape; the gospel is embrace. Kin with the King.

> Our greatest fear is abandonment, and our greatest need is attachment.

Kin.

Kin actually comes from the word *kind*, and God is more than always good, but He is always *kind*—because He is our *kin*! God can't be anything but kind to *His very own kin*!

The kingdom of God is actually a *kin*-dom, and *in Christ*

we are grafted into a *family*-dom, and we are more than servants in the *kin*-dom, we are the child, the bride, the beloved of our King who has adopted us, wed us, to be nothing less than *His*! Earthly marriage and adoption cannot ever fully image the tri-une God's heart for humanity, but they do image the ways the triune God makes His way toward us, to covenant to be with us in suffering, and wherever we go, He goes, and wherever He goes, we go, and *as long as nothing gets in the way of us being together, everything on the way is going to be okay.*

KIN

A kind Chinese official brings over two red ink pads, bends forward over the paperwork to try to explain to me in gestures that I will need to press my thumb right here into this ink pad, then impress my red thumbprint right here over my signature because my name alone will not be enough to seal this adoption. Only a red-stained hand will seal the deal.

I press my thumb into the red ink pad, then over my signature, shake my head: It's His covenant of *hesed*-love, signed with His red-stained hand, that makes every Red Sea Road.

And that's what I can see in my mind's eye, that Red Sea Road cutting right through towering walls of water; and that scene flashes, too, that strange scene from Genesis 15, maybe one of the most significant scenes of the Old Testament, when God tells the father of the faith, Abram, to cut the heifer, the ram, the goat, in half—and then after the sun sets and darkness sets in, God cuts a deal, a covenant, to always *hesed*-love Abram. God alone, blazing like a pillar of fire, passes between the red-stained pieces of sacrificed animals. Abram doesn't enact the covenant. Abram doesn't walk through the red-stained sacrifices, because he knows he can't keep the deal to always keep company with God, but God says He Himself will keep the covenant of love for *both* of them.

And when God cut the waters in two and carved a Red Sea Road through the waves, that is exactly what is happening: *God is cutting a covenant with His people.*

Like the presence of God was "a smoking firepot with a blazing torch [that] appeared and passed between the pieces" (Genesis 15:17), just like the presence of God was a cloudy flaming torch that passed through the cut waters at the Red Sea, the hands of God were cut with nails and fastened to the cross, and the rocks and the veil in the temple split in two, as we passed into the open arms of God, who cuts through every sin, every storm, every story, every sea, and makes a *hesed*-covenant of intimacy.

This is the whole of the gospel, this is the Way, this is every Red Sea Road. God always comes the whole way through *for* us, to be *with* us.

What God is saying, when He cuts the covenant as the smoking firepot in Genesis 15 with Abram, when He cuts the Red Sea for the people of Israel, when He cuts the temple veil because of His sacrifice at the cross for us right now, is nothing less than:

> *Not only will I cut myself off if I don't keep My covenant of* hesed-*love to you forever; I will pay the penalty and let Myself be cut open if* you *can't keep your love covenant to* Me. *Even when you fail and fall and all the dreams and hopes fracture, and you don't and can't keep your covenant of* hesed-*love, I'll*

> *keep the whole covenant for you, and I'll be the One who loves*
> *you to death and back to the fullest life, to make you Mine,*
> *kin, for forever.*

With much motioning and Chinese words I can't understand, I'm asked if I can take off one of Shiloh's shoes—then
her sock. The official holds out the red ink pad to her bare foot.

Ah, of course.

I hold her up and press her tiny bare toes into the red ink pad.
She doesn't have to know what any of this means. She doesn't know
yet how we're going to swing in the hammock together, reading our
favorite dog-eared books on late summer afternoons, or eat cherry
tomatoes in our pajamas in the kitchen garden as the sun comes
up. She doesn't yet know how we will bike down our country gravel
road at sunset, her in the carrier behind me, her hands raised in
the air like she's swooping and soaring, and she'll watch our flying
shadow stretch across the fields and she will sing as she soars,
"Look, this is usssss together! This is usssss, togetherrrrrr!"

She doesn't know yet how we will pray it together every night
under the stars over the farm, "Our Father who art in heaven,
hallowed be Thy name, Thy kingdom come . . ." because this is
our Abba Father's world and we "are adopted children of God—
adopted by grace through Christ,"* and we are His kin, safe in
His kin-dom, and because this is *His* kingdom, all *His* safe ways,
not our ways, be done. She doesn't know yet this is a covenant to
kinship, to family, and her Father and I will keep the whole long
covenant regardless of what happens, what hurts, what the road

---

* "Lord's Day 13," Heidelberg Catechism, Christian Reformed Church,
accessed November 14, 2021, https://www.crcna.org/welcome/beliefs/confessions
/heidelberg-catechism.

holds, what she ever can or cannot keep, we keep our promise to be family. Her foot is stained bright red.

Every real exodus only happens where we just enter right into Christ.

Every crossing, through the cross, and through the sea, is through God's act of covenantal love, an entering into belonging to God for forever.

God does not bring us out—does not make a way for our own exoduses—for us to go our own way or have our own way. Rather, God says, "Let my people go, that they may serve me in the wilderness" (Exodus 7:16 ESV). And the Hebrew words for *serve* and *worship* used throughout Exodus 7 are the linguistically related words *abad* and *avodah*, which mean "keep in bondage, be bondmen, bond-service."*

The WayMaker's saying, "Let My people go—so they will fuse to Me. Worship Me. Be bound to Me." The WayMaker doesn't make a way for us to go our own way.

> The WayMaker's saying, "Let My people go—so they will
> attach to Me."
> The WayMaker's calling us out of bondage—*avadim*—to
> Pharaoh—to bondage, to *bonding*—*avadim*—to Him.**

---

* *Strong's Hebrew Lexicon*, s.v. "H5647 *abad*," accessed November 14, 2021, https://www.blueletterbible.org/lexicon/h5647/nkjv/wlc/0-1/.

** God says of the Israelites' bondage to Pharaoh, "I brought you up from Egypt, and brought you forth out of the house of bondage" [*avadim*] (Judges 6:8 KJV), and then God says of His own people: "For they are my *avadim*, whom I brought out of the land of Egypt" (Leviticus 25:42 NKJV). "The word used, *avadim*, is the very same word used to describe what the Israelites were to Pharaoh" (Lewis Warshauer, "What Is a Slave?," Jewish Theological Seminary, May 2, 2002, https://www.jtsa.edu/torah/what-is-a-slave/). God had freed them from bondage in Egypt to an all-consuming, all-encompassing *bonding to Him.*

The WayMaker makes a way for us to be free to be bound to His heart.

Every exodus out of *bondage* is for *bonding*.
Every exodus isn't for an escape out of a situation but for
attachment to a saving Savior.
Every exodus is for *connection*.

You know you're walking a Red Sea Road through when you're bonding closer to Him.

God leads us out—to lead us in. To lead us to the home of Him. Shiloh doesn't know yet how we will fly home and someday say those words from the Heidelberg Catechism, together around the farm table after the soup bowls are cleared, what may be the most tender, transformative lines in the whole history of Christian theology, and how she and I will reach for each other's hands:

> You know you're walking a Red Sea Road through when you're bonding closer to Him.

What is your only comfort in life and in death? That I am not my own, but belong—body and soul, in life and in death—to my faithful Savior, Jesus Christ. He has fully paid for all my sins with his precious blood, and has set me free from the tyranny of the devil. He also watches over me in such a way that not a hair can fall from my head without the will of my Father in heaven; in fact, all things must work together for my salvation. Because I belong to him, Christ, by his Holy Spirit, assures me of eternal life and

makes me wholeheartedly willing and ready from now on
to live for him.[5]

Right there beside my own red fingerprint, I lay the red sole
of her foot.

We're walking right through.

Not having any idea what we're walking into.

chapter twelve

CLEMATIS

Christ is not valued at all unless He is valued above all.

—AUGUSTINE

Seek God, not happiness—this is the fundamental rule of all meditation. If you seek God alone, you will gain happiness: that is its promise.

—DIETRICH BONHOEFFER

I am sitting on the farmhouse kitchen floor that first morning home with her, Darryl and all the kids circled round, and we can't stop laughing wide-eyed wonder at her, her catching bubbles, her giggling, her falling into our arms, us falling into her.

"I've got you, little girl, we've got you, Shiloh . . ." Darryl whispers it gently as she trips over his legs, stretching for a shimmer of bubble, and he gathers her close, curves his large arms tenderly around her.

The leafing vine of the clematis, growing in the very center of our potager, begins to curve and curl and unfurl in early spring, the weeks after I fly home from China, and farmers go off to the fields.

ATTACHMENT

I'm not sleeping deeply at night. The wee curl of Shiloh's tucked in beside me in this crib extension that's literally attached to the side of our bed. Night after night, in the inky pitched hours when the stars blink over the farmhouse and fields, she jars, terrified, scrambles to find me, sits bolt upright, and screams. This ain't China anymore, and we aren't her *ayis*, and we smell like old coveralls and spring dirt, not gingko trees and chow mein.

I reach through the dark, pull the tremble of her in close to me, try to caress away her ache, hush-comfort her howls. No need of an oximeter to know it: Every single one of these cries of hers will be plummeting her oxygen down into some steep valleys, her half a heart literally struggling to work and breathe through her fears. Darryl rolls over close, slips his arm around my waist, like he's tenderly holding me up through the crashing waves.

Wild with fear, she frantically shoves back his hand. *Breathe, baby, breathe. Breathe, marriage, breathe.*

"It's okay, Shiloh, it's okay—no one's taking your mama away from you." He's half asleep, tries to rub my tired back too.

She's having none of it. She yowls louder, bats at his hand, lips bluing with her crying.

"She just—she just doesn't know you yet." I'm feebly trying to find him, enfold him too. I wish I could say I curve in close to Darryl, cleave my fears and doubts in toward the willing rib of the man, which could have cleaved all of the fears right in half. But I am actually starting to feel the edges of me curl in on myself, my whole body tender, dangerously torn, trying to reach for her, trying to hold on to him, missing how the stretched places can be thin places to see God because I'm slowly turning inward. Is this what Augustine said of what it means to be human? We are *homo incurvatus in se*—every human turned and curved inward toward oneself.[1] It's what all the limping and bent saints who have come before have said of the curved journey—Augustine, Luther, Barth, Lewis. *Incurvatus in se* curves us away from the heart of God— until our attachment ultimately breaks and our own hearts break.

Come misty spring morning, as Darryl's taking the last sip of his steaming cup of coffee, before he heads out with seeds to bury in the earth, he leans over to kiss me—and Shiloh, perched in my arms, she pushes his face back.

He arches back.

Taken aback. Hurt. He doesn't want to be, I know he doesn't want to be because he more than feels, he *knows* how she's just lost her whole world, and she needs to know how she's attached and still has a world of her own. But I can read woundedness in his eyes. Does he blame me? He never says that once. Maybe it feels like he's quietly retreating? Maybe I'm just missing his connecting turns at every turn? He's busy, I tell myself, we're both busy. He's starting to stay out in the fields later, under that early spring moon. And I don't even know when my days start or end, heartsick babe in arms, waiting for an appointment with the cardiologist, waiting for her next breath, waiting to read some epiphany about attachment in the books that I'm burning the midnight oil to read. Is he tired of me? Maybe I'm tired of being me. Or maybe we're both just really dog-tired.

As painful as it is, it's easier for me to bear witness to all of this, if it will spare even one other soul from bearing the weight of what happens next. Keep burying how you feel and you'll end up digging your relationships a pretty big grave. If you don't speak your fears and questions aloud, they only grow louder in your soul. I needed to say all the fears out loud, to him, to me, to God, but I didn't. I curved around all my aches like I could self-protect—not knowing this was how you begin to self-destruct. *Incurvatus in se*, indeed.

When baby Shiloh's still howling after midnight, heart racing and oxygen plummeting, I slip out onto the front porch so as not to wake the whole sleeping house, and she and I, wrapped in a blanket, rock in the porch swing under a full spring moon; this rocking rhythm that mothers can naturally know calms trauma, what I'd confirmed when I'd read what the brain and attachment researchers say:

> Repetitive and rhythmic somatosensory activity . . . elicits a sensation of safety. Rhythm is regulating. All cultures have some form of patterned, repetitive rhythmic activity as part of their healing . . . rituals. . . . in part because [rhymthic movements] are tapping into the deeply ingrained, powerful permeating associations created in utero.[2]

As wee Shiloh wails, I rock and sway. Life is waves, and we are rocked and regulated by the swelling and falling of waves, and, if we let it, if we let go and let come what comes, the rhythm of waves can rock us into the deepest, healing safe. *What is in the way is making the way.* Surrender. Waves don't have to drown us; waves can rock us into a healing peace.

Long after she finally drifts off, her face lit in my arms like a jewel in the pearl-orbed light of the moon, I keep turning these pages about attachment, like there has to be a way to tether all our hearts and find more of love's way through.

I would read how pyschology professors Todd and Liz Hall defined attachment as an invisible bond "supported by a literal brain-to-brain linkup between parent and child" and what the three characteristics of the invisible bond look like:

1. Proximity and staying close—or, in the reverse, becoming "distressed when they are separated from their attachment figures (separation distress)."
2. The attachment figure is "a haven of safety in times of distress and a secure base from which to explore the world," offering emotional comfort and regulation.
3. The attachment figure offers "a sense of mutual knowing, influence, and belonging."[3]

Rocking the front porch swing through a sea of shimmery stars, I would memorize the invisible bond of attachment, of heart bonding, as four movements:

1. Closeness
2. Craving presence

3. Cruciform reach
4. Cleft in the rock

Babe in arms, under the milky light of an early spring moon, I'm orbed by God who encircles and beckons us across the waves to attach hearts to Him by just that: to stay close, to crave His presence, to live a cruciform reach toward Him for comfort, to turn to Him countless times a day as the safe cleft in the rock for our souls.

I think of this, as I comb Shiloh's silky black hair in the morning light, as I stir honey into her steaming porridge, as I trace her face with the tip of my finger and feel this child as part of me, as I rock her through the nights and all the waves like a bonding, a making of a Red Sea Road between our hearts.

At the doctor's office, when she suddenly looks up from a pile of books, looking for me with a rising wave of panic.

"Mama?" Shiloh turns. "Mama?"

"Right here, baby girl. Your mama's right here." The soul is made to fit into a cleft in the rock and proximity always eases anxiety.

When she stacks one of her last wood blocks onto the top and looks up, eyes dancing sparklers of celebration, I'm right there, smiling pure delight over her existence, christening her with a kiss. When she burrows her head in the crook of my neck, I try to make my arms, my heartbeat, all the moments of my day make the invisible bonds of attachment visibly clear.

> The soul is made to fit into a cleft in the rock and proximity always eases anxiety.

When your world slides off base, you have a base.
When your world needs to feel safe, you have a haven.
When your world feels rocky, I'll be your
    cleft in the rock.
Closeness. Craving presence. Cruciform reach.
    Cleft in the rock.

"Secure attachment means someone in this world has signed up to look out for you, to always be *for* you."[4] And it's true, whatever I may have inked on those adoption papers, my signature said: Always and forever, to look out for you, to be for you:

If you're ever lost—I'll make your way through.
If your heart ever breaks in two—I'll give you my own.
If you're ever alone—I'll make a way to hold you.
Because as long as there's a way for our hearts to stay close,
everything's going to be okay.

Was it really any different when I signed on the dotted line of my marriage papers? *My heart for yours, my walk with yours, my life bound to yours, till my last breath, then always and forever.* So why in the aching world was the suffering of the marriage covenant infinitely harder some days?

DETACHMENT

"You got time for a coffee?" Darryl asks tenderly one night after we've finished dinner, finished murmuring our weary prayers around the table.

But the words that come crashing out of my mouth like a tidal wave catch me off guard: "Coffee? Time for a coffee? Where in the world *are* you most of the time? Where *are* you anymore?" *Ayekah?*

Sometimes you don't know where you are till the words out of your mouth actually find you. How can all these words hiss with a pain that I hadn't even been aware was really there? How often was I actually slowing to still and pay SACRED attention these days?

"Look, wherever in the actual hades you are?" I'm whispering the pain. "It doesn't feel—like you're here, right here, with me. Doesn't feel like you're processing this whole attachment road with me, that you're up all night rocking Shiloh Shalom, or researching her heart condition or attachment or adoption trauma? I feel like you've kinda withdrawn into your own shell and you're not carrying this at all." Subtext: You're not carrying me.

Deeper subtext: Sometimes your own *incurvatus in se* means you're seeing the world through a lens curved toward self.

And yet still: Inside all of us is a tender child who longs to be gathered to someone's side and carried. Held. The heart-cries we have as a child grow with us into adulthood, and we seek from our partners what we sought from our parents: someone to hold us.[5] Someone to rock us safe. Is this why Scripture paints the two metaphors that most fully express our relationship with God as Father, close parent, and as Lover, covenantal partner—because both are about being held, both are about dependence, both are about intimate emotional bonding, about withness and witness and attachment? And like a child who feels her person has moved away, abandoning her, I'm crying to my person the very echo of God's first recorded question: "Where are you?"

Ayekah? Why aren't you here with me? Draw near to me. *Hineni.* Say, here I am. Say, come let me always be with you; come let me hold you. The cry in all our anger and ache is for attachment. And emotional isolation is its own kind of wilderness desolation.

So why am I leaving Darryl alone in his?

He's still listening to me, but he's reaching for the stack of dirty dishes. Not for me. I push my chair back from the table, and we're both putting a million hurting miles between us, and my fears slam him like waves of anger that keep throwing him back, so we are nowhere close to each other, not reaching for each other, not seeing or making connecting turns toward each other, not being a cleft in the rock, safe haven, sure base. How did we get here so fast and why is distance so terrifying and how in the world do we find a way back to each other?

"Nothing I do these days seems right enough for you, Ann." He's not wrong. The only thing he's safely pulling closer is that stack of dishes. "You're on edge." His eyes are begging mine. "And when you're on edge, how exactly can you expect me to be close? I don't want to be that close to the edge."

I hear him, I do, but I do have expectations of attachment. I do. "Well, that is actually where I am—on edge—but maybe if you'd hear me, come near, that would literally pull me back from the edge?"

"Look." He's standing there at the edge of the kitchen table, hurt and honest. "When I try to get close to you at all? You just snap my head off, and I'm just kinda done with it, Ann. Done. It's all too much. Way, way too much."

Too much? What exactly is he saying is too much? Me? Or is he saying my feelings are too much? Is he trying to say that he can't handle what I'm feeling because it draws him into feeling, and that terrifies him?

Maybe what we all are most deeply afraid of is feeling.

"I just really need—space." And he turns.

He turns and walks away, leaving me fighting a dark undertow of thoughts, standing there in the kitchen, alone. Exactly the one thing I was desperately trying to say I couldn't bear to be anymore—alone.

Throw in a load of laundry. Fold a pile of towels. Say nothing. *Space?* I can give him space. *Difficult?* That looming one word from those ancient counseling files that the therapist forecasted for our marriage. Maybe she was right—or maybe, more accurately, *I'm* difficult? Difficult and on edge? I'll just edge my difficult self off his radar entirely, make myself invisible and small and not say anything at all. Subtext: *Incurvatus in se* bends your head in ways that might be eye-roll-laughable from the outside if it didn't start derailing your whole life from the inside out. I've got this down to a tender fine art: *In my own hurting way, I tried to say I needed you—and you rejected me—so now I'll prove I don't need you at all.* Strange how the trauma from our early stories lives on in our bones and bends the way we see the world. We may have buried my sister after she was killed in front of my mama and me, but the trauma of witnessing her brutal death scrapes its way out of the grave to live on in me as this fear that I'm never safe. That trauma can bend the way I retreat and try to self-protect.

For us, this is our disorienting dance:[6] Early life trauma can leave you bruised tender, so when the everyday ordinary brushes a tad too close, you end up lashing out and bruising someone else. (It's more than your heart getting things wrong; it's also that there were terrible wrongs that broke your heart.) And that early trauma of seeing my baby sister crushed under the wheels of a truck and lying dead in our farm laneway left me, at times, soul-sensitive to even a breath of pain, and he would graze-touch my fears of being abandoned, which touches off all kinds of soul agitation, which he reads as anger, which drives him away, which I read as further abandonment, which leaves me more afraid—and alone. Round and round we go.

Peel squash for soup, clean out the sink. He comes and goes, and we are two souls drifting further apart, forgetting the falling in love parts of our story. Why didn't I cup his face close and stare into his eyes until I found the glint of that grinning Farm Boy who swept a young girl right off her feet? Marriages drift not because there is increasing conflict and anger but because there is increasing distance and decreasing attachment. Why didn't I remember it, like a mother does with her child: The moment you want to push away could be your sign to find a way to draw closer. I stay quiet all day. Traumas can bend us away from reaching for, or trust taking, any comfort from anyone. Nobody tells you that the shields you throw up to protect your heart end up being more like a prison that leaves you alone.

What I wish I'd known sooner?[7] Communication of feelings brings regulation to feelings. *Emotion* literally means to move. Emotions are meant to move us toward each other and God, move us to be responsive to each other, move us to vulnerably share. Coregulation soothes agitation. Sharing the weight of your feelings with another soul regulates your feelings, bringing balance to your soul.

> The moment you want to push away could be your sign to find a way to draw closer.

One night after I've kissed kids' foreheads goodnight and they've all burrowed under blankets and I turn out the lights, what's deep into the dark places of my mind, what I think he thinks, on replay, in all the ways: *I am too much. I am too much. I am too much. And I am not enough, not enough, not enough. Somehow, who I am will have to disappear.*

This is the way of how many women?

Feeling like you're not enough can be just one way of saying you feel like you're too much. Why can't he want more of me, instead of less of me? Why can't I be more for him, what he needs? Why doesn't he cup my face and whisper, "You're never too much to be loved and you are always more than enough to be loved"? Why can't I lean into him and say, "I want all of you and trust you with all of me"? Why does it feel like we're losing the promised land and waking up back in Egypt, choking dry sand in our mouths?

BONDAGE

I'm undone by the chain of events that then happen, how, as I'm curving my life toward Shiloh, attaching my heart to hers, I'm slowly curving away, detaching from my husband's heart, drifting in this distancing from God's heart, and in the season of growing things, I begin to curve toward a fragrance heavy with the scent of . . . comfort, any comfort, anywhere, to avoid any suffering. I'm not even fully aware of how I'm pulling away from Darryl, so I can reach a hand out to find all the comforting distractions that soothe any pain and ache. This is the way *incurvatus in se* moves . . . I curve and bend, detach and turn inward in ways that physically pain me even now as I try to find words to describe the ways and curves I chose.

It begins inconspicuously. I'd read it later, how, if a pilot leaving from Los Angeles "adjusts the heading just 3.5 degrees south," the plane will land in Washington, DC, instead of New York City: "Such a small change is barely noticeable at takeoff—the nose of the airplane moves just a few feet—but when magnified across the entire United States, you end up hundreds of miles apart."[8] Fear that I'm too much, fear that I'm all wrong, fear is driving a lot of my wrong turns and sharp curves, and it turns out that wrong turns compound. One small wrong turn here, one slight wrong curve there, leads to largely different destinations. Ever so imperceptibly shifting habits begins to dramatically shift who you are. Shortchanging meaningful time with the Way Himself here, turning and skimming the surface of the way there, is turning and changing who I am. It starts small at first, just here and there, not taking up my SACRED rule of life, just mustering up some (pretty pathetic) justifications why I don't have time first thing in the morning to take a SACRED way and curve toward God—and it's easier to bend back toward the worn ruts of Egypt.

Shiloh's been up all night wailing, and I'm struggling through an aching brain fog to keep my eyelids open. Dragging out of bed too late, I tell myself I don't have very much time to still and *yada*-know the bare heart of God.

Later, I grab a verse from the Word in a devotional lying out like a begging on an end table. I keep a running mental list of gifts, fleeting thoughts of thankfulness flashing across my radar. But late into the night, I research attachment, read studies of adoption trauma, devour adoptee stories, and study her medical condition and the outcomes of hypoplastic left heart syndrome surgeries. I wake late again next morning, and the next, and Facebook distracts with drama, so I don't begin my day quietly in the Word, gazing upon the face of my Beloved who never made a child He thinks is too much. Sure, the praise music's cranked, and we bow our weary heads around the dinner table, and we never push chairs away from the table until we've opened the Word. But, if I'm searingly honest, this is a season when my heart is not arced toward Him like I've been, and I'm not keenly attentive, not desperately hungry for a fresh revelation, not deeply stilling my heart to know that He is God and He is mine and I am His.

What I am doing is this: I am a fool going through the motions, and these are not justifications of how I started to slide off the map and get my sense of direction all wrong—these are simply the devastating facts of how my SACRED compass begins to slip out of my hand and I let those SACRED spiritual disciplines of stillness, attentiveness, cruciformity, revelation, examine, and doxology slip as priorities, and if you lose your rule of life, your way of life, you lose your way. Life is about direction. To be human is to be relational and directional. All of life turns on the turn. Life isn't about how far you've come, or how far you have to go; it isn't about detours, roadblocks, wrong ways, wildernesses, deep valleys, steep mountains, or the overwhelm that has you between a rock and a hard place. Life is about distance, in relation to God, and living constantly in the direction of God. No measurement in the world matters but the distance between us and God.

True, I'd only moved my feet just a few inches, just a bit further away from the Way Himself, raised my nose a lot sooner out of the Word, and I tell myself I just don't have that flicker of time to pick up a journal and pen to orient and direct the way of my soul, that it's just as effective to snack on a verse and a prayer here, like navigating at 120 miles per hour, on the fly. But the stark reality is?

For a plethora of deceiving reasons that I try to convince myself are reasonable—ruthless busyness, deep weariness, and upheaval of rhythms because of a new child—I obliviously start to inch-turn away, curve away, from the safe intimacy of my SACRED sure base, and I forget, I falter, I fail. While farmers work late in fields, and the clematis in the garden twines and curls, and our baby girl clings to me in sleep, her fingers wrapped tightly round mine, my heart takes the way of *incurvatus in se*, this curving in toward self—self-sufficiency, self-protection, self-comfort, self-interest. It's the bent way of being human: We're wired for attachment, for dependence on God, but our inclination toward *incurvatus in se* turns the direction of our dependence toward destructive things, and our attachments go awry. All addiction is an attachment in the wrong direction. Name your pain, name the way you try to make the pain go away, and you name your addiction. Name your default direction. Name the way you turn for comfort—a glass, a screen, a plate, a sweet, a drug, a page, a voice, a click, a hit, a rush, a bottle—go ahead and name what you curve to, to comfort your ache, and you name your Egypt that looks like ease.

I've named it and confessed it, my painful *incurvatus in se* to my people, but to name it here on paper could lead you, fellow WayFarer, away from naming the way your own *incurvatus in se* is curving and bending your own heart right here and now. For each of us, in our own tender, hurting ways, "there's a way of life that looks harmless enough; / look again—it leads straight to hell" (Proverbs 14:12–13 MSG), and the only way through is to find the curve and bend of our own hearts and come bend the knee to a realer and better love. All my wrong directions aren't shared for distracting speculation but rather as an open invitation, a blank space, to fill in with yours—so you might begin to feel your one sacred life turn right around.

I've sat with this long, in prayer, in the Word, in therapy, asking through tears: *Why, why, why did my own* incurvatus in se *curve me this way, and that way, and away?*

And maybe the bruised and battered and better explanation is: At the heart of all kind of addictions is a broken attachment that left a broken heart.[9] The food addict, the screen addict, the game addict, the pill addict, the bottle addict, the porn addict, the gambling addict, the person addict, the shopping addict, the comfort addict—all the addicts carry a hurt in the wrong direction, looking for a way out of pain. Addictions entwine us when motivations aren't strong enough to turn us toward a more fulfilling, though harder, direction. But when we curve and turn inward, toward other comforts, and act like we aren't made to be in relationship with God, that God doesn't exist as God to us, then parts of our own soul cease to exist. *Incurvatus in se* may say the way out of our heartbreak is to simply curve inward, but the way out of pain is to reach out, cruciform.

> The only way through is to find the curve and bend of our own hearts and come bend the knee to a realer and better love.

Bonding or bondage, those are always the two ways to choose in every moment.

I watch it all through early spring and the waxing and waning of the moon, the clematis out in the kitchen garden attaching and curling up the wind vane trellis, winding and twisting and covering it under all these leaves unfurling. And so my addictions curl around my wounds, whispering that they will comfort, heal me of any pain or suffering, if only I keep the curve of my heart hidden. And I do. And so I am consumed. Like all wrong turns of distracting comfort, to avoid suffering, mine hiss the lie that I'm in control of all the things, and it's not in control of all of me, and my inner world tangles into a garden of wrong curves and tangled turns.

I can hardly breathe it, but it's true, what Augustine said: "To forsake God and to exist in oneself—that is, to be pleased with oneself—is not immediately to lose all being; but it is to come closer to nothingness."[10]

I can sense this. The only thing I am coming closer to is nothingness.

In being bent inward toward self, we bend to self, becoming the egotheists. Rather than atheists, we are the egotheists, delighted mostly in ourselves. And like the small-minded and egotistical, it's our egotheism that makes our souls, our very lives, small. In this curving inward to enlarge ourselves, we actually belittle ourselves.

The clematis seemed to be kind of sleeping, and by late spring, it was creeping, but now, by early summer, it's leaping, seeking, sweeping, overreaching, competing against other growth in the garden, curving and curling up the wind vane trellis, till the rotating arrow of the wind vane is choked and swallowed silent in vine. All direction all self-consumed into—nothingness.

It is summer, the time when farmers come in from fields, when one could get deathly drunk on the comforting scent of clematis blooms.

chapter thirteen

OPEN HEART SURGERY

"GOD, your God, is leading the way; he's fighting for you. You saw with your own eyes what he did for you in Egypt. . . . this same GOD who goes ahead of you in your travels to scout out a place to pitch camp, a fire by night and a cloud by day to show you the way to go."

—DEUTERONOMY 1:29–33 MSG

Lying on the couch with her in warm shafts of summer light, she in her onesie zippered pajamas, and I in old sweats and a ball cap, she turns and crawls up on me, pajama legs straddling my shoulders, and leans close, her baby breath smelling all milky. Glory be, the land flowing with milk and honey is wherever she is.

Her tiny fingers press these frog stickers down my cheek and across my mouth and she can't stop giggling—"One froggie . . . two froggie . . ."—and I can't stop laughing through sticker-sealed lips—"Ribbit! Ribbit!" The ugly frog's being kissed to life by the giggling princess, and what's charmingly endearing is simply her, the riveting miracle of her, wherever she breathes.

And wherever she goes, she wears this buttercup yellow, handknit crown, and her strapping Dutch brothers lie on the floor and roll out homemade purple playdough cookies with her, and she tickles her sisters' bellies and bare toes with squealing glee, and they laugh till their sides ache happy just to hear the cascading musicality of her giggle. She holds court over the whole swoon of us. We are made kin by the King.

Her big brother whisper-tickles in the curl of her ear, "You are the very best part of our story, Shiloh Shalom Yu Xin." I can almost read that very page when she brings a book and lays it bravely in Darryl's lap at the end of a long day, and he leans near to look her in the eye and ask gently, "You want your papa to read to you?" And he's hard-earned tired, but he scoops her up, swings her in the air, and when she laughs breathless, reaching out to grab hold of his neck, he sings softly, "Your papa's always gonna take care of you." I wonder and want that to be true too. How and whom we trust is what changes us.

When my phone rings on a Wednesday morning, I reach for it. Heart surgery. Booked for Friday. Friday?

How and whom we trust is what changes us.

Friday they will lay our Shiloh on a rattling metal bed. Friday they will saw our baby girl's chest open. Friday they will reach down and hold the brave beats of her heart. Who is going to hold mine? I can feel it like a pained ache emanating across my chest, like my too-much heart's cracked broken and curved all wrong.

Yes, no foods or liquids, yes, we will be at the admitting desk at five a.m. for open heart surgery, and yes, I signed the consent papers that state all the risks or even the possibility of death— yeah, my head can't even go there, and please, *Abba Father, don't take us there.* Yes, she's only eighteen pounds, and she fills our whole little world with full color.

Cut my heart open instead.

She's screaming wild when the women in gloves and masks carry her through the OR doors. Frantically clawing at air, clawing to get back to me, her cheeks blue-purple with terror, with lack of oxygen, she's gone from us in a heart crack through the swinging OR doors. Long after I can't see her flailing through the glass window slots, I can hear her crying far down the hall, "MAMAAAA! MAMAAAA! MAMAAAA!"

Oh, Shiloh Shalom Yu Xin. *Peace, peace, please, God, give her perfect peace.* And then there's only mocking silence. Somewhere in the inner chambers of the surgical labyrinth, they're readying to splice open her heart. My heart fissures. There's no way for me to get to her.

"I don't think I can take this." I choke the words out, but Darryl's half-turned, one eye watching the weather blaring on one of the pre-op room TV screens. We are in the middle of a drought. Don't I know it. Don't I know he's a farmer looking for rain, that he needs rain for thirsty, cracked ground, that he keeps looking at the horizon for rain, but he's got to know how parched and dry we are over here and how the serpentining clematis at home in the garden is choking everything out.

"Why in the world did the midazolam have the opposite effect?" I'm shaking my head, trying to compete with the ignorant TV weatherman. "Paradoxical effect. Making her wilder instead of calming her. Isn't this some beginning. What if this is the first in a string of things that don't go as planned?" And yeah, don't I know all about that. I've been the fool, in how many ways, but particularly the one who did what you aren't supposed to do and googled much of what can go wrong when they take the fine, sharp blade of an oscillating saw and cut through our baby's sternum, cracking her chest wall to get to her underdeveloped heart with only one ventricle instead of two, on the right side of her chest instead of the left. Yet maybe my heart's the underdeveloped one, me curving in on my own heart.

"It's okay, Ann, it's going to be okay. God has her." Darryl turns from the screen. But what does that even mean, God has her, has us? You tell me: This whole hospital is stacked with twenty-one floors of sick kids, 453 hospital beds of babies, and how many times since we've been here have we heard the hallways erupt with *Code blue! Code blue!* because some baby's literally turning blue with death? What if the next code blue is for our baby? What if her heart stops midbeat in some surgeon's hand and our baby girl doesn't find a way out of here alive?

Sure, there's shalom in storm, sure, there's laying my *korban* down to draw nearer, and yeah, sure, there's a sacred way down a Red Sea Road to bonding with Abba, King of the universe, but you tell me first: Do you really trust that that King has us and will take care of us when our baby just went through those OR doors and they're going to razor open her one heart to keep her from death's door? What if this is the last unexpected stop, and she doesn't get a life, or the life of her dreams, and none of her hopes ever get to even be and we're stuck parched and withering over here in the land of the suffering?

When Darryl's leaning down to sign us into the surgical waiting room, like he's signing some covenant, I want to grab his pen, get him to look me in the eye: *What if I am never loved the way I want to be loved? What if I die never having been loved the way I dreamed? Is there really anyone who is literally taking care of us, or is all this metaphor, and who is truly taking care of me if not me?*

These are not rhetorical questions. These are the questions that scream in the inner chambers of cracking hearts. It seems somebody better crack open an ocean of aching doubt and make a way out.

He finds a seat at the back of the waiting room. Our little Shiloh's chest will be bare by now, ready for the saw to whirl through her flesh and bone. And here we all are, hurting in all kinds of unspoken ways.

Things had gotten unexpectedly messy between us. Ugly.

"I don't think you like me." I'd hardly whispered it to him.

"I don't think you like me very much either." He hadn't turned.

I don't say anything, that I love him, or like him. He doesn't either—that he wants me or needs me.

He just kept looking out the kitchen window, past the

clematis twining and twisting over everything he'd once smiled and gently kneeled down to help me plant.

As the sun has the power to thrive or shrivel a leaf, so relationships can either heal trauma or actually cause it.

I curl up in a chair in the corner of our bedroom and weep. He eventually comes, finds me, but before I even let him begin to apologize, I'm shaking my head, a wave of selfish words rising, swelling, breaking, and breaking us both.

"You say you're done with it all being too much, that it's all far too much? Well, you know what? I hear what you're saying, loud and clear. I hear you saying that *I'm* far too much. I hear you not saying that you like me. I hear you not saying that you love me. Well, guess what? You win, Darryl, you win. You? You maybe don't need to be stuck with me after all."

He's too hurt, wounded—stunned—to say anything. Doesn't want to get too close to my edge.

And I walk out the door, wishing I could find a way out of *me*.

I drive up to the lake. I walk around water, but the truth is I am blind to my own refusal to still in my soul. When you don't still, you react. When you don't, first and foremost, purpose to utilize the strength of stillness—there's no way to pay attention to who God is, or to your location, or to what your soul deeply wants. If you don't pay attention to your one sacred life, you will pay with your life. Where there's no cruciform, truly reaching toward the one true God and others, but only *incurvatus in se*, this curving inward, there is always only going wayward to a hell of your own making.

And as to revelation? Where there's no seeking a fresh revelation of God, but a hoarding of old manna gathered from yesterdays in the company of God, you can count on that manna growing stale and rotting and nauseating your life. Go ahead: Examine everyone else's soul, but don't examine your own, and it's your own failure that will end up suffocating you while you sleepwalk through your days. Don't covenant your life to daily doxology, and the dark of entitlement will devour your one and only life and you won't even know it. You will be the quietly enraged, entitled, living dead.

This is the death of me to say.

This is my story. This is how you profane holy things.

Walking the same lake that we walked on our honeymoon, I stand on the edge of the water on an empty beach in the early morning fog and listen to the crash of the begging waves at my feet. But if I don't take care of me, who will? Curve in toward yourself long enough and you will trip yourself.

HOW WE STOP BELIEVING IN MIRACLES

In the surgical waiting room, I watch the clock. The surgeon should be placing the pressure line on Shiloh's superior vena cava open right about now, preparing to access her central venous through her femoral veins. Increase the dopamine. Clamp the veins. Elevate the arterial pressure. I've got to get out of this room of parents waiting on the edges of their seats, got to walk some dimly lit empty hallways, got to help myself to any kind of distraction, some kind of comfort, that will ease or numb or soothe even a bit of this pain.

Right now, somewhere down this labyrinth of hallways, a surgeon's bent over our daughter's naked chest, taking a scalpel to Shiloh's right pulmonary artery, completely dissecting it from its base, splitting it straight through where it divides into the lobar branches.

I reach for my phone to scroll and click and numb out with any rerouting comfort.

It is after the exodus out of the slavery of Egypt through a God-breathed Red Sea Road, after weeks and several hundred kilometers, with thousands of men, women, and children traveling by foot across the desert, fed and watered and cared for by God, it is after meeting God at Mount Sinai where God weds Himself to His people with the ten vows of love,* after spending months building the tabernacle so God could travel with and dwell intimately among His people, that God finally sends twelve spies to canvass the promised land He promised to give to them (Numbers 13:1–2). Only to have the people shrink back in fear that the inhabitants of the land are stronger, greater, and tougher. They don't trust God to make a way.

To be clear: They don't trust the God who breathed back the entire sea with the breath of His nostrils, they don't trust the God who held back the waves into towering walls by the word of His mouth, and they don't trust the very God who visibly descended from the heavens in a pillar of cloud, a cloud that was actually on fire, who then personally moved ahead of them and led them with their own eyes through a sea of water, on a dusty, dry Red Sea Road, straight through miraculous waves of impossible. They don't trust the God whom they witnessed releasing those walls

---

* "The covenant at Sinai is often thought of as a wedding between God and His people, between God and the bride He chose for Himself." Ray Vander Laan, "Lesson 9.5: I Led You Like a Bride: A Wedding at Sinai," *That the World May Know with Ray Vander Laan*, streaming video, 1:15, accessed November 14, 2021, https://www.that theworldmayknow.com/i-led-you-like-a-bride.

of waves to swallow up Pharaoh's pursuing army of Egyptians whole.

Why trust the God who gives water from a rock, who makes manna miraculously fall out of thin air, who blows in a dinner train of quail on the daily? Why trust the God who takes care of them and takes care that the angel of death passes over their houses but not the houses of their oppressors? Clearly: You can be a firsthand eyewitness to God's work and still not trust God to take your hand and make a way. You can say that if you saw miracles you'd trust God, but we have, and we don't, and the Israelites had, and they didn't, and seeing is not believing, knowing is not living, witnessing is not trusting.

It was more than the Israelites not trusting God to take them to where they dreamed: They didn't trust God *to take care of them*. What broke God's heart was that the Israelites didn't trust God *to take care of their hearts*. They didn't trust the God who took care of them once and brought them through to take care of them and bring them through to His safe arms again.

> You can be a firsthand eyewitness to God's work and still not trust God to take your hand and make a way.

Life deals in trust, relationships deal in trust, and the currency of holistic change is wholly trusting. Trusting the process, trusting the work, trusting the road, trusting the Way, trusting the WayMaker, trusting the kindness of God. "In God, whose word I praise, / In God I have put my trust" (Psalm 56:4 NASB). The word translated *trust* from the Hebrew, *batach*, literally means "to cling or adhere to something"—or attach to someone.[1] Life is waves, but there is One who walks waves on whom you can cling. Who says, *Trust*

Me! Trust Me! Wind your arm right around His, trace the thin blue vein at His wrist and the way your name's etched right into His palm,* lace your fingers through the fingertips that can carve stone and pin the stars to the night sky, then wrap all your trust around God, clinging to Him like a belt, to keep your whole life from falling down around your ankles, tangling you and drowning you in it all. "'For as a belt is bound around the waist, so I bound all the people of Israel and all the people of Judah to me,' declares the LORD" (Jeremiah 13:11). "You must . . . cling to him" (Deuteronomy 10:20 NLT). You are on the way of Jesus only when you need to cling to Jesus the whole way. The only way to hold on for dear life is to cling to Him who whispers, *Dear child, I've got you.*

How long has our child been under the knife now? Are the surgeon's gloves clamping Shiloh's pulmonary artery right now, is he glancing up, waiting to see the fluctuations in her oxygen saturation? Or has he already split open her superior vena cava and skeletonized it from where it joins with the innominate vein, straight up to where it meets her heart? *Breathe. Beat, heart, beat.* I turn down another hallway, farther and further, murmuring all the way.

I'd have fit right in with the Israelites, the children who slapped their Beloved in the face with their lack of trust, taking His years of tried-and-true faithfulness and throwing it back in His face. Could anything be more insulting than shirking back from your beloved's outstretched hand and murmuring, "I don't trust you. I don't trust you to love me, I don't trust you to take

---

* "See, I have engraved you on the palms of my hands; your walls are ever before me" (Isaiah 49:16).

care of me, I don't trust you to have my best interests at heart, I don't trust you to be there for me, I don't trust you to bring me into any promised land, I don't trust your ways at all." I'll cling to my comfort of choice instead.

And God's broken heart howls: "How long shall I bear with this evil congregation, which murmur against me? I have heard the murmurings of the children of Israel, which they murmur against me" (Numbers 14:27 KJV). God's heart aches over this "evil congregation," which means, according to the Hebrew word used to express "evil" here, the "evil of consumption, an evil that comes from letting natural desires consume you."[2] Which is exactly the dark that Augustine wrote of: our deep *incurvatus in se*, the curving in the heart of every human toward self, consumed with desires to take care of self, comfort self, preserve self. And it is a curving that causes us to murmur, or *layan*, which means "to remain" or "to stay"[3]—which is to say: a refusal to move forward on the way. Murmuring is stopping to *rail* against God, which is the antithesis of *stilling*, which is slowing and paying attention to God, and where our soul is in relation to Him. Murmuring is what gave the Israelites forty years in the desert.

These may not be popular, meme-approved, societal truths, but they are deeply spiritual, Scriptural truths: Self-care is not the same as resting in *God's* care. Trying to self-protect can be how we self-destruct. Trying to save oneself can be how to *lose* oneself. The independence of *choosing* my own way can be what *destroys* my way. When we try to take care of ourselves, we can take away the care *God* means to give. What sends you out into the wilderness is being stressed out and refusing to stay in relationship with God. This isn't about the wise care of taking a long walk or a long bath, but rather about wisely considering how there are ways that taking care of self can take away the joy *God* has in caring for us—and the joy we can only experience *when we let Him*. Is that what I have done, what I keep doing, in all kinds of diverting ways? When I don't expect God to take care of me, *I exile myself to the wilderness*. When I doubt the WayMaker's taking care of me, I curve toward my own wilderness-making. When I don't fully expect *hesed*, I can fully expect I've made my own kind of barren desert way.

"There are only two kinds of people in the end," wrote C. S. Lewis: "those who say to God, 'Thy will be done,' and those to whom God says, in the end, 'Thy will be done.' All that are in Hell, choose it. Without that self-choice there could be no Hell."[4] What has the final say in a life, and in our days, is whether we say to God, "Thy way," or we demand He say to us, *Thy way*. One is trusting. The other is terrifying.

The drugs of heparin and prednisolone will be running through Shiloh's veins by now. Her superior vena cava clamped. Someone will have raised the head end of the operating table, so Shiloh, in her two little pigtail sprouts, breathing heavy under her oxygen mask, will be on an incline to better allow her venous to drain through her collaterals and azygos vein, before the gloved hands of the surgeon slide in a bidirectional shunt of polypropylene from her superior vena cava to her pulmonary artery. And all eyes in that operating theater will turn to watch the screens to monitor her superior vena cava's pressure.

My eyes can't stop watching the time, not at all managing the wild pressures in my own hardening heart. Turning at the end of the hallway, I run right into Darryl.

"Ann." His eyes read confused, hurt. "Where have you been?" *Ayekah? Ayekah?*

Don't worry. If you think I'm too much, I won't share much. And, honestly, I haven't the foggiest notion of where I am anymore. I just know I ache everywhere, and that ache is that I'm just beginning to know how I have wildernessed myself. This is the way you end up when you've cut yourself off from your own cleft in the rock, your own base, turned from your own safe haven, and headed stiff-necked back down into Egypt.

It feels a heart-stretch longer than six and a half excruciating hours since Shiloh was peeled screaming from my shoulder, before Dr. Caldman, still in his surgical cap, finally waves us out of the waiting room and into the hallway.

"She's through."

Waves of relief. Utter mercy of parted waves. We want a way through, when God wants to get through to us, that the way is always to trust. To cling to Him, like a vine, like a belt, like a sure hand across water.

Through—she's through. Bidirectional cavopulmonary connection. Ligation of the pulmonary artery. Flow of deoxygenated blood rerouted from upper extremities to lungs, bypassing heart.

Red Sea Road. Our baby girl still breathes.

Who takes care of her and the sparrows, who catches every teardrop in His bottle, who was still holding the world in His hands when my little sister fell to the ground under that crushing wheel?

God is the Word, the Author of our story, and He keeps writing the story until the last line is good. No page is the whole story, and no dark gets to write our last line. The Word writes the last line, only Love Himself does. So we stay in His story, dwell in the Word Himself, stay and cling-trust that there is only one Word who can restory and restore all our broken hearts with His.

Do I believe? Do I more than believe with cranial matter—do I trust in the clinging matters of the heart?

"We'll keep watching her pressures and oxygenation over the next few days, see how long her recovery is, monitor how her heart adjusts to the shunt, how her lungs and body handle this rerouting circulation, but looking at things right now, this surgery looks like it sets her up as well as can be hoped for her next heart surgery."

I don't ask when the next heart surgery is, only ask when we can see her.

"Are you her mama?" the nurse asks me when we are called back to ICU.

I'm trying to find little Shiloh somewhere underneath a circuitry of tubes, wires, electrodes and drains and oxygen mask. "Yes. Yes, I'm Shiloh's mama." *Kin.*

> *My heart for yours,*
> *my walk with yours,*
> *my life bound to yours,*
> *till my last breath, then always and forever.*

"When she started to stir, when we were extubating her back in OR, the first thing she cried when we pulled out that tube from down her throat was just that: 'Mama! Mama!'"

Oh, baby girl. Everything blurs. *Mama's here, right here.*

Abba. Abba's here, right here.

Cry out for your Abba.

Shiloh moans for me. I stroke her fingers, her hair. Nurses measure how much bloody fluids are draining from her chest tubes. Screens beep. I never leave her side, sleeping in a chair beside her all night, cardiac ICU nurses standing by. Darryl grabs a few hours of shut-eye at his sister's an hour north of the city.

Things go south early the next morning. Malakai's running a fever at home. Malakai, newly diagnosed with diabetes. Thirteen-year-old kid who's never had to navigate being his own manual pancreas while also managing being sick. How do we accurately monitor his blood sugar levels, his ketone levels, and avoid diabetic ketoacidosis, a serious complication of Type 1 diabetes that can develop suddenly when battling the flu, leaving one in a coma—or, alternatively, dead?

"I know, you've got to go home to Malakai, I know." I'm telling myself Darryl isn't just looking for a way out of this medical labyrinth, this metropolitan maze of streets and people and lights that makes a farming man antsy, a way to take gravel roads back to the safety of the farm with red maples lining the lane and the comfort of cornfields and big sky and all the love he knows. Or am I the one always looking for a way to push him away?

"You don't want me here anyways."

"You don't want me."

Hissed, hushed words.

Alarms scream. Code blue, code blue, somewhere in CICU.

Breathe, baby, breathe. Breathe, marriage, breathe. We are all dying here in our own sterile ICU.

I can see it in his eyes, feel it across my chest: We both feel utterly abandoned. It's not a lack of hot passion but a lack of being each other's safe haven that makes for unhappy marriages. And why can't we be the safest refuges for each other, the way we are the safest refuges for our children?

He leaves me for Malakai. And I don't go with him for Shiloh. Life's complicated, and it can be confounding to know what to do, which way to go, but all of life is relational and directional because all of life is about the way the heart bonds—in a healthy attachment, or in *incurvatus in se* addictions. Across this whole blue spinning marble in space, there is not one heart that beats with self-sufficiency, and any notion of separateness is mirage; we are all bonding or in bondage, all our hearts dependent in ways that flourish us or wilderness us.

He walks out quiet and hurting through the swinging CICU doors.

Something in me breaks.

chapter fourteen

THE WAYMAKER

He can deal gently with the ignorant and wayward.

—HEBREWS 5:2 ESV

If there is anywhere on earth a lover of God who is always kept safe, I know nothing of it, for it was not shown to me. But this was shown: that in falling and rising again we are always kept in that same precious love.

—JULIAN OF NORWICH

hiloh's not home twelve months after her first bidirectional heart surgery, and her cardiology team doesn't yet have her next heart surgery even on the calendar, and out in the kitchen garden, the clematis is growing in a wild mess of curving directions again, when I take the screeching elevator up to the operating room of our little country hospital for what should have been a straightforward surgical procedure of a feminine nature.

I hand the check-in nurse the consent forms and paperwork my doctor sent with me and glance down at my phone to see how late I am for what's slotted as a twenty-minute uterine ablation.

"Uh. What exactly is keeping you standing right now?" The OR nurse, pen in hand, looks up from my paperwork, wide-eyed, reaches over and touches my arm as though she can help keep me upright.

"Exactly how long have you been walking around with hemoglobin in the low sixties?"

Which is to say: I'm walking around at half of the 125 g/l normal baseline. Which is to ask: How are you getting enough oxygen to your brain?

"Well, maybe that explains a whole lot of things." I'm laughing like a blushing fool, like it's funny, like I only wish the last year and my *incurvatus in se* was even mildly amusing, instead of destroying good and right and lovely things and leaving me smiling thinly while clawing on the inside for a way out of a parched, wilderness pit of aloneness, this rock and hard place of my own making.

"Who's been monitoring your iron levels, your ferritin levels, your hemoglobin levels?" She's poking the piece of paper like she can drill down to whatever's going on.

"Well, I did know I had low iron levels." Feebly, I half defend, trying to explain how I know I'm not enough and too much and . . . but she cuts me off.

"Whose care have you been under? What I'm asking is, who's been taking care of you?"

She wants a doctor's name, but the walls of my claw-scratched canyon ring with the howling truth: I have. I have been trying to take care of myself.

The doctor called in to look again at my blood work pulls out her stethoscope to listen to my heart. My heart? I'm—I'm just here for a uterine ablation.

"Okay, you've got to know. You have a systolic heart murmur. You're so severely anemic—your heart's compensating for the lack of red blood cells getting to your body's tissues by pumping faster and pumping more diluted blood across your aortic valve, creating a heart murmur, a turbulent flow." *Turbulent flow?* She has no idea.

I'm laughing embarrassed and dying on the inside.

"Guess it looks like somewhere along the way, my body's slowly acclimated to lower hemoglobin levels, iron levels, and oxygen levels to the old noggin, eh, Doc?" I'm awkwardly choke-laughing, but: When we move our way toward self-focus slowly enough, it masquerades as healthy normalcy.

Before my little day surgery, they get me into one of those flimsy hospital gown getups, and then, after a consult out in the hallway, they decide that before I go under the anesthetic, they'd better drop two units of blood into my willing, needled vein. Try to turn my pounding, murmuring heart around. How long has my heart been murmuring like an Israelite? Since I started turning inward, to take care of me, to avoid suffering, and lost all sense of direction, of connection?

> When we move our way toward dysfunction slowly enough, it masquerades as normalcy.

The red drip trickles, the thin bedsheets pulled up over my milk-bottle-white knees, and as I watch the blood run into me, I think of how all our precious *incurvatus in se* starts out as turning inward to comfort an ache, instead of cruciformly reaching out with our ache to find healing in communion with God and in community—until self squeezes the lifeblood right out of our souls. Blood transfuses. And I'm feeling this interior transformation, like a strengthening, an awakening: Every single temptation I've ever known to take my own way has spoken the language of entitlement. My entitlement—or God's enthronement. Living feeling entitled to a story—or entrusting the story to God. And if I don't *trust* God enough to form a deep *attachment* to God, I get lost and turn to trust all kinds of other things with my needs, and those attachments can grow into craving addictions because they can't deeply satisfy.

All our addictions are wrongly directed attachments, and all addictions are healed with rightly directed attachments.

The clematis in the garden is a knotted tangle and I've wildernessed myself and lost the way back to Darryl, or us, or all we dreamed to be. I could weep.

The bag is emptying down.

It all comes down to this: Your wholeness is more about the *health of your attachments* than the *hellishness of your adversities*.

Any reprieve of peace or comfort from pain found in distractions, in screens, in food, in bottles, in drink, is only for a fleeting moment till we crave the hit of more. The reorienting truth is this: Relationship is the only rewarding reality that lasts for all eternity.

The way through is always about moving in the direction of connection. Waves part, and there's a Red Sea Road anywhere we move in the direction of connection with our Abba Father, and His people, so hearts are deeply seen and *yada*-known.

Deep adversity is offset by deep intimacy.

Am I ready for my own heart to turn? Reroute? Curve toward Love Himself?

After the blood bags drip dry, they roll me in under the glare of the OR lights for this womanly procedure, and I'm feeling like an exposed, splayed duck. The last thing I remember before going under is: *Please, help.*

TIME TO ADMIT

Two days after the twenty-minute surgical procedure, I'm in bed at home with a fever of 102.6 and doubled over with cramps.

"Ann." My mama's standing in our bedroom, her brow knit, shaking her head and her white crown of glory. "We? We are not playing here anymore. I'm still your mama. And you? You are going straight to the ER. Get your shoes on, girl." She hands me laceless sneakers I can just slide on. Things in me are loosening, unraveling—and yet just beginning.

In the waiting room, I lie across chairs, head feeling too heavy for one thin, aching neck, joints aching, like embers smoldering in each socket. Mama strokes my hair back. I close my eyes.

By the time they get me into an ER bed, I'm a teeth-chattering mess, feverishly huddling under a stack of warmed blankets, and a nurse pokes around with a needle to start IV antibiotics in one arm for whatever infection is spreading. Feels like? My precious *incurvatus in se* toward self has turned, curved and curled, a kind of self infection wrecking all directions and relations and sacred connections. Dr. Mapleton orders another two units of blood for the other arm, because I'm still registering ridiculously low hemoglobin levels, and she calls out into the hallway for abdomen and chest X-rays and for someone to call the lab and draw blood so they can somehow track down the source of infection that is spiking this raging heat through my bones. Do I tell them I already know the source of my soul infection, I already know?

They decide to admit.

Am I ready to admit? How I've turned inward, self-ward?

They wrap me again in another shroud of warm blankets, wait for tests, antibiotics dripping into my vein late into the night. I toss and turn with the feverish ache of things, staring out the hospital window long after Mama kisses me on the forehead and heads home. *Where is Darryl? Where am I? Ayekah?* Where is the way when you've curved your heart all wrong? I listen to machines all dripping, watch car lights wind down streets, all the black sky lighting up. Suffering can be the friend who drives you where you didn't know you needed to go. I dare to believe: Life's detours and deconstructions mean God wants you to run right into His arms so He can reconstruct your heart.

I've had it all wrong. I thought what mattered was forward, always forward. If life gets hard, if your health tanks, if love feels like it up and ran off, if the tax man's hunting you down and the dog puked on the carpet and you've broken your leg and the whole bottom falls out of things, I would always say, *Forward! Just keep moving forward, keep looking forward, keep pressing forward.*

Every breath hurts; every joint aches. Don't I know it: Because all of life is directional and relational, hollering "*Forward! Forward! Always forward!*" from the helm of life's ship, like you're some Christopher Columbus. But forward doesn't get you where you want to go if your road's curved inward. If your heart's curved inward, moving forward is going wayward.

Because the whole of life is directional and relational, the rallying cry of a soul on the way is *Toward! Toward God! Toward hope, toward grace, toward love, toward cruciform, toward home!*

Instead of focusing on moving forward, what matters is what you are moving toward.

Not inward, not wayward, not forward, always *toward!*

Trying to roll tenderly in the hospital bed, to roll toward the window, to the lights, trying to breathe through the ache, it strikes me, an epiphany in the middle of the night in a hospital bed, in the middle of trying to breathe through every painful breath: Suffering is not our main stress. Estrangement is. The estrangement that began in Eden with a broken trust and broken attachment with God is what keeps breaking us.

Humanity's greatest problem is not the problem of suffering but the problem of sin because, as Lutheran theologian Eberhard Jüngel startlingly noted, it is sin that leaves us "without relations,"[1] that leaves us estranged, that leaves us alone. Sin is putting things in the way of the WayMaker coming to me, and letting things get in the way of me going to Him. Ultimately sin is our way of keeping God away.

> Suffering is not our main stress. Estrangement is.

More than the stress of any suffering, sin that keeps us estranged from God is the cause of our deepest distress.

The place we are all ultimately seeking a way out of is *aloneness.*

By the time the sun bleeds up the sky in rose and scarlets, I'm still awake, in wild distress, bent over on the edge of the bed, hacking up a horse. Cough-racked, it feels like a steely vise is crushing my ribcage, flattening my lungs.

I'm sent for a second set of chest X-rays. Now my lungs are filling like two empty buckets under an overflowing eaves trough. Is this what it feels like to be drowning alone in a sea of yourself?

"Okay . . ." The doctor's pressing the stethoscope across my back, and I'm throat-raw with the hacking and ribs aching. "We are—trying to figure out what's going on. You came in here with an infection lurking somewhere from your surgical procedure, an infection that we're still trying to find . . . yet this morning, your lungs are filling up with fluid—frankly, your lungs look like, well . . . serious junk. Looks like postoperative pneumonia."

Thirty minutes later the doctor's back in my room, instructing a nurse to hook me up immediately to a heart monitor. *A heart monitor?*

"So. This is where we are." *Location, location, location.* Pay attention. Figure out where you really are first.

"We just called down to the city hospital—to speak with a cardiologist. And what has become clear is: You're in heart failure."

Heart—failure? Maybe that's actually been clear—since before Shiloh had her heart surgery, back when I started to withdraw and turn inward, looking for distracting, nonhealing comfort in all kinds of diverting directions, and the clematis started to grow wildly every which way?

"And the reason you have postoperative pneumonia is because you're in heart failure and your heart can't keep up. Your heart can't pump the fluids we've been giving you to fight whatever this infection is, and that is why you're hacking like you're dying. It's because you've tipped into heart failure."

I know. I'm struggling to breathe because I've lost all attunement with the rocking safe beat of my Abba's kind heart, and I'm hacking like I'm dying, my heart's failing because all of life turns on the turn, and Augustine said:

> Man has undoubtedly the will to be happy, even when he pursues happiness by living in a way which makes it impossible of attainment. . . . And hence the falsehood: we commit sin to promote our welfare, and it results instead in our misfortune. . . . What is the reason for this, except that well-being can only come to man from God, not from himself? And he forsakes God by sinning, and he sins by living by his own standard.[2]

Why did I think I could trust myself more than trusting and forming an attachment with an endlessly lovingkind God?

I'm brimming. Dr. Mapleton reaches out and touches my arm.

"Ann. It's okay, it's okay—this isn't your fault, honey, it's your lack of iron that's caused the heart murmur, that's tipped you now into heart failure, which is causing the postoperative pneumonia." Dr. Mapleton's eyes try to reassure.

But she doesn't know what I know. Without the iron nails of the cross of Christ in the veins, fastening the heart to Christ—the heart fails.

She whips out her pen, leans over to write it in block letters right there on my chart, like a neon marquee for the obvious:

TIPPED INTO FAILURE

Right there in indelible ink.

But what she doesn't know: I haven't just tipped into heart

failure right now; I've been falling in failure for too long, failing my darling Darryl, failing my marriage, failing my sons and daughters, failing the kindest of friends and long-suffering family, failing in bruised relationships, and failing God. I've curved inward instead of turned, blamed instead of owned, controlled instead of calmed, dismissed instead of peeling back everything and lavishing attention on souls just yearning to be seen. When you don't know if you're really wanted—you can end up wanting things, doing things, breaking things—that leave you with a story you never wanted—and becoming a way you never dreamed you'd be. How do you find a way through, how do you find a way to forgive yourself for all the ways you've fallen so far short?

"Seeing God's greatness is not our deepest need, but seeing His *goodness*," wrote theologian Dane C. Ortlund, who then points to the words of the vulnerable and venerable Jonathan Edwards, who said, "One glimpse of the moral and spiritual glory of God, and supreme amiableness of Jesus Christ, shining into the heart, overcomes and abolishes this opposition, and inclines the soul to Christ."[3]

Dr. Mapleton tells the nurse to book me for yet another CT scan, another ultrasound, another set of chest X-rays. A technician rolls in an echocardiogram, and she's helping him hook electrode leads to my chest.

I lie there, listening to the rhythm of me. They say that a heart murmur literally sounds like *rushhhhh* and *hussshhhh*. I can hear the hurry and the worry within, and all the ways I thought I had to make a way to take care of me—that's taken me to about the end of me.

Is that what's happened? My heart's curved inward, and the rhythm of SACRED ways, the rhythm that handed me a compass, a way of life, a rule of life, that gave me the direction to the most meaningful relations, has all broken down. I'm in a state of de-SACRED. *Desecrated*.

Lying there under a thin hospital sheet in the dimmed room, listening only to the stillness—and then the sloshing, slogging chaos of my failing heart, there it is: By stillness, sanity is found. By stillness, sense is made of things. By stillness, the roar of the enemy is stilled, and the soul can listen to the whisper of its Maker. You have to make time to be still—in order to make a life. Why had I needed a literal heart failure to find a long, long stretch of clarifying stillness? Had I needed to fall into heart failure so my actual life wouldn't fail? What's in the way is making the way, and He is always taking care of us.

> By stillness, the roar of the enemy is stilled, and the soul can listen to the whisper of its Maker. You have to make time to be still—in order to make a life.

Lying in a hospital bed, in heart failure, listening to an echocardiogram—*rush . . . hush . . . rush . . . hush . . .* that is all I can think: You only get so many heartbeats before here is over. You only get so much time. You only get so much time to forgive, to wipe slates clean, to make things right when you've gotten things wrong, to love, to love, to love. There is only so much time to make love your life. That is all time is for, that is all life is for: To take your days and find ways to say to Love Himself who made you, "I love You too."

This is the one and only expectation.

Expect nothing but the *hesed*-lovingkindness of God here—and accept everything here is a way to love Him back. You were born for this SACRED romance. Before time here will run out, before it's too late and your heart will stop its brave beating, before there will be no more time here to love, to change the story here, to make a way for your life to say all the love that you feel.

I have got to somehow breathe.

RUN HOME

I lie awake all night, coughing and choking on the past. Screens blinking, tracing my failing heart, and I cough up at the stars, like I can cough up my sins and all this curving in on my heart. Alveolus fill, pleura fill, Spirit fill. I just keep seeing it flash, all the scenes: Young Farm Boy's first tender kiss. The covenant, there on my wedding finger, the cross inked there on my wrist. The way Darryl hugged me and swung me around the day he said yes to Shiloh. Him reaching for me in the dark, reading me like braille in the dark until he *yada*-knows me and doesn't let go, like the waves have been storm-cut in half, and the two who have cleaved have been made one. I blink it back in the room's shadows, everything slowed down and stripped away to just my struggling beating heart, my every desperate breath.

Who of us hasn't been like the prodigal?

I've been like the foolish prodigal who said, "Father, hand over now the share of property that should be coming to me. Because we may be kin, Abba Father, but I'm thinking of acting like parts of us are dead to each other so I can have what's coming my way now because, maybe, in some ways, I don't really trust Your ways—don't trust Your ways to take care of me, don't trust Your ways to grow my joy large because Your ways aren't just higher than ours; sometimes Your ways seem straight up–high and right stoned that take us down a road of suffering." The soul's greatest lack is lacking confidence in God.

So I up and took the grace that He gave and curved my way down into a far country and squandered it all in my own kind of self-focused living where I thought I could avoid suffering, until now, when my heart's literally failing and I can't breathe.

Run away from your past, from rejection, from fear, from failing, go running and looking for self-comfort in all the wrong places because you think you can write a better story than God, take care of yourself and your people better than God, wanting to be a kind of god unto yourself—and you become a prodigal, an Israelite who wildernesses yourself: Not Your way of taking care of me, but my way of taking care of me be done, *and be done by me.*

"And when he had spent everything, a severe famine arose in that country, and he began to be in need" (Luke 15:14 ESV). Breathe. Can the vine of your wrong-clinging clematis twine around you until it collapses your lungs? *Breathe.* Breathing is a rhythm, and that's what I've lost; I've lost my SACRED rhythm.

> "I will set out and go back to my father and say to him: Father,
> I have sinned against heaven and against you. I am no longer
> worthy to be called your son; make me like one of your hired
> servants." (Luke 15:18–19)

It's not the only time in Scripture those words are spoken. The only other time is when Pharaoh says the same words to manipulate Moses to get his own way (Exodus 10:16). How often have I been like the prodigal who isn't actually repenting of his ways but is devising a way, like Pharaoh, to manipulate and twist the father's arm to earn things, make things happen, his own way? The text doesn't say the prodigal returned to the father in actual repentance; the text says the prodigal would "arise and go to my father" and make his way—his own way—back to the father.[4]

And the prodigal in the muck and the mire of the pigpen knows the Jewish tradition of the *Kezazah* ceremony that cuts off any Jew who loses the Jewish family inheritance to a non-Jew, a ceremony in which the community fills an earthenware jar with burned nuts and corn and then breaks the jar at the prodigal's feet to symbolize the estrangement, the severed attachment.[5] The prodigal knows he's deserving of the severed attachment, the cutting him off from relations forever because he's done exactly that—lost the family inheritance, lost the precious things his father has given him. Focusing and trivializing the problem as the lost inheritance—and not the lost *relationship*—the prodigal knows the only way now to avoid the *Kezazah* ceremony of shaming and estranging him, breaking all bonds and cutting all attachments, is to find a way to earn back every single cent of the inheritance he's lost.

The prodigal thinks he knows the best way: "Make me a hired servant so I can earn it all back, so I can *earn* my way." How often am I the prodigal trying to find a way to work and earn my way back, work for Abba instead of be with Abba, perform impressively enough for Abba, instead of passionately living with Abba, in Abba? Turns out you know you're a prodigal when you merely play at doing things God's way while actually expecting that God will do things your way. You can look like you're going God's way while your heart is still going its own way. You can want God's ways—but you can want your own ways more.

Cough-hack under a night black sky. I have sinned against heaven (*cough*). I have sinned against Darryl (*cough*), sinned against how many beautiful souls who deserved better and more (*cough*), sinned against a Holy God who made a way out of Egyptian bondage to intimate bonding with Him (*cough*). All because I thought I knew all kinds of better ways to take care of me, and I've curved inward and away from relations with Him, with others, cutting myself off from the attachments, wildernessing and performing the *Kezazah* on myself.

I try to pull myself up in the hospital bed because I feel wide-eyed-wild for an exodus out of my own story and skin, and every single breath feels like the clematis is twining tighter and tighter around my chest. *Oh God, ayekah?*

While the prodigal is yet a silhouette in the distance, when his heart's still yet far off and distant, it's Abba Father who is out on the porch waiting, neck craning greater than any *incurvatus in se* curves the heart, the Logos who loves us beyond logic; it's WayMaker Abba who flies off that porch, defying the shame of baring His legs by hiking up His robe, to be the WayMaker who runs for us, who covers all the distance, to cover all our mess by personally taking the public shame of running to hold His child who's smelling like hogs. It's WayMaker Abba who knows just by the silhouette how His child walks when she thinks she can find her own way, and He comes running the whole long way to get to His child first and make things right before the community's *Kezazah* ceremony cuts off the attachment to His beloved kin forever. How is this anything but a rescuing love story that is sacred on your lips?

The prodigal may have had a plan of manipulation, but the father has a plan to take all the prodigal's humiliation so there can be complete reconciliation. The prodigal may have had a plan to negotiate—but the father has a plan to extricate, reinstate, and celebrate the prodigal. The prodigal has a plan to take things into his own hands—and the father only wants to take the son into his arms. *Hesed* holds. No created thing can sever us from the love of God who knows that our deepest fear is abandonment and our deepest need is attachment and resolves both by being the deepest love who never leaves our side ever.

Before even one word is out of the prodigal's mouth, Abba Father falls on the prodigal's neck and kisses him with grace. *Abba Father runs like a mother to not rain down wrath upon you but shower you with kisses.* This is the romance that will outlast all of time. This is nothing short of revelatory, a revelation story, which is to say: This is nothing short of apocalyptic, which is what revelation means—*apokalupis*—and there is never any revelation of God without an apocalypse in us. Every revelation from God is more of a cataclysmic deconstruction of our kingdom to rebuild us into more of God's kingdom, and I feel this revelation of Abba Father God's reckless prodigal heart, and I am utterly wrecked and remade. Sacred revelation.

All we all can say now is the prodigal's unprepared speech of heartbroken confession: "Father, I have sinned against You and against heaven. I am no longer worthy to be called Your son." But any talk of becoming just one of the servants to earn our way home is tenderly kissed away by the kinship of God.

In a darkened hospital room in the dead of night, every filling of my lungs burning with pain, heart monitor beeping, I don't hear *rushhhhhh* or *hushhhhh* in my murmuring heart, I don't hear: "My child who was lost has come all the way home." All I hear is Abba say what He says over every prodigal: "My son who was lost is *found*."

> We never find our way back, we never find the way through, we never find the way out.
> We don't find the way. The Way Himself finds us.

We never find our way back, we never find the way through, we never find the way out.

We don't find the way. The Way Himself finds us. The Way found me. The only One who is the Way, the only One who can find the way, the only One who can make the way, can be trusted to make the best way.

Oh God, ayekah?

Hineni.

Here I am, Ann. I'm right here.

Breathe.

Before the sky out the hospital window even starts to lighten with hope, before I take the incentive spirometer again and suck air into my lungs like an apocalyptic explosion tearing through my chest and my eyes leak for the pain, I have got to call home, even if it's four-something a.m. I've got to talk to Darryl. Now.

"Ann?" He's half asleep, confused, but there's concern more than anything in his voice.

"Darryl, I can't sleep. I can't breathe. And it's got very little to do with double pneumonia, but maybe more about actual heart failure. I just know—I can't keep living like this."

I heave through another strangling breath.

"I—I need you. Can you—come?"

Gripping the steely cold edge of the hospital bed rail, I brace myself through another roaring wave of pounding coughs.

And in the wake of the crashing wave of coughing, his voice is quiet, steady: "Yeah. Yeah—I think I can see my way through."

chapter fifteen

SIGN

The sweetest joys and delights I have experienced, have not been those that have arisen from a hope of my own good estate, but in a direct view of the glorious things of the gospel. . . .

I felt an ardency of soul to be, what I know not otherwise how to express . . . to be full of Christ alone; to love Him with a holy and pure love; to trust in Him; to live upon Him; to serve and follow Him.

—JONATHAN EDWARDS

She comes running through the door for me first, like she's some prodigal's father, widely wasteful with lavish love.

"Your heart brave, too, Mama? Your heart brave like mine?"

Shiloh's crawling up in the bed to kiss me, hiking up her t-shirt for me to see the raised scar from her heart surgery that parts her chest like a Red Sea Road, scars always a memory made into skin, a memory you can touch.

"Ah, baby girl, Mama doesn't have a brave heart or scar like yours." I'm smiling, but my eyes are searching the face of her papa coming in tentatively behind her. He's the one who bears all my scars. I want to trace every one of the scars I've made, whisper sorry, beg mercy.

"But Mama? You got heart lines though, Mama, see?" Shiloh's tracing lines and leads from screens to my chest.

"Shiloh? What's Mama's heart always tied to?"

And in one supernova explosion, Shiloh breaks into this dazzling smile, like she's a morning star rising after a glacial dark.

"I knowwwww, Mama, I always know." And she dances her fingers on her chest and then flings both her hands toward me. And I'm laughing, mirroring her, fingers dancing on chest, then stretching both hands toward her, she and I both saying it in unison, same rhythm, same heartbeat: "My heart is always tied to your heart."

She throws back her head and laughs, like she is soft light dancing over a singing brook, and I'm drenched in the loveliness of her. Hearts tied, hers and mine.

Attached, we are free to love.

"Darryl?" I stretch my arm out toward him standing in the doorway . . . pat the side of the hospital bed. "My heart is tied to yours too . . . my heart is yours too."

My heart for yours,
my walk with yours,

277

my life bound to yours,
till my last breath, then always and forever.

He shakes his head slowly, his eyes desperately sad, wounded. Shiloh's pulling out books and crayons from her backpack, half-singing to herself, her half a heart beating steady between surgeries. My heart is in all kinds of failure. Darryl's standing here, the way a man can, though his heart's breaking slow.

"I'm sorry. I am unspeakably sorry." I can feel it, embodied in me, with the weight of my pneumonia lungs and how hard it is to breathe: "Wide is the gate and broad is the road that leads to destruction," says the Word,* destruction literally meaning narrowness, while straight is the gate and narrow is the way that leads to the expansive life. The way of sin is wide-open and easy, but it narrows until life becomes crushed. The way of life is narrow, but "it broadens out into the spaciousness of life."[1]

> The pathway of least resistance leads to the least life. It's the narrow pathway of great resistance that leads to the great life.

The pathway of least resistance leads to the least life. It's the narrow pathway of great resistance that leads to the great life.

What can I even stammer but this: "I have sinned against heaven and you. I am unspeakably sorry for all the ways I've turned my own way, gone my own way, failed in all kinds of heartbreaking ways. Ways that kinda actually broke your heart."

"Oh, Ann." He sits down on the edge of the bed. "You're not

---

* Matthew 7:13.

alone . . . every single one of us has wanted our own way, gone our own way, in different ways."

I drop my head to his chest. And I break, a dam, and everything runs liquid, free.

I've been addicted to me.

My addiction is to self. It is an excruciatingly painful thing to cut open your heart and see: My addiction is me.

I have committed idolatry.

I have broken the first commandment: "I am the LORD your God, who brought you out of Egypt, out of the land of slavery. You shall have no other gods before me" (Exodus 20:2–3).

Instead of laying myself down on the altar as a living sacrifice before God, I've put myself, my needs, my wants, my dreams, before God, before Darryl, before my love-covenant to both. Instead of trusting God to take care of me, I have turned and gone looking for all the lying ways of this hurting old world to comfort me. Instead of entering into the sufferings of Christ, who keeps His covenant to suffer with us, I have kept looking for the way out, any way out, always looking for an exodus out of pain. And where we keep looking for a way out of our heartbreak, we only drag a whole lot of beautiful souls into more heartbreak.

I bear heartbreaking witness to the way of my ways: Nothing destroys a life like idolatry. Nothing destabilizes a life like centering self. Nothing will turn your life into a colossal mess like turning inward. All your *incurvatus in se* will leave you begging for a cure.

Though the roads will look different for each of us, always: The only way out and through is to enter into the sufferings of

Christ. Only the One who keeps His covenant to suffer with you can carry you the whole way through.

Always: The only way out is to turn outward, love reaching out to God and others.

And always, always, always: If you don't set yourself apart for a SACRED way with God, you set out to tear your own life apart.

I'm wild to go home and tear out that clematis, that was my own wayward, turned-inward heart, that was just about the death of me, and I am desperately ready to die to self to wake to the one SACRED life I always dreamed of.

When I look up, everything is swimming and blurring, and my chest feels like a narrowing vise.

Instead of gazing on the beauty of God Himself, we've all kept gazing on a way, a dream of another life without suffering that we've made into some kind of god to us. Instead of turning toward God, we all keep returning to the garden to go our own way and eat the damned apple, and then try to convince ourselves and all the world that it tastes divinely sweet, when the truth of it is, we have never chosen to taste and see the eternally satisfying rich goodness of God.

Each of us has curved our own way and away from God, rejecting His ways through suffering, His way of wooing us through heartbreak, His way of taking care of us through everything, when it's only His way that will make the most fulfilling way.

I brush my cheeks with the back of my hand, look up into Darryl's eyes, and I can read God. God doesn't break attachment and abandon those who break His heart in a thousand ways. We break God's heart, and God calls us beloved; we've gone our own way, but God won't let us go. We run, and God seeks romance.

I loved him . . .

    I took them up by their arms . . .
I led them with cords of kindness,
    with the bands of love,
and I became to them as one who eases the yoke
    on their jaws,
    and I bent down to them and fed them. . . .

How can I give you up, O Ephraim? . . .
My heart recoils within me,
    my compassions grows warm and tender.
I will not execute my burning anger;
    I will not again destroy . . .
for I am God and not a man.
    (Hosea 11:1, 3–4, 8–9 ESV)

There is no way God will ever abandon us; there is no way He will ever give up on us. He can only give us *hesed*-lovingkindness. The way the WayMaker's heart beats toward every struggler, and sufferer, and straggler wandering is nothing less than: "My compassion grows warm and tender" (11:8 ESV).

"God in whose hand are all creatures, is your Father, and is much more tender of you than you are, or can be, of yourself," assured Puritan John Flavel.[2]

The clematis may curve and attach this way and that, and our hearts may curve away and grow cold toward God, but God says, "I am God and not a man, the Holy One in your midst, and I will not come in wrath" (11:9 ESV). The WayMaker's ways are not our ways, they are *higher*, with stratospheric covenantal commitment, meteoric compassion, heaven-high *hesed*-lovingkindness. It's not our perfect ways that persuade God's heart, but it's our imperfect ways that make His heart passionate for us. The WayMaker works in ways far higher and *kinder* than ours, and He never stops working to take care of us in ways that are working more good for us than we ever dreamed: "With God on our side like this, how can we lose? If God didn't hesitate to put everything on the line for us, embracing our condition and exposing himself to the worst by sending his own Son, is there *anything else he wouldn't gladly and freely do for us?*" (Romans 8:31–32 MSG, emphasis mine).

"I desire steadfast love [*hesed*] and not sacrifice" is what God says (Hosea 6:6 ESV). "For trust did I want, and not sacrifice and knowledge of God more than sacrifice."* God, who gives us *only hesed*-lovingkindness, desires faithful, *hesed*-attachment love *from us*—that we trust the ways He takes care of us, that we acknowledge how He is more than a good Father, that He is a loving, kind Father, and that we are safe to go His way.

Cheap faith says one has only to believe. But the truth is: Real Christians aren't merely the believers. Even the demons believe (James 2:19). Real Christians are actually those who turn, faithful followers who keep turning and turning, to be the faithful *trusters*. Christianity is never only the mental assent of faith in Jesus, without requiring the lived attachment, trusting faithfulness to Jesus. Why in the aching world don't we give our trusting, *hesed*-faithfulness back to a God who *hesed*-loves us like this? Because we don't intimately *yada*-know Him. To truly know Him is to truly trust Him. To bear witness to an honest revealing of God's heart is to only find God's heart for

---

* Robert Alter, *The Hebrew Bible: A Translation with Commentary* (New York: W. W. Norton & Company, 2018), Hosea 6:6.

you appealing. It is a "misapprehension of God [which] is at the root of all hostility to God in the human soul."[3] If we really *knew* God, how could we ever have a divided heart?

How often do we want God to divide some Red Sea for us, yet we are the ones with a divided heart?

CONFESSION

"Ann?" Darryl's voice is gentle at my ear, as I lean against him through the exhausting coughing. "Can—can I ask . . . how . . . when did this happen, that we started moving apart?"

"When I heard that I was too much . . . I just wanted to take all of me and just . . . go another direction and not be a burden, not be an obligation . . . just . . . not be *at all*." The heart monitor is quiet.

"Whatever was said, can you hear me now, really hear me?" Darryl's voice is hushed but earnest, honest. "You feel much, see much, love much—but you aren't too much."

He's stroking my hair. "Remember? Remember what that Messianic Jewish teacher, Arie Bar David, once asked you, like a test, what Jesus said was the beginning of the greatest commandment of all?"

"Yeah . . . and I had tentatively offered the commandment that echoed the Shema, the most important prayer in Judaism: 'Love the LORD your God with all your heart and with all your soul and with all your strength'" (Deuteronomy 6:5).

"And our guide had interrupted you," Darryl's nodding.

"Yes, and he'd used both hands while he was talking," I'm remembering, like he was giving me clear directions.

"Listen. In the original Hebrew," our guide had said. "Jesus quotes the most important prayer to God's people, the Shema: 'Love the Lord your God with all your heart—with all your feelings and affections—and with all your soul—with all your life-breath, your whole self—and with all your very, very, much. *With all your very muchness.' Me'od*—muchness." Our Messianic Jewish teacher, Arie, had smiled. "Love the Lord your God with all your very, very much."

All your very, very much—was made to love God much. To *hesed*-love God. *Hesed*-love in the right direction.

You aren't too much, like the stars are never too bright, like the moon is never too large or luminous, like the wonders of the world are never too much.

> You aren't too much, like the stars are never too bright, like the moon is never too large or luminous, like the wonders of the world are never too much.

You aren't too much to the people who choose to see all of you. You do not have to disappear. You will not ever have to disappear. Your muchness may make you feel like not enough, but your *muchness is your strength.*

"Mama!" Shiloh calls from her crayons and books from the window where she's been singing lispy to herself as she draws and colors all these pages hues of her favorite reds and blues.

"Look! I drew a picture of all of us, of you and me and Papa!" She holds up her scrawled drawing and then points so we don't miss it.

"See the way we all have big hearts, right in the center of us?"

"Oh, oh—just a minute!" She quickly kneels down on the

floor and drags her crayon several times across the page, then jumps up to show us.

"See? I drew a line from my heart, to yours, to Papa's, and back to me."

I'm nodding, brimming.

"All our hearts, always tied together!" She's grinning, eyes dancing.

Attached. Invisible ties of deep bonding, all of us and God. I take a long deep breath through pain, and Shiloh leans over to kiss my cheek—and then her papa's.

"Let's all just get home here together." Darryl smiles, kisses both of his girls on the head. Let's all just get home. That's the only way every broken heart needs to find: the wellness of home in Him, the shalom of God.

Just come home.

We're all just needing to find a kind way home that we don't have to walk alone.

FREE

After six hacking hospital nights, Dr. Mapleton announces that I'm finally free, free, thank God Almighty, free at last, and she discharges me from the hospital with a litany of pills, including a twice-daily dosage of Lasix for the pulmonary edema that's causing the rapid shortness of breath, and a warning from Dr. Mapleton that this old ticker's going to need some regular echocardiograms to track function, that the body will need time to recover. The journey is always long and the choices we make can delay. *Do not delay on the way.*

Darryl tenderly brings me home to the farm, and Shiloh sings around me, like a serenading, hugging legs, hugging us all together, and all the kids have strung up a Welcome Home banner, and I want to envelope them all and then directly go tug out the clematis in the garden, right at the roots.

I want to say I recover quickly, easily, but narrow is the way that leads to life, and that is the only way I am ever going to purpose to take again, to *hesed*-love back the WayMaker who takes back His wayward ones, and straight after I take my pills in the early dark every morning, I am hungry to take the SACRED way of life that I am holding on to now for actual dear life, the way to be set apart and consecrated to Him.

I know it now with every fiber of my being: *If you don't set yourself apart for a SACRED way with God, you set out to tear your own life apart.* Where there is a divided heart, the waters will not part.

And I begin again, scratch it all down, the unvarnished and honest, in my SACRED way journal:

> *Stillness:* Deep breath . . . "The LORD will fight for you; you need only to be still" (Exodus 14:14). And after you still the waves within, the roar of the interior storm, the thunder of the overwhelm, simply by turning and gazing the soul on Him who suffers with you and who fights for you, you hear the Lord not in the roar, not in the storm, but in a low, still, quiet whisper (1 Kings 19:12): "Peace! Be still!" (Mark 4:39). God holds us still.
>
> *Attentiveness: Who do I say that You are?* You are the Holy One who still *hesed*-loves the unholy. *Where am I coming from and where am I going? If I am brutally honest?*

I am Moses who has struck the rock and who wanted my way more than His. I am the prodigal who doesn't know how to live with herself, forgive herself, and every curved way is done in plain view of God, and every wrong way that leaves us undone is done ultimately to Him—and is it possible to find a way forward when all you're wild to do is go back and undo the ways that you thought were better than His, ways that should never have been done?

I mean: Who can believe that David threw around his weight and status until he crushed a woman under the curve of his full-bodied lust, and yet he wound his way back on stinging skinned knees to the feet of God, to feel his failure finally lifted off flattened lungs—to exhale the expansiveness of grace that is weightless.

Who can believe that Nebuchadnezzar's proud ways defied God till he was laid low on all fours, foaming at his boasting-now-bovine mouth, chewing on grass ripped from the earth with his bare teeth, for more than two thousand naked days under the beating elements, until he came to his surrendered mind and willing feet and was returned to humble power from the humiliation of the pasture, even more able in His ways than he had been before, his needed cud-chewing years ruminating him toward restoration?

Who can believe Peter scorched his own soul with his repeated denial of Jesus, the hostility around Caiphas's fire absolutely terrifying, only for the resurrected Jesus to light a fire on the beach and Peter to turn, to truly turn, filled with the burning scent of shame, and hear Christ's humbling hospitality to come eat, to come, there's a way, come be entrusted still with work in the kingdom to humbly feed Christ's sheep?

Who has the gall to believe there is a way for everyone who trusted their way more than His, who has wanted their way more than God's?

Not me.

I scrawl it down: *Not. Me.*

How do you find a way to believe that wreckage can birth resurrection?

Even when I can't see, I trust the SACRED compass to keep curving me daily toward God: Stillness, attentiveness, cruciformity, revelation, examine, doxology every day, and when I feel my heart curving in, that's my sign to turn toward my cleft in the rock, my base, His Word, let His *hesed*-heart whisper truth to mine, revelation upon apocalyptic revelation. I just keep cling-trusting the WayMaker and a daily SACRED way of life to grow a deeper attachment to God because it is turning again and again toward healthy attachments that heal harmful addictions.

I'm weak from my wandering heart, and my body's slow and exhausted, winded, and I have to learn how to be tender with all the broken parts of me and life. Malakai has a blood sugar low that sucks him into eye-rolling seizures, then limp unconsciousness, and we're bent under the white lights of the ER praying our diabetic kid lives. We drive another child to the city hospital to have a thyroid radiated and embark on this daily and relentless calibration of meds for Graves' disease and being a manual thyroid for life. We keep giving Shiloh her blood thinners daily, keep our cardiologist appointments to monitor what her palliative half-a-heart needs, and we never stop begging God to give long life.

But in countless ways, I stop.

I stop comparing where we are compared to everyone else. I stop living like I have no agency. I stop living without boundaries. I stop thinking I deserve more than I simply need to serve. I stop turning and curling and curving and cling-trusting to anything but God.

And I start. I start living sacred, set apart for God, rerouting in all the ways.

I start therapy. I start spiritual direction. I start grad school. I start paperwork with Darryl to sponsor a second refugee family from the Democratic Republic of the Congo, as our first sponsored refugee family from Syria has flourished into self-sufficiency. I start a partnership to create a fair-trade store to empower marginalized women. I start hacking away at my own *incurvatus in se* by living cruciform, reaching outward, by caring and curving toward other people's needs because the way to happiness is always to bless and bless and bless. I start to live it in every way: The only way to do the right thing, when it feels like an impossible thing, is to choose the cruciform thing. To surrender, to live given, with arms vulnerably outstretched, palms wide-open. In Christ, we can live like Christ. Cruciform is the shape and form of attachment, arms outstretched to God and people, and *cruciform* is always what *transforms*.

I start walking outside every day, what the Japanese call forest bathing, what I call my daily glory soak—because the whole earth is full of His glory, and I need to soak in His glory to change the affections of my heart. I start running and rowing because moving the body keeps the stress moving through.[4] I start to cut off every interior conversation with fear and worry and angst with the prayer, "Into Your hands I commit . . ."

I try to forgive myself because Jesus already has, and why can't I believe that His grace is sufficient? I start every day counting His gifts, count all the ways He loves me, count all the ways His *hesed*-lovingkindness takes care of us and holds us close:

> . . . *thankful my heart's pounding alive today.*
> . . . *thankful for the dog sleeping at Darryl's feet.*
> . . . *thankful we all are safe and fed and there's a stack of*
> *plates in the sink.*
> . . . *thankful that when morning breaks, it breaks all the*
> *mistakes of all the yesterdays, breaks our dome of dark so*
> *all His fresh mercies can flood in, and we will welcome*
> *them right in and start again.*

I start again and again and again, every morning, to practice a SACRED way of life.

Maybe: Life is a long repentance in His direction. This is the only SACRED way my lungs, my heart, don't hurt to breathe: stillness, attentiveness, cruciformity, revelation, examine, doxology.

It takes time, but change can take hold—*if we let God hold us.* Change happens when *identity* changes and our identity is attached to *whom* we are attached, and how they see us, treat us, act toward us. Our God is the God who stays *with* us, exactly so we can see ourselves the way *He* sees us—beloved, cherished, wanted, chosen—because this is what changes our *identity*, and it's changing our identity that changes the whole of life. Healthy attachment cures harmful addictions because when we attach our identity to already being loved, there is no more to need. Turn the pages of His Word, turn toward Him, turn and live, let Him love you through a SACRED love, set apart for Him, and your whole life can turn around.

Put one step in front of the other—in the right direction—and you can have another life.

Easy way. Empty life.

Hard way. Holy, fulfilling life.

Narrow way. Hard way. Holy, fulfilled life.

FOUND

It's at the very beginning of Lent that I begin fasting and praying. Morning after morning I sit with my SACRED journal, cruciform and flat-out begging God, in His *hesed*-lovingkindness, for a clear sign that He is our WayMaker still. Even though we keep crashing into walls, and our people keep crashing and burning, and the waves keep breaking and crashing, and our hearts keep being busted and broken, is He really still our WayMaker?

After weeks of grieving and fasting and praying, "Show me that You're our WayMaker, some sign that You. Are. Still. Our. WayMaker," I find myself lost in all kinds of ways, driving a rental car down some winding cow path, through valleys, and up around mountains, in the fine verdant state of Tennessee, thousands of miles from our home farm, trying to find my way to a women's prayer gathering. Pulled over on the shoulder of the road, I'm gawking over my shoulder to make sure no good ole boy in a pickup is about to come flying over that hill before I can swing a quick U-turn because my GPS—and my Expectational Positioning System—has been begging me with its "rerouting, rerouting," and that's what I'm trying to do with all I have.

And this is the moment the miracle begins.

But like most miracles, you can miss when it begins if you're not paying attention to the manna in the moments. Tucked away in the center console, my phone, straight out of the blue, Bluetooth connects to the rental car speakers. I can't get that to happen even at home behind my own steering wheel, when I'm valiantly trying every hack under the sun to finagle some kind of elusive technical pairing between vehicle speakers and recalcitrant phone—let alone the phone just spontaneously, seamlessly connecting on its own to the speaker in a random rental car I've never laid eyes on before in my life. But here is my phone, connecting with these speakers, and the audio devotional that I've tried half a dozen times to download this whole long day of traveling now suddenly decides to connect and download, booming at full volume the devotional text of John 14:1, 3–4: "Do not let your hearts be troubled . . . If I go and prepare a place for you, I will come back and take you to be with me that you also may be where I am. You know the way."

God. Hear me. That is exactly the point: I'm a middle-aged woman desperately trying to know the way through a life that's not going the way she dreamed because I am not the way I dreamed, and I keep trying to find the way.

I'm making my U-turn just as the speakers blast Thomas's words to Jesus that are the cry of all the prodigals: "How can we know the way?" (v. 5).

His question isn't even yet a complete thought in my mind, when I curve around a bend in the road, and there it is, *there it actually is*, a literal sign, a billboard in bold letters:

Jesus Is the WayMaker

And at that very *exact* same instant, full blast through the speakers of the rental car, come the very words of God: "I am the way and the truth and the life. No one comes to the Father except through me" (John 14:6).

The WayMaker never stops working in ways beyond anything you ever dreamed.

I hit the brakes, pull off to the shoulder in front of the sign, lean over the steering wheel, and weep.

I am the prodigal who wanted my own way. I'm thousands of miles from home in another country. I've been fasting for days at a time, for weeks, wildly hungry to taste the shalom of God, and I'm lost, and I've turned and—WayMaker Abba's just run the whole way to me, fallen on my neck, and kissed me with *hesed*-lovingkindness, whispering who He is to me over and over again: WayMaker, *hesed*-Lover, Abba Father, Kind Kin till the end of time—and you are beloved, held, chosen, mine.

Come let Me love you. "Come. . . . Get away with me. . . . Walk with me and work with me. . . . I won't lay anything heavy or ill-fitting on you. Keep company with me and you'll . . . live freely and lightly" (Matthew 11:28–30 MSG).

Come home to Me, the One covenanted to suffer with you. There is nothing to fear. Only doxology, doxology, doxology.

Kissing God with my praise, my awe, my worship,* my heart splits with this Red Sea Road of thanks to God Himself when I call Darryl to tell him how God comes.

---

* *Proskuneó* (worship) literally means "to kiss the hand to (toward) one, in token of reverence," as in Matthew 4:9 and Psalm 2:12. *Thayer's Greek Lexicon*, s.v. "4352 *proskuneó*," BibleHub, accessed November 15, 2021, https://biblehub.com/thayers/4352.htm.

"I don't—I don't even know how to explain this?" I'm crying and who is a God like this, and I want the SACRED way, to be set apart for a romance like His. "In His grace, He gave . . . He gave me the sign that He is always our WayMaker. He is more than some sign pointing the way to get somewhere; He is the Way who is a *Person* who gives us Himself so we can know a whole new way of being . . ."

Doxology, doxology, doxology.

"Did you expect another way?" This is a SACRED world and what profanes it is wanting our own way.

I'm choked up. Maybe I'd had . . . expectations? But: Jesus is the Way Himself, more than a genie making our fantasy life; He is the way to a new way of being and life of intimacy with the triune God. Because this! *This:* Intimacy is the very point of history—*and our story.*

> Intimacy is the very point of history—*and our story.*

"Ann?"

I know. I know what he's going to say, know it along the fractures and fissures of my heart—and his.

"What is in the way—is still always making a way." A way for us to have closer *hesed*-attachment with God through suffering.

"Ann? You okay? Breathing? Your heart?" His concern for me in the weeks since being released from hospital finds me a thousand miles away. Never too much, always enough to be held.

"Yes, yes—my heart is more than okay." Wherever hearts are tied together, they're free to be secure.

Cutting Shiloh's heart open again would test that in ways we'd never dreamed.

chapter sixteen

MOSES WAY

Desire only God, and your heart will be satisfied.

—AUGUSTINE

Nothing created has ever been able to fill the heart of man. God alone can fill it infinitely.

—THOMAS AQUINAS

Before dawn on the third Friday of Lent, they're ready to saw through Shiloh's sternum and go back in. You do whatever you have to do to get to a broken heart. You always have another chance.

In the three a.m.–something-dark, he and I reach for our identical shirts with "Heart Strong" emblazoned across the front because this is what we are doing: Between a rock and a hard place, between her half-a-heart and the unknown, between Egypt and the sea, he and I know: We are as strong as we are bonded, and the strength of our attachments is our truest strength. In our twinning shirts, we look like signs. *Heart Strong*, hearts bonded with God. Like signs, we get to be waymarkers, pointing beyond ourselves to the *WayMaker Himself*. In the predawn blackness of our bedroom, before we wake Shiloh for the long drive to the big city and the OR lights and the surgeons waiting, Darryl slips his arms around me, bows his head, and we reach for God:

> *God, give us the grace to embrace*
> *mysteries we don't understand,*
> *the cruciform openness to live a tender surrender,*
> *into Your ways wiser and kinder than ours,*
> *and the deep shalom of simply being*
> *with You here,*
> *right here,*
> *with us.*

We begin centered, in a SACRED and set-apart way of being, being loved, held, known, safe.

This time, this heart surgery, it can be a different way because we have a new way of being. None of us ever get do-overs, but we all get to keep writing on, we all get to write new lines and dreams and love into our tattered and crumpled stories, and we can truly keep on trusting that our stories won't end till the last line is a good line.

I directly ask Darryl what he needs of me, wants of me through this heart surgery to feel seen, safe, secure, known so I don't again scar the arteries of his own vulnerable heart as we face the question marks of our baby girl's life.

"Just . . ." His big Dutch hand reaches for mine. "Be present to me, be honest with me, be care-full with me—and grab a coffee with me." He winks, grins. "Oh, and how about kiss me now and then? What do you think?"

"I think . . . I think I can do that." And I prove it, long and slowly and tenderly.

And then I close my eyes and am brutally honest.

"I think I am scared of surgery again—facing an ocean of unknown and all that can go wrong—that I'll get it wrong, be wrong—be too much." There. I said it.

"Hey?" He lifts my chin. "Remember?"

I nod: *You can't be too much, like the stars can't ever be too bright, like the moon can't ever be too luminous, like the very ways of God can't ever be too much.* I see him: He's a waymarker pointing to the WayMaker, and all the feelings and fear and grief and unknown that feel like too much, these are all signs in wildernesses pointing toward God, to take it to God, to love God with all the muchness, to be fully, honestly, vulnerably, closely with Him in it all—because withness is the only real way through anything.

Before we even wake Shiloh for heart surgery day, he and I've done this tender heart surgery of our own, detaching from all kinds of misdirecting expectations and curving lies, and reorienting to the way of being heart strong and secure, attached, with this liturgy of intimacy:

**CLOSENESS *TO* EACH OTHER,
CRUCIFORM REACHES FOR COMFORT
FROM EACH OTHER,
CRAVING THE PRESENCE *OF* EACH OTHER,
AND BEING CLEFTS IN THE ROCK
FOR EACH OTHER *THAT WE CAN COUNT ON*, AS WE
KEEP RETURNING TO THE ROCK HIMSELF, OUR
ALWAYS WIDE-OPEN SAFE HAVEN.**

When I scoop Shiloh out of her bed to begin our long trek toward that scalpel that we pray will save her, Shiloh's wearing what she laid out weeks before, for this pilgrimage she's prepared for, which she knew was coming: There, over her pajamas, Shiloh's wearing a blue and red cape with *HERO* embroidered in white right across it. I curl the sleeping girl onto my shoulder, kiss her forehead, and she's warm against me, she's alive in this moment, and how can one tiny human being fill your heart with this much aching love? She is a brave sign, too, a waymarker, pointing to the Hero Himself in all our love stories who comes the whole long way to rescue us and save us from the aloneness of ourselves. I keep stroking back her falling hair.

Darryl's waiting at the farmhouse back door, our coffees already made and in hand. He's already cupped me in intimacy.

He nods, seeing her sleeping, seeing that I don't want to ever let her go.

"Ready to begin?"

I nod, take a deep breath.

The only outcome that matters is that we come to Him. If death is the outcome, we still get to come to Him. If pain, or shame, or flames, or chains, or graves are the outcome, we still get to come to Him. True freedom is to be free of outcomes and come into Him.

When the waves swamp, it can come, this desperation to surface, to find the way up, the way out, the way up to the life expected. But the way through is not to strain and strive upward, but to still and go down and into the depths of God. The way through is down into God. Down in the depths of God, all is still and calm. With babe draped in cape, we stumble out into the dark, pilgrims on our way, going down, down deeper still. Let whatever waves come.

"Mama?" Shiloh whispers it in my ear as we wait in pre-op. "You and Papa be brave with me, Mama?"

"Yes, baby girl, the way Jesus is with us gives us all a new way of being—of being brave." I swallow hard, kiss her cheek, little waymarker pointing toward home. Darryl's rubbing her back and I'm rocking her back and forth, and we are softly singing how Jesus loves us, oh how He loves.

Darryl winks and gives Shiloh a thumbs-up when she plunks her favorite red plastic fireman's hat on his head and adjusts the shield because "We're both gonna be super brave, okay, Papa?!" There's this lump burning in my throat. He's still wearing the fireman's hat when Shiloh's pre-surgery sedative lets her drift off in my arms, me leaning against him for support as I sway with all the weight of her, as I sing at her ear, "My heart for yours, my walk with yours, my life bound to yours . . ."

She is my heart, and she is the *korban* I never want to lay down but I must, to draw nearer and love God with all my heart's very muchness. I am Hannah and I have come with my Shiloh, offering the child I have prayed for back to God because sin is any dream that wedges its way between the heart and God.

THROUGH THE WAVES

She hardly stirs when they take her from my arms. I turn and fall into Darryl's. He still hasn't taken off Shiloh's fireman's hat, and we're aflame with a surrendered passion for the WayMaker and whatever way He wants to love us, take care of us. The flames forge and form not just the soul, but the road to God. *Into Your hands, we commit our spirit, our lives* (Luke 23:46).

> The deeper I trust the sovereignty of God, to accept and receive whatever He gives, the deeper my intimacy with God.

The deeper I trust the sovereignty of God, to accept and receive whatever He gives, the deeper my intimacy with God.

This is the great paradox, the great surprise that shouldn't be a surprise at all: God's sovereignty over everything is due to His *Kingship*, and my intimacy with Him, through everything, is due to His *kinship*.

This is our Father's world and the ancient words of the Belgic Confession lace His complete sovereignty with a deeply comforting intimacy:

This doctrine [of God's sovereignty over all things] gives us unspeakable comfort since it teaches us that nothing can happen to us by chance but only by the arrangement of our gracious heavenly Father, who watches over us with fatherly care, sustaining all creatures under his lordship, so that not one of the hairs on our heads (for they are all numbered) nor even a little bird can fall to the ground without the will of our Father.[1]

And I feel it, what has always been true, how the Maker and calmer of waves, He answers every one of our prayers like waves. Sometimes He takes the pain away, like an ebbing, all the suffering receding like the waves drawing back, washing all our ache out to sea like an exhaling reprieve.

But more often than not, He doesn't sweep the suffering away but surges with more of Himself, comes with a crest of *hesed*-lovingkindness to raise us into the next breath, an upsurge of grace that carries when we can't see any way to keep going.

Coming like the certainty of waves, God may not sweep the pain away to sea, but He sweeps in *to carry me*. Sure as waves, God may not wash our heartbreak back out to the ocean, but He always rolls in like an ocean of carrying strength. And always, no matter what, like waves, He rocks all our ache, like a Father singing a lullaby till the peace finally comes. *Whatever way, whichever way, just always the WayMaker's way—because His ways are more than good; His ways are loving and kind.*

My old failing heart beats with the old words of Saint Thérèse of Lisieux: "I had to pass through many trials before reaching the haven of peace, before tasting the delicious fruits of perfect love and of complete abandonment to God's Will."[2]

Darryl slips his arm around me while our Shiloh is slipping again under the knife. We put one step in front of the other. This time we remember what we each need to be heart strong: Closeness to each other, cruciform reaches for comfort from each other, craving the presence of each other, clefts in the rock for each other, and this time we pray aloud because unless we are a threefold cord, everything unravels. This time we pace halls together, his hand never letting go of mine. This time I turn and curve thoughts around God.

I'm reading the right map now. The way of Jesus always runs through the valley of suffering, through Gethsemanes, and right through the door of hope *that is Him* (Hosea 2:15). I am finding that too: Driven and motivated to always feel okay is not a steadying way to navigate your one life. If your only way to navigate your inner landscape is to manipulate, control, and dominate your outer landscape, you've lost the map to joy. Life isn't a linear, forward march but a circuitous, God-toward maze, and the road that seems to be winding the wrong way can also be making the way closer toward Him and home and Christ dwelling within. Just because the road doesn't seem to be upward and onward, doesn't mean it isn't making the way closer toward God. The way of Jesus is never about upward mobility but always about the way deeper down, toward God-intimacy. Every real map will point the way: Gethsemanes are places of intimacy. At every crossroad the call is to remember the direction of the Way Himself whom we follow, and He always carries a cross and is going the way of suffering toward a place of dying. Why expect another trajectory when you're following Him? Cruciform is always the healing trajectory of intimacy. The Suffering Savior wants nothing less than to be with us, and suffering is the way He is for us, near us, and in us. If you want the WayMaker to make a way, know that His way always runs through suffering; He has no other way. Not because He doesn't love us but exactly because He does.

If our WayMaker makes a way through unbelievable suffering to be with us, how can we not believe that whatever suffering we face, it is never because He's abandoned us? His forever *hesed*-lovingkindness forever proves that whatever our suffering, He is in it with us, and not just as kind kin but as the wisest King who controls everything.

> If you want the WayMaker to make a way, know that His way always runs through suffering; He has no other way. Not because He doesn't love us but exactly because He does.

How could we ever be conformed to the image of our Suffering Savior if we never suffered? If God had created a world without great suffering—would this be a world without great souls? Isn't suffering the ink of all the unforgettable love stories and epic quests? Eliminate adversity and you obliterate bravery. Hadn't she been strong in my arms, so little, choosing to be so brave? Take away overwhelming suffering from the world and you take away the overcomers of the world. It's changing my every trajectory to ponder what theologian Martin Luther wrote: "God's glory is manifested in our suffering, better than in any other way."[3] If the chief end of man is to glorify God, and God's glory is most manifested in suffering like Him, how did I think God would make a way that doesn't run through suffering in the end? And how did I so misunderstand the fool spoken of in C. S. Lewis's *The Great Divorce*:

> That is what mortals misunderstand. They say of some temporal suffering, "No future bliss can make up for it," not knowing that Heaven, once attained, will work backwards and turn even that agony into a glory.[4]

The way through this world is suffering, following a Suffering Savior, that makes a way into all the glory of the world to come.

"You want to head down to the vehicle, put away her fireman's hat?" I smile faintly, nod toward his big Dutch hands, wandering these hospital halls, holding his Chinese daughter's red plastic hat.

He shakes his head.

"Nah." He takes a deep breath, exhales. "Feels like a way to keep carrying her." The way a man carries his cross can look like the glorious way of Jesus. When a man knows he signed up for a love that suffers, he becomes a sign that points the way to the realest love.

SACRED COMPASS

Six interminably long hours of a surgeon working painstakingly in the chest cavity of our daughter, six hours of pacing, six hours giving thanks because giving thanks is what gives us strength to carry our crosses. And as we keep walking through the stress, to keep moving the stress through, my heart keeps taking the SACRED way, always the exodus through, and into a sacred bonding with Him because if you don't have an anchor to center you, any wave will throw you for a curve.

Stillness: I can do this anywhere. Breathe in, breathe out, lungs rise, lungs fall, breathe, and life is literally waves and when we learn to still and breathe, even the sound of our very breath saying His name YHWH, we learn to ride the waves, walk on water. Always first: Be still so that you can know who God still is, and you don't think your way into stillness, like you breathe your way into stillness. Breathe slowly and you will slowly still. I can do this. Stillness in the heart happens with slowness of the breath. I was but dust till God kissed me to life with His warm breath—and when my breath turns slow—I slowly return to the calm stillness before the sovereignty of Him.

Attentiveness: Wherever the feet are, the sacred interior work is to pay attention to what you're paying attention to. How many times has my therapist, Curt Thompson, said what he writes about in his book *Anatomy of the Soul*: "What you pay attention to, is what you will remember, and what you remember is what you will anticipate in the future"?[5] Pay attention to lovingkindness and you will remember it, and anticipate lovingkindness coming to meet you with arms wide-open tomorrow. When I keep paying attention to God's questions of the soul, God's own questions in Scripture, I am paying attention to Love Himself beckoning me: *Who do you say that I am? Where are you coming from and where are you going to? What do you want?*

We climb flights of steps in a back hall to pass the waiting, Darryl climbing ahead of me. My heart ascends, preaching truth to my soul, locating my soul in relation to Him so I can have relationship with Him:

> *I say You are sovereign King and intimate kin, and I am coming from being one of the prodigals to being Hannah, and I want to be free of all the bondage and bond with You in real shalom. And—yeah, don't You know it: I want to hold Shiloh Shalom Yu Xin again.*

Cruciform: This is always the thing. The shape of anything that is real and lasting is always cruciform. Reaching out—to

God and souls—transforms within. Surrender precedes saving. Letting go makes a way to be fulfilled again. There is no way for transformation without cruciformation—without surrendering the form of what is to the form of Christ. Surrender your *korban* to draw nearer to joy, to people, to God. It is everything I keep returning to: Cruciformity cures *incurvatus in se*. If you live cruciform, *the obstacle becomes the miracle, the obstacle becomes the miracle, the obstacle becomes the miracle.*

> There is no way for transformation without cruciformation— without surrendering the form of what is to the form of Christ.

Darryl turns at the next landing and leads our descent down, and none of this is futile. Yes, that: *The way of Jesus is never about upward mobility, the way up and out, but always about the way deeper down, deeper down, and higher in, toward God-intimacy.* The way we spend our waiting, the way we live our dash from birth to death, is exactly where we wage our way deeper down into our own epic love story with Love Himself. So, Lord, here is my *korban*:

> *I surrender to You all our tomorrows, I let go of all my wrongly turned loves, I cruciform the form of all my dreams; draw me nearer, nearer, nearer, come let me love You. Into Your hands, I commit all of me.*

"Maybe soon?" Darryl checks his watch again at the bottom of the stairs. Half a dozen hours of heart surgery for a palliative heart repair, the way of cutting to heal.

"You want to grab a coffee?" He reads my eyes, grabs my hand.

Darryl orders. I swipe open the Word on my phone and drink, drink, drink.

Revelation: This Word is not only an early-morning book, not just a compartmentalized book, a "quiet time" book, but an anytime-everywhere book, that is always your secure base.

When you can't see your way through, move closer to the light. If we don't set apart time with God—can we expect to see the way God is parting waves? Unless we are poring over His ways more than we are poring over any other informational streams, are we truly wanting God to make a way? We say: Show us the way—and He says, *Yes, here I am. I am the way.* We say: Tell us what road—and He says, *Yes, here I am. I am the road.* We say: Show us which way to go—and He says: *Yes, come here, right here.*

Darryl hands me my coffee, and I read it out loud:

> God is a safe place to hide,
> > ready to help when we need him.
> We stand fearless at the cliff-edge of doom,
> > courageous in seastorm and earthquake,
> Before the rush and roar of oceans,
> > the tremors that shift mountains.
>
> Jacob-wrestling God fights for us,
> GOD-of-Angel-Armies protects us.
> (Psalm 46:1–3 MSG)

"Exactly." Darryl blows gently on his steaming coffee, points to my shirt. "Heart Strong. What is there to fear?"

How in the name of all things good does God work for us and keep us safe when the dreaded phone call detonates, or the shrapnel of shame shreds everything that looks like hope, or the sky lashes round and swallows your dreams whole, or the claw of death guts deep, and how do you stagger forward hiding your bloody entrails? Evil hisses that if God really is love, then we better get roads without any suffering. And we shake off the lie and crush it with truth: Because God really is love, then we get roads with Him, and because God really is love, we are always soul-safe. "Though the cherry trees don't blossom" (Habakkuk 3:17 MSG); though the bank account, the bed, the chair, and the calendar are empty; though the grave dirt may be heaped; and though the lungs ache with the weight of breathing through the drowning waves, in Christ *what matters forever, is always forever safe.* God is safe to trust because, whatever the way, we are always soul-safe in Christ! "There's nothing [anything or anyone] can do to your soul, your core being" (Matthew 10:28 MSG). Hell can try to work us over, but God works even the hellish things into good. *God is the Word, and the Word only works everything into a good story, so the last line is a good line.* God isn't transactional, making deals with us of no pain in exchange for faithful love; God is *relational*, making the way to be *with* us through pain because He *is* faithful Love. God doesn't keep us from suffering; *He keeps us through it.*

> "Every detail of your body and soul—even the hairs of your head!—is in my care; nothing of you will be lost. Staying with it—that's what is required. Stay with it to the end. You won't be sorry; you'll be saved." (Luke 21:17–19 MSG)

Nothing of you—the real you, the soul you, the you that will last forever—will ever be lost. Stay with it, the staying with Him, and all is soul-safe.

Examine: Exactly. What exactly am I afraid of?

When we make it back up to the OR waiting room, I see her surgeon walk in, looking for our faces. I try to read his. He's talking about how it didn't go as planned.

"Well, the plan was a lateral tunnel Fontan." I'm nodding—yes, he explained that during her pre-op appointment.

"But when we got in there, her right artery, contrary to what we had thought, wasn't actually big enough to do a lateral tunnel." The surgeon is sketching on a piece of paper, and I'm trying to pay attention, but I just keep staring at his hands: His hands held her broken heart. Those hands.

"Is she—is she going to be okay?"

"Well, we had to find another way right there in the OR and decided to dissect her two hepatic veins from her right artery, unroof her coronary sinus and augment with pericardial patch, and then oversew her right artery." He's trying to draw us a map of her heart, of all of its cuts and conduits and breaks.

"And then the two hepatic veins were anastomosed, connected, to the PTFE graft." He looks up. "And that part was a success."

All three of us break into smiles, waves of stress break. "This surgery to finish rerouting the blood flow of her single ventricle heart should last us decades before we have to think about the next step. Heart transplant."

Doxology: Give thanks, give thanks, give thanks.

"Now we just wait and see if there are any complications with recovery."

Whatever may come, and no matter what comes, or seems to come in the way, thank God. Kiss God: doxology, doxology, doxology.

COME WHAT MAY

After surgery, all the days bleed into streams of nights. Shiloh is a pale and fragile maze of wires and lines. *Life is not a linear, forward march, but a circuitous, God-toward maze, and the road that seems to be winding the wrong way can also be making the way closer toward the home of Him within.* I keep stroking the back of Shiloh's hand, watching her eyes because we're all looking for eyes looking for ours and every fighter deserves a witness. Every life needs its lifers. When anyone has to bear pain, they deserve someone to at least bear witness to it. We're here for it, here for all of it, and we're but one of the bleary-eyed huddles of parents barnacled to the side of a child's bed in CICU.

"Tell me what you need," Darryl whispers to me after midnight of the second night. "Why don't you grab a few hours' sleep and let me take this shift?"

"Oh D, no . . . no." I lean my head on his shoulder. "I can wait up here a few more hours. Why don't you get a bit of sleep first?" Come, let me love you, after all my wandering ways, come let me do at least that for you now.

"Well, if I take the first shift, I'm just going to sleep right here in one of those chairs in the family room just outside the door. Leave my phone on, set my alarm for three." His lips kiss-brush my forehead. "Text me if there's anything—and there's going to be no arguing: I'm on at three. Then your turn." We keep learning the art of turning.

"Hey?" I whisper loud when he's almost at the door. He turns, eyebrows raised, ready for—anything.

"Just—you . . ." I smile, try to set him at ease. "You on day two . . . three . . . or whatever of wearing that same shirt? You're still looking mighty fine." He grins, winks.

"You too." Never mind I have coffee stains on mine, and I ain't smelling fine. "The shirt . . . becomes you." *Heart Strong*.

I shake my head, and he blows a kiss as he creaks open the door, and we are becoming the signs pointing to the dreams we've been looking for.

In the darkened room lit only by monitors, I pull up a chair by her bedside, stroke her little fingers as she heaves and sleeps and breathes under her oxygen mask, kiss every single one of her fingertips. *What if our hands had fumbled about our whole lives and never found yours? What if your laughter had never filled all the empty spaces in our story? What if we'd never held each other so close that our hearts finally heard the rhythm of home?*

No, baby girl, adoption isn't maybe the right word to describe how our worlds found each other. Because you are more than an adding to us, more than an option to us. Maybe it's always more than an adoption story—maybe it's always more like a story of grafting.

We are all the grafted. Cut and wounded. Joined at the places of loss. United and always growing together. Hearts scarred and bound and carved into one. One strong heart beating together as we go down deeper and deeper into His love. Let whatever waves come. It's just after one a.m. when the next wave crashes, and Shiloh's surgically traumatized heart jolts into a wild gallop of an arrhythmia, her room screaming with alarms. More than a dozen of the cardiac team swarm into the room and around her bed, and Darryl is bleary-eyed and all there.

Over the alarms, the doctor on nights tries to explain the risks of this charging arrhythmia, her heart slamming out of control at over 150 beats per minute in her little body . . . versus the real risks of the medications to rein it back into its steady pace.

"Honestly, we don't know which way this is going to go." She's shaking her head at the waving lights on the screen.

"Whatever you need to do . . ." Darryl is quiet, certain.

Father, into your hands we commit our dreams and nightmares. Take our hands. Hold us. Hold us in Your hesed-*lovingkindness, and no matter how the road goes, You are our road, You are our way.*

The only way to survive waves is to keep the beat of your heart in rhythm with the One who walks on water.

I keep stroking her hair back, keep hoping for morning with her, with us.

I dare to believe, no matter what: There is no heartache that heaven can't heal,[6] but there is no heartache on earth that isn't felt more up in heaven. Because God is Love Himself, He is the greatest and longest sufferer of the universe. And suffering has to have enough purpose in the world if God Himself daily purposes to endure all this suffering *with us.*

When the sun rises, she's here, right here, with us—*doxology, doxology, doxology*—thanks be to God for her taking the next breath and the next heart wave on that screen—even if none of the medically induced shocks have actually changed the pounding pace of her heart.

THE WAY HOME

Shiloh's cardiac team keeps trying to determine the why and ways of Shiloh's heart, keep experimenting with different meds to find a way to slow it down into a rhythm of shalom. And Shiloh keeps moaning and coughing with pain through the days, keeps crying and begging with fear through the nights.

"Home! *Hommmmme! Goooo hommmmeee!*" For hours, night after night, she howls the cry of all our hearts, tears at her oxygen mask, like she just wants home where she can just breathe. *I know, baby girl, I know.* Darryl crawls in beside her in her hospital bed, gathers her in, rocks her, and all her lines, to sleep in his arms. *In the arms of our Father, we're already home.*

When cruciform surrender is our way of life, the waves of life, one after another, can be but a rocking rhythm that balances us in the rest of God.

The waves in the way are making the way.

Deeply traumatized by surgery, exhausted and afraid of the constant stream of technicians, specialists, nurses, Shiloh wrestles to control the one thing she can: The child refuses to eat. For four days, she eats nothing. I cajole and beg. Ice cream? Yogurt? Darryl whirls forks of food around her like acrobatic planes. Rice incoming! Shiloh, ashen and scared, closes her eyes, turns away. Our hearts ache.

Through the mess and maze of wires, Darryl scoops her into his lap, strokes her hair as she moans, the surgical drain tubes heavy and pulling at her incision. He reads her stories, *Winnie the Pooh and Piglet*, sings her songs, "Jesus Loves Me," and whispers that she is being so brave, *Child of God*. He rubs lotion on her feet. She falls asleep, head on his chest, breaths rising and falling.

On Day 5: Darryl is swooping and soaring long green beans from Shiloh's tray and singsonging in this high-pitched voice: "And Papa Bird's found a long green worm that will taste the juiciest for his Little Baby Bird—and he flies the worm throughhhhh the aiiiiirrrr—Swoop! Dive! And Little Baby Bird opens wideeeeeee her mouth for Papa Bird."

And Darryl opens his own mouth under the long green string bean, and then drops it in his mouth—*gulp*.

"And Little Baby Bird gobbles that little worm right up! YUM!"

I'm chuckling, marveling, as big Farmer man, trying to lure his little Shiloh into one bite, just one bite, playing this Papa Bird and Baby Bird with bean after bean, flying and dipping and diving and opening wide.

"And then . . ."

And then, noon of Day 5: Shiloh opens her mouth!

And: Drop! Pretend little green bean worm right into Baby Bird's mouth! Papa for the win, and Mama can't stop laughing happy, and Shiloh smiles shyly, and Papa leans in for a grinning kiss.

Later, as he finishes gently washing around Shiloh's large steri-taped scar incision during a warm bath meant to calm and soothe, I watch him from the other side of the bed where I'm massaging Shiloh's little hand, watching him washing her down so tenderly. I can feel it, the curvature of my heart.

"Hey?"

Darryl looks up, washcloth in hand, eyebrows raised with this half smile, looking sheepish, looking like that sixteen-year-old Farm Boy I once knew.

"I just wanted you to know—that I don't know if I have ever been more in love with you, watching you like this, big Dutch farmer, serving his brave little Chinese daughter in a million little ways." Nothing is more attractive than sacrifice. Nothing makes and saves a love story like sacrifice. Cruciform is the form of love.

But he's shaking his head, whispering it quietly. He doesn't look up, washing the heels of her feet.

"She's—she is always and only my daughter. And this is just love."

I nod, blinking it back, and I was wrong, wrong in so many ways, and he is right: Grafted family.

> Nothing is more attractive than sacrifice. Nothing makes and saves a love story like sacrifice. Cruciform is the form of love.

Bound and joined and attached till we become one. And all I can do is this dance of fingers over my chest, this curving over the bed with all my heart, to stretch my arm out, over Shiloh, toward his chest.

He sees what I'm doing, smiles, dances his fingers across his chest, reaches his arm back toward me.

"My heart—"

And before I can finish . . .

"Is tied to your heart."

And Shiloh, under her oxygen mask, she stirs—and we watch her move her hand to dance fingers over her bare, scarred chest, and then she stretches out her little arm to reach out to our held hands, and Darryl takes her hand.

"Until my last breath, then always and forever." Her father takes her, hearts tied, hearts strong. *Here, right here.*

There is no shame in this needing each other; need is our greatest need. This is how we live the love story of our dreams. This is the way of all the epic love stories: Dependence deepens attachment. Vulnerably tying hearts to each other isn't tying us down; it's pulling us out. And this is true too: Dependence on God is what deepens attachment with God, and dependence is nothing less than a trusting that knows it can depend on the bridge to hold, for the arms to take our whole weight, for the heart to always open, for our person to be the One we can count on to take care of us the whole way through. Which is to say: Dependence is having faith. Need is our greatest need because need curves us in the direction of dependence, of faith. And there is no deep love without dependence, there is no love without faith; there is no love without being able to rely upon, depend upon, lean upon. This is what God seeks: hearts to have faith in Him, and for hearts to be faithful to Him. Deep calls to deep, dependence to dependence, *hesed* to *hesed*.

It is changing me, that

> the Greek word for "faith" is *pistis*, which, like almost any word ending in *is*, refers to an ongoing, dynamic reality. A more accurate, though perhaps clumsier, translation might be "faithing." Or perhaps we may translate it as "faithfulness." In historic Christianity, faith is not understood as a single, absolute certainty, based on a one-time experience of salvation. *[Faith] is an active, ongoing movement toward and with God.*[7]

The whole of the Christian life is more than a single act of faith at the foot of the cross; the Christian life is a moment-by-moment *movement of faithing* toward God, with God, of trusting in God to take care of us, a depending on God to carry us out, to carry us deeper in, of *faithing* in God, which grafts our hearts to God. Faith isn't a noun; faith is a verb; and faithing is an act, a journeying with no map but God alone. Faith is not being sure which way, but going always toward Him, in Him. Faithing is the journey of clinging trust. And then this is deepest true: All sin is anti-faithing. Sin is refusing to trust God, to attach to God, curving away from any need of dependence on God, which is to say: Sin is relational and breaks more than laws; sin breaks trust, it breaks attachment. Sin is anti-attachment.

Father, into Your hands, I commit Shiloh's sutured wild heart. Please, not my curved way, but Your kind way.

When I don't understand God's timing, my heart will keep SACRED time with God's heart.

"Mama?" Shiloh stirs, reaches for me in the middle of the night during my watch, reaching for me from the hospital bed. "Mama, how we get there? How we get there?"

I'm not sure what my baby girl missing her two front teeth is asking. After our coaxing her all day to eat, to take another step, to shuffle with her IV and oxygen and monitors down the hall toward the goal of this wing's playroom, is that what she's now murmuring aloud through her dreams, in the midst of monitors and leads and oxygen, is to get down the hall to the floor's communal playroom?

"How do we get where, Shiloh?" I lean in close. "The playroom, baby? Just—one step at a time—one step at a time." Forward—*toward.*

But Shiloh puts her hand on my cheek: "No, Mama. How we get there? How we get out of here and get there—how we get to *hommmmeeee?*"

Oh, baby girl. That is always the question, that is always the quest: How do we get out of here and get to there—get home. Her eyes are begging mine. She looks so fragile, she looks so strong. My eyes brim.

Faithing. The faithing that is attachment, moment by moment . . .

I cup her face.

The whole long way of SACRED faithing alone will lead us home.

"Shiloh, soon I promise—we'll be home." My eyes try to calm hers. A strong heart is the bonded heart: *already home.*

"You make it go faster, Mama? Please?" Her eyes wildly search mine. I kiss her forehead gently. Oh, baby girl, I know, I know— but that's the thing: You don't have to go faster to get home, to get up and out of all this—your heart literally has to slow down, still, go down deeper, deeper into Him . . . *trust.* SACRED faithing: *Stillness. Attentiveness. Cruciformity. Revelation. Examine. Doxology.*

Shiloh's finally fallen asleep, and my mind's making its interior SACRED way, step by vulnerable step, moving home, toward God, while I slip out and make my way down the stairs to grab a coffee. Darryl had whispered to me to take a break, go get some air, something to wake me up, and he's pulled in close beside her.

As I'm passing beside the hospital's children's library on the ground floor, on the way to the relief of my short flat white coffee, my eye just happens to catch it: There on the front display of this government-funded public hospital library are six books, six books out of thousands of library books, sitting on book easels in the front, cover out. I stop. The hospital library is featuring not Beatrix Potter, or Paddington Bear, or Winnie the Pooh, but six children's books on the Passover and the exodus of the Israelites out of Egypt and right through the Red Sea.

It's like a sign, God being a being of communication and revelation, and everything's a sign pointing the way to Him when there is no way, everything meant to be a sign pointing toward the home of intimate communion in Him.

Hushed, on holy ground, I step toward the display, tenderly pick up the first book, then the second—flip the pages of these children's books to see it in full-blown, full-spread color: The children of God crossing through the towering walls of water of the Red Sea, exodus to enter in, bondage to bonding. This isn't a children's fable—*this is the children of God literally faithing.*

My hands run awed across all these pages, hungry for this story we all keep living: There's the red dust clouds of Pharaoh's chariots storming across the desert floor—and the expanse of an endless cerulean sea crashing at their feet. I spread out the next book: Tribes are bickering. Tensions are whipped into a frenzy. Terror rising like a tsunami. Time seems to be running out. Next book of illustrations: The people are railing at Moses and wailing at God. The former slaves were still enslaved to not seeing possibility, though the Egyptians may have outnumbered the Israelites ten thousand to one. But fear is a phony con artist that stretches things, the clever magician that always dupes, and the Israelites see the approaching hundreds of Egyptians as an entire horizon erupting into a monstrous horror. But there's Moses standing still, attentive to God, arms stretched out cruciform— and God, in a tempest of love, with a blast of His nostrils, splits the sea in two to make a way out of bondage and into bonding, and the people of God reject the notion of drowning in fear, the paralysis of questioning, the bitterness of feeling abandoned, and they walk one fierce faithing step after the other, deep faith calling for deep waters, and you only find a way through waves when your faith, your trust, your relying, isn't as fickle as waves but is in the Way Himself.

I turn the pages of the next book, and there are the people of God passing right through the impossible, no-way sea, and I'm ringing with the words of Martin Luther, facing his own no-way:

> [When facing] a body of water which I must traverse, and I find no crossing, no bridge, or no ship, I must either drown or remain on this side and retrace my steps. Similarly, even though I led a good life here on earth and pursued a good course, still, when the hour is at hand for me to depart this life, I must have a different way and path on which to cross over. Now this is none other than the Christ who suffered and died for me, that through Him I might attain eternal life . . . the One who is and remains constantly at our side and within us, particularly in the hour when this life comes to an end, and who is so close that He alone is in our hearts . . . the Savior who has passed through death unto the Father for me, in order to take me there too. Then [I know] I am on the right Way, the Way we must take and travel from this to the life beyond. This journey begins in baptism.[8]

The way always is a baptism, a going down, going down, always the direction of deeper into the waters, into being immersed entirely in Christ.

I don't think it had ever struck me so powerfully before, holding all these paintings and colorful visual renderings of these Red Sea Roads, that this is what all the people of God are doing: The exodus through the Red Sea is going down, way down under the waters, like descending into a grave, dying to self, submerging their entire beings into God, then rising, resurrected, transformed into a new way of life, a new sacred way of being, a new way of faithing. The Jews called this Red Sea crossing a *mikvah*—literally, a gathering of waters for a spiritual cleansing—*which is like a baptism.* A renewing and remaking, *mikvah* is derived from the same word in Hebrew as *hope.*[9] Every Red Sea Road is a *mikvah,* a going deeper down and dying in the depths of Christ—to rise, rising into hope! Was our baptism any different than our own Red Sea Road, a going down into the waters, burying the old self in the perfect sacrificial love of Christ, and rising remade, resurrected to the dance and romance of the triune God?

There it is, right there in the next book: Miriam, Aaron, Moses, after hours of faithing through the depths of the sea, walking through their Red Sea Road to the other side, and there's the dancing, there is Miriam with her tambourine because when the Israelites had to flee Egypt in the middle of the night, taking nothing with them, it's the women who remembered to grab their tambourines, ready for the dance. Because even though they were facing a no-way Red Sea, their faith actively trusted that there is always a way to give thanks to God for His lovingkindness, their faith actively trusted and relied on God to take care of them through all things, and their faith actively trusted that through great walls of waves and great suffering, one can have great expectations in God romancing with His *hesed*-lovingkindness.

I'm a fool laughing at all these children's books open to Red Sea Roads, and I want to grab a tambourine and sing and dance: *doxology, doxology, doxology.*

Giddy awake now, I forget the coffee, gather up each of the books like manna in a waiting wilderness, and carry them back to Darryl and Shiloh in the hospital room. In the midst of the beeping heart monitors and lines and leads, I open up the books beside our little girl—and I'm looking at the miracle right here in living color. A blink and a turn ago, I was the wandering WayFarer, back in the Farmer's pickup truck, and I'd said it aloud, like a lost WayFarer, that there was absolutely no way for us to find a way to adopt a baby named Shalom Yu Xin from China with a literal busted heart. And now, here in a fourth-floor hospital bed, Shiloh trying to recover from a brutal heart surgery for that same busted heart, Darryl is turning the pages of all these children's books of Red Sea Road illustrations with his beloved daughter, Shiloh Shalom Yu Xin, and all I can hear is Ellie singing down all our Red Sea Roads:

> *When we can't see the way*
> *He will part the waves*
> *And we'll never walk alone*
> *Down a red sea road*

On a child's tilted hospital bed, Shiloh looks like a shaft of light flooding us with glory, and Darryl is a wave of grace that catches me when I'm falling, and there is the triune God who carries us through every Red Sea Road with the scarlet red love of His cruciform passion, who romances us as we dance. All that is needed for the Way is allegiance to God, attachment to the Lover of our Souls, faithing in the One who will *hesed*-love, adopt, and protect us, dwell with us forever, loving us with His life to life.

On Day 14, when the cardiologist gives the green light for Shiloh to head home with a three-times-daily beta-blocker, a heart Holter monitor, and directions for us to pause and be still to check her brave little ticker's heart rate at set intervals throughout the day, like set-time prayer, we're this teary mess of laughter, and Shiloh rises in her bed with hands waving, "Now, Mama! Now we get to go home! *Home! Hommmmeeee!*"

After tenderly buckling giddy Shiloh into her car seat, we exhale with these wild sighs of relief to drive out of the darkened basement hospital parking garage and up into the light and fresh air emancipation of going home.

"Hey, D?"

"Mhmmmm . . ." He's watching, waiting for the first light to turn green, and words come that I've waited decades to say.

"The way you've stayed with me these last fourteen days . . . and the way you've stayed with me . . ." My voice trails off. I turn toward him. "The way you've loved our Shiloh Shalom Yu Xin during these last fourteen days . . ." I swallow down that burning lump in my throat.

"Just—the ways you have given love the last two weeks in a hospital has given me more love than any old honeymoon." It's always cruciform love that romances through any circumstance.

The light turns green, but he turns toward me.

"Because—I love you. Because I really love you and I really love Shiloh."

And the GPS navigates in her hifalutin accent, "rerouting, rerouting." She's trying to find a way to steer us through a maze of construction around the hospital, down streets unknown to us. I reach over, lay my hand on Darryl's knee as he navigates. Maybe all the mazes that seem to be leading us further away are actually rerouting us in ways that bring us closer.

"Ann?" Darryl's pulling into the right lane at the next street-light, smiling a mile wide, shaking his head.

"Look up. Look up at the name of the street that the GPS is taking us down now."

And I look up and can't believe, but completely do, what I am reading on the green and white street sign by the lights:

MOSES WAY

chapter seventeen

HONEYMOON

Let your religion be less of a theory and more
of a love affair.
—G. K. CHESTERTON

The Believer after all is someone in love.
—SØREN KIERKEGAARD

Marriages are fragile things, not an accomplishment to be
proud of, but a miracle to give thanks for.

He and I, we fly across an ocean of waves, fly away to a
tropical isle alone together for the first time in our lives, for our
twenty-fifth anniversary—for a second honeymoon. There may
be no do-overs, because all our scars become us, but we get to be
over the moon that we stayed and weathered waves, that we're

living it. That first vow was "I do." Now it's "I'm here, right here." Where two hearts repair a heartbreak by grafting together, they can be the strongest right there at the break.[1]

What I find is a one-room cabana on an island pineapple farm for my farming man and me. It has French doors that open right up to the lapping ocean and pineapple fields with flocks of clucking hens, and if he needs to go work, they've got good dirt. Maybe he will feel at home—or at least have a way of escape? Maybe if I feel rejected—lost—I can find solace in waves?

After we land, we rent the only economy car left on the lot, a blue Kia, tentatively wind our way to the far wild end of the island, then turn down an empty, no-exit road toward the farm and only us for the next seven days. I take a deep breath, nervous. Underneath the grove of palm trees leading toward the farm, our host farmers have left the cabana's front porch light on. We smile like fools. This is a kind of wayfaring and returning, a homecoming to the light that's always left on. Love is an endless coming home.

We walk out to the edge and dip our toes in the ocean straightaway. We've held on and only made it because the WayMaker's *hesed* always holds us. He slips his arm around me, fingertips tracing the curve of bare shoulder, and we watch the sun set ember across waves, fireball sinking down into its own Red Sea.

"This week? What's—your dream?" I turn to face him, like I need to somehow be enough to hold a man's attention. "I've made a list of all the different things we can do that you love. They've got ATVs just down the road, and Sea-Doos for rent, and I think there's sailboarding somewhere?"

He tilts my chin to read his eyes. "No renting. No reserving.

No—adventures or accomplishments. What I'd really love? Is just being with you. I just—want to be with you."

I nod, chin trembling a bit. I can change, he can change, people can change, things can change, stories can change, our ways can change, the way we see and be and are can all change.

We keep the French doors open to the ocean, to lemon breezes and the scent of seaweed and waves coming, all night long. We lie awake, listening to the sea, and we find each other and amazing grace finds us and we don't sleep. Our bodies speak for our souls.

We trace and we touch, and I lay my hand on his weathered cheek, and his eyes, like fine art framed with decades of wrinkles, they don't leave mine. He knows. *Yada*-knows. He knows all the edges of my story that bruise when touched, the places that are fractured and fraught, the spaces within me that ache tender with emptiness. He knows what shames me. He has seen all of me. And I don't mean the sagging and the cellulite—I mean ugliness and spewed words that can't be stuffed back into any bottle, sins that have marred and scarred long stretches of my soul—and his.

Our eyes hold each other. There's an old love that sees with a kind of holy double vision—that remembers a young lover in all their seeming infallibility, and sees your aged lover in all their beautiful humanity. This must be what it is to be naked and unashamed.

Passionate love is far more than falling in love. *Passion* literally means to suffer—which means: Lovers are the longsufferers. Which is to say that the old lovers are the most passionate of all. It's the old lovers who have suffered tenderly through crises and kids and the countless blur of days and untold heartaches, who live the most genuine nonstop passion. It's the old lovers whose willingness to suffer for each other has made all their other suffering bearable. It's the old lovers who have passionately suffered long for each other, with each other, who have grown the most passionate, companionate love of all. And it's the suffering, passionate, companionate love—the easy laughter and sure reliability and steadiness of companionship and friendship and withness—that makes for the happiest love of all. And it's the old love that is the most suggestive love of all because it suggests that the whole of us is actually seen and known, and we are still wholly loved. It is only in being really known, in ways that we wish nobody ever knew, that we ever really know what it means to be loved.

What could be more risqué than risking aging with someone and being worn down to your bare souls?

The sun comes up, we cleave and we covenant, we need and we are needed, we want and we are the wanted. We are no longer the ashamed; we are the saved. The surest love stories are always rescue stories, saved from living alone in our own souls, curving in on our own hearts. Our skin renewing our vows renews us again and again.

He and I are writing another line in our love story that I never want to end, though I'd almost ended it all, and this is one of the truest things I know: Our addiction to turning, always turning, toward novelty in a thousand ways—to all the new shiny things, the new distractions, the new things to buy, to eat, to read, to watch, to click—makes our souls sick, too sick to see the beauty in the old things, the familiar things, the tried-and-true and profoundly sacred things. I trace the curve of his arm, outline the palm of his hand. I know this man. It's familiarity that incubates the kind of real love all kinds of distracting novelty can only dream of.

"How do you still make my heart skip a beat?" I whisper it quiet, our legs tangled in sheets. I'll take the boring love of decades of him helping with the dress zipper there at the nape of the neck, the sharing of the same table and passing down the pitcher of water night after night, and then washing up the white everyday dishes and turning out the light because the truth is: The real romantics are the boring ones—they let another heart bore down deep into their own until the two become one.

If our addiction to turning to fall in love with all kinds of diverting novelties makes us soul sick, then this is the truest too: Wholeness is falling in love with the same old sacred rhythms, the same old places, the same old miraculous people every day all over again. This is the way of Love Himself. The One who is Love can't stop loving the same sun dancing across these same skies, day after day, can't stop wooing this same world around in the same spinning choreography of moon and stars and space and infinite grace.[2] It never grows old for Love Himself to keep falling in love with His same old loves.

"And you . . ." He tucks a few silver strands of mine behind my ear, grins. "How do you keep growing more beautiful?"

His smile's slow and easy—familiar. He's grinning like we're young kids, and I laugh because the Farmer thinks he knows about growing, and I close my eyes. Marriage isn't about always being happy—marriage is about always *growing in the right direction*. Life isn't about avoiding trauma and suffering; life is about *growing* through it. And even the oldest love, the hardest

> Wholeness is falling in love with the same old sacred rhythms, the same old places, the same old miraculous people every day all over again.

days, can know slow growth, in our own singular ways, for those who have eyes to see. Any ecosystem that remains always the same—never changes—is stagnant and dying. If a relationship isn't changing, growing, even slowly—it's dying. Pursuing an unchangeable state of happiness will lead you to a stagnant state of despair. Happiness-centered marriages implode—because that shifting center won't hold. There's no such thing as unchanging happiness—happiness comes and goes like waves—and the only thing that is unchanging is change itself. Healthy relationships have a healthy relationship with waves, with the rising and falling, and believing that there will still be another way to rise. The two become one to become stronger, to persevere and suffer and change and be sanctified and grow, rising to a new life together.

> It is not the absence of infatuation that makes any marriage unhappy but the absence of deep attachment.

This is the unspoken miracle of marriage: You vow to keep loving the same old person who keeps growing in their own way into a stranger.

God knows, this is the deeper vow: "I'm here, right here." It is not the absence of infatuation that makes any marriage unhappy but the absence of deep attachment.

What turns a marriage, a life, around is choosing in a million small moments, instead of turning toward some distraction, some screen, some addiction, to turn toward the face of the other. Making your spouse your person is what can make your marriage happy. Falling in love is only the wild rush before the soft landing in a deep canyon of companionship through any pain and suffering that leads the way into real bliss. The fall into love is an exhilarating part of it all, but it's the staying loving that makes a love story.

The passion of the Christ is the ultimate passionate love; stay in Christ so it's possible to stay in love.

My eyes don't leave his. His don't leave mine. And we don't ever want to stop seeing each other with this kind of holy double vision.

"You okay?" His voice is tender as he gathers me in, arm around me, my head lying there on his chest. I can hear his heartbeat. Strong.

> The passion of the Christ is the ultimate passionate love; stay in Christ so it's possible to stay in love.

"Every time you say just those two words—'You okay'—I hear: 'I see you. I am for you. I care where you are. How do you need me? How can I give myself to you so you know you are deeply safe?'"

The way through anything is knowing we are beloved in everything.

He kisses my forehead gently.

"Perfect. That's exactly what I wanted to say." His heartbeat's right there at my ear.

After we throw back the sheets, before we walk out to the ocean and the waves always coming in, I slide into this long, full skirt he picked out for me himself, in Israel, the Farmer laying down his hard, dirt-earned dollars in the Holy Land for this silk skirt of painted roses by a stream winding its way through a garden. I can't ever remember him doing anything as wildly lavish like that before. There are crystals sewn into the flower garden there at the skirt's waist.

He steps up behind me at the cabana's tilted mirror, slides

his arms around my waist, whispers at the nape of my neck, "You know? Morning with you—still feels like the garden of Eden."

"After everything?"

"Especially."

His lips brush my cheek. It was back in the first garden of Eden that we all rejected God's way, but in that garden of Gethsemane, the Son of the triune God bows His head and says, "Not my way be done, but only Your way be done." And then He goes to the Tree of Calvary to lead us toward our home of the restored garden of Eden at the end of time, with its "pure river of water of life, clear as crystal, proceeding from the throne of God and of the Lamb. In the middle of its street, and on either side of the river, was the tree of life . . . The leaves of the tree were for the healing of the nations" (Revelation 22:1–2 NKJV), where there will be communion and consummation of the love story beyond dreams. There will never be another turn away, never another tear, never anymore fear, never another way but the kindness of His. "No longer will there be anything accursed, but the throne of God and of the Lamb will be in it, and his servants will worship him. They will see his face, and his name will be on their foreheads. And night will be no more" (vv. 3–5 ESV). And we will wake to all our dreams come true: We will be fully known and know the fullness of God. Everything will be the way it was made to be, even, especially, us. The dream is almost and already; He's already claimed us and named us as His own: beloved.

"Can I ask . . . ?" I murmur it to him, down on the beach, his lips finding mine, as a photographer kneels down in the sand, trying to capture us in frames to commemorate our last two decades and a half of marriage.

"Why didn't you kiss me like this on our wedding day, when the photographer tried to grab pictures of us after our vows?" The hem of my garden skirt is being caressed by waves.

"Guess I've had more practice now," he teases, nuzzles my neck, and, surprised at his brazenness, I throw my head back, laugh too loud, the happiness of us choosing us to keep practicing our faith. And we're swept up in an ocean gust, and he's emboldened and kisses slow up the side of my neck with no shyness, no shame.

"Like the roar of many waters" (19:6 ESV), joy will sweep in then too, when time rolls up and we will all rise in waves of adoration that finally Jesus has come for His bride, that "the marriage of the Lamb has come, and his Bride has made herself ready" (v. 7 ESV), and we will have practiced the whole of our sacred lives for this kiss of doxology, doxology, doxology. The dowry for the bride has been paid in full at the cross, by the Lamb whose blood covered the doorposts down in Egypt to make a way for the angel of death to pass over us, by the sacrificed heart of the Lamb who is Jesus, the only One who has ever loved you to death and back to the realest life.

"The angel said to me, 'Write this: Blessed are those who are invited to the wedding supper of the Lamb!' And he added, 'These are the true words of God'" (v. 9). No truer words have ever been written. We've read the last page, and we know the way our story ends—our story ends being loved without end, the last line always a good line. The metaphors of this world will give way to the marriage of forever. The hard ways are being made into a way to the holy wedding. For every way that seems like no way, God makes a way "through the sea . . . through the mighty waters" (Psalm 77:19), a pathway to the love feast that will in no way ever end.

We've read the last page, and we know the way our story ends—our story ends being loved without end, the last line always a good line.

Our happily ever after is certain: There's a wedding with Love Himself after everything.

The coming consummation overcomes whatever comes.

After everything?

Especially.

We are held; the dream will be fulfilled. Keep faithing that this is always the way of His universe, the only way that matters in the end.

Darryl takes my hand and leads me right out into waves, and the water feels like a washing, like a renewing, and his body steadying mine feels like an anchoring, and me and my Holy Land garden skirt are being baptized in the sea. The first exodus through the waters, with God's outstretched arm, was to save not just from all that enslaves but to make a way to be with Him, He Himself testifying:

> "You yourselves have seen what I did to the Egyptians, and how I bore you on eagles' wings and brought you to myself. Now therefore, if you will indeed obey my voice and keep my covenant, you shall be my treasured possession." (Exodus 19:4–5 ESV)

When the new and last exodus of Revelation comes, all who keep trust-faithing in the Way will be "standing beside the sea of glass" to "sing the song of Moses . . . and the song of the Lamb" (Revelation 15:2–3 ESV), which is but one epic love song in two sacred movements, a love song from one way out, to the forever

way in. When Moses crossed through the Red Sea, he led all of
Israel to sing this love song to God:

> "I will sing to the LORD, for he has triumphed
>   gloriously;
>   the horse and his rider he has thrown into
>   the sea.
> The LORD is my strength and my song,
>   and he has become my salvation;
> this is my God, and I will praise him,
>   my father's God, and I will exalt him."

> "At the blast of your nostrils the waters piled up;
>   the floods stood up in a heap."

> "You have led in your steadfast love [*hesed-*
>   lovingkindness] the people whom you have
>   redeemed;
>   you have guided them by your
>   strength to your holy abode."
>   (Exodus 15:1– 2; 8; 13 ESV)

Then "Miriam the prophetess . . . took a tambourine in her
hand, and all the women went out after her with tambourines
and dancing. And Miriam sang to them: 'Sing to the LORD'"
(vv. 20–21 ESV).

To this day, Jews rise and sing these exact words every morn-
ing, this Song of the Sea, this Song of Moses, a serenading of
God's *hesed*-lovingkindness from that day to this. And to this day,
I keep a collection of tambourines just off the kitchen, because

there are still women who grab their tambourines in the middle of their Egypts and hold on to their tambourines when they are between a rock and a Red Sea, faithing that there will be a way through and God is always worthy of thanks, *doxology, doxology, doxology*. And someday, soon and very soon, we'll be the ones singing the love song of Moses with the Song of the Lamb before our wedding supper at the end of time, when we will be His, there next to Him at, as Spurgeon wrote: "the feast of love; there, love is at home."[3]

Every tropical morning on this second honeymoon, he and I feast on a quart of fresh blueberries and a tub of Greek yogurt from Ram's Grocery off Bay Road, sharing a bowl down at the ocean. We watch the daily rain clouds rupture out over the waves, and this gold sunlight falls with the rain, and we grin from ear to ear, laughing, with a full rainbow arcing over our graying heads. God can set flame to the rain and shoot a bow of love, of shalom, straight into storms, and all week we keep the French doors of the cabana wide open.

Our love's making the metaphor. Soon, the reality.

HOME

I hang that wild Holy Land garden skirt on the back of our bedroom door when we get back home to the farm so I don't forget the foretaste of forever. A tambourine hangs ready and thankful on the wall.

Darryl and I sweep up Shiloh and wander some beckoning Sunday afternoon down to the farm river. Shiloh's singing like a crooning crown up on Darryl's shoulders, and I'm holding his hand, holding this moment in mind like a picture frame, and we linger under the ancient boughs of our gnarled willow trees there at the edge of the waters.

Shiloh leans down over Darryl's head, pats her papa's cheek, points across the shallow river, waters lilting softly over stones.

"Papa, you take me across?"

I know what he's thinking before he even answers her because I know what he's said to me, to God.

"For you, yep, anywhere, any way."

That's the way through, that's all I need to turn and say to my First Love, to Abba WayMaker, no matter what no-way place I'm in, no matter the crashing waves ahead: I'm here. I'll go whatever way with You. Whatever the way, as long as You're with me, and I am with You.

The Way is a Person, and the only way to be a whole, fulfilled person is to embrace His SACRED romance.

I lean against the willows and smile like a love-drunk fool over the father carrying his laughing daughter through the waters singing its steady song. And maybe the farm river is coursing with the Song of Moses, the Song of Miriam, the Song of the Sea, and the Song of the Lamb—and that clueless young bride I was who got married with the preacher talking about "Annie's Song," she now knows who she is because of Whose she is, because He made a way to wed her, and her new heart beats, in this faithing, trusting way that sings a love song of its own:

> *Come, I'll let You love me anyway You want to love me,*
> *Come, make Your way to me,*
> *To take me, and make me—*
> *Your child, Your bride, Your own.*

What other SACRED song can I sing in response to the WayMaker who never stops working all things into love?

And the waters of the old farm river run on with this song of the *hesed*-heartbeat of the WayMaker that never stops:

> *I am here, right here, and you are already home.*
> *You are already held.*
> *You are already loved.*

Shiloh and Darryl turn midstream in the river, grinning like they're walking on water, and Shiloh waves for me to *Come!* Darryl nods, smiling wide. And I laugh and step into the beckoning water—and yes, I'll come—and take the sacred way to the other side.

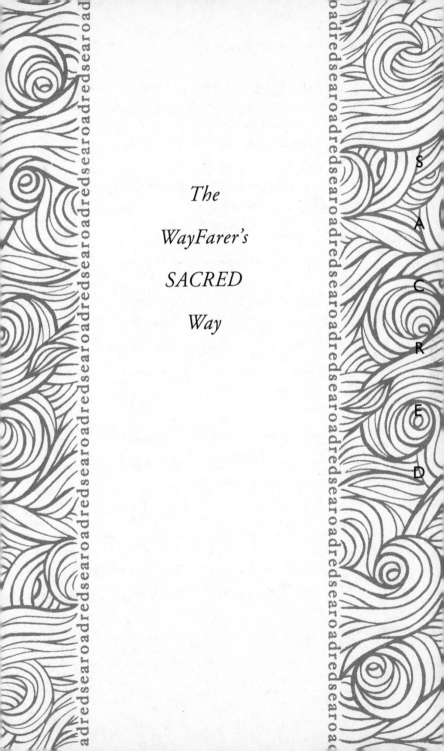

The

WayFarer's

SACRED

Way

THE WAYFARER'S COMPASS
A *SACRED* WAY OF LIFE

S TILLNESS *TO KNOW GOD*

How can I slow, still, and breathe in a place of trust with God today? (Psalm 46:10)

_____

_____

A TTENTIVENESS *TO HEAR GOD*

Who do I say that God is today? (Mark 8:29)

_____

_____

Where am I coming from and where am I going to today? (Genesis 16:8)

_____

_____

What do I want today? (John 1:38)

_____

_____

C RUCIFORMITY *TO SURRENDER TO GOD*

What do I need to do or surrender to live cruciform today? (Luke 9:23)

_____

_____

EVELATION *TO SEE GOD*

How did I experience a fresh revelation from God in His Word today? (Psalm 119:105)

_____

_____

XAMINE *TO RETURN TO GOD*

What am I afraid of today? (Mark 4:40)

_____

_____

OXOLOGY *TO THANK GOD*

What can I thank God for today? (1Thessalonians 5:18)

_____

_____

THE WAYFARER'S MANIFESTO

Today, I am on the Way when I still and trust:
Strong winds blow
Red Sea Roads.

Today, I am on the Way when I still and trust:
No fear,
Always loved,
Always withness,
Turn, turn,
He'll always carry me the whole way through.

Today, I am on the Way when I still and trust:
What's in my way leads to the Way.
(You know you're walking a Red Sea Road through
when you're bonding closer to Him.)

Today, I am on the Way when I still and trust:
What's clouded in mystery is a flame to light
the Way.

Today, I am on the Way when I still and trust:
What matters is not merely moving forward, but
what I am moving toward.
Not inward, not wayward, not forward,
always *toward*!

Today, I am on the Way when I still and trust:
Jesus is my person.
(*True freedom is to be free of outcomes and come into Him.*)

Today, I am on the Way when I still and trust:
I only cross through the waters
when I surrender to living like the Cross.
(Incurvatus in se *may say*
the way out of heartbreak is to simply curve inward,
but the way out of pain is to reach out, cruciform.)

Today, I am on the Way when I still and trust:
The pathway of least resistance leads to the
      least life.
It's the narrow pathway of great resistance that leads
      to the great life.
(*Easy way. Empty life.*
Hard way. Holy, fulfilling life.
Narrow way. Hard way. Holy, fulfilled life.)

Today, I am on the Way when I still and trust:
The obstacle is the miracle.

Today, I am on the Way when I still and live it:
Doxology, doxology, doxology.

THE WAYFARER'S PRAYER

God, give us the grace to embrace
the mysteries we don't understand,
the cruciform openness to live a tender surrender,
into Your ways wiser and kinder than ours,
and the deep shalom of simply being
with You here,
right here,
with us.

ACKNOWLEDGMENTS

As God's children walked through the Red Sea as a community of people, so the way of this story through waves has been a healing journey in a community I am earnest to thank.

To Darryl, who chose me how many moons ago, you have been an anchor in Christ through storm and crisis and waxing and waning of moons, and I love you to the moon and back and round a hog's hind leg. You have been like Jesus to me, looked me in the eye, and whispered, "No shame." You are my shelter, my safe place, my most cherished gift from the hand of God Himself. Even if everything falls away, because of the Way Himself, there is no way our love will ebb away, so I am not afraid; everything is going to be okay. My heart is welded to yours as one. I can never thank you enough, Darryl, for the gift of this life with you.

To the beautiful, brave hearts of the women at Morning Star Foundation in China, who loved Shiloh Shalom Yu Xin with all their hearts, you forever have my highest esteem and deepest gratitude. Your sacrifice to wholeheartedly love, even in the face of heartbreaking loss, is nothing less than the fragrance of Christ. To Shiloh's birth mama, there is never a day that goes by that I don't think of you, pray for you, ache-wish that we could find you, thank you, marvel over the daughter whom you carried.

To Ellie Holcomb, Nicole Witt, and Christa Wells, who gathered up a line from one of my blog posts, wrote the song "Red Sea Road," and gave us an anthem of hope when there seems to be no way.

To Arie Bar David, Ji Yun, Kyle Strobel, and Curt Thompson, from the shores of Israel, to the great state of Texas, to both shores of the United States, you each ushered us into more of the heart of God.

To Lisa-Jo Baker and John Blase, you came this story's whole long way, the steady and sure, the honest and true and kind. I'd walk a thousand more miles with faithful pilgrims like you. You can't know what you each have meant to me.

To Bill Jensen, Don Jacobsen, Damon Reiss, Debbie Wickwire, Carolyn McCready, Sandy Vander Zicht, Tom Dean, Mick Silva, and Sara Riemersma, each of you is like Aaron and Hur, you held me up, you prayed on your knees, you are like family. I am indebted to you for grace beyond measure, and when you stand before our Lord, my hands will sting from my wild applause for your crowns laid down at His feet.

To Molly and John and Mama, my kin. We belong to each other for always, never alone, and when there seems to be no way, the WayMaker makes His way through hell to get to us and whisper, "Mine." We are re-fathered and held until the end of time and then for forever. I love you more than you can ever imagine. We are going to make it because we have a WayMaker.

To Caleb, Joshua, Hope, Levi, Malakai, and Shalom, for making my heart split with joy just because you are, for all the times you sacrificed and forgave and rose again with true grit and lavish grace and pressed on, I couldn't love you more. You are half a dozen of the most captivating human beings, and being your mother, giving you witness and withness forever and for always, no matter what, has been the greatest privilege of my life. I cannot wait to see the wondrous, wholehearted stories you write with your lives. Your mama thinks you each are something else.

To Shiloh. My daughter, cherished, chosen, and beloved. There are not enough pages or ink or words to express how I love you, how being your heart mama is sacred ground, how whatever you ever need, you have our promise to make it our life's holy vocation to make you feel deeply seen and known, profoundly safe and secure. Your whole family thinks you're about the best thing that ever happened to us; we are dazzled by you, smitten with you, here for you, and our hearts are tied to yours for always and forever.

To the WayMaker. At the bottom of my most hellish pits, I discovered Your hands didn't reach down for me; Your arms have always been under me. At rock bottom, You are the rock who has always held me, and, Jesus, You are not mere belief to me, You are breath to me, not some theory but all my gravity, not a lens for my life, but You are my life. Triune God, my very WayMaker, You are not one sphere of some multi-dimensional life—You are to me like my very own atmosphere, terra, lung, and my only way not to suffocate in self.

Here I am, Lord, You have all of me—have your Way.

We are all tethered to Love, and He is always the way.

NOTES

Chapter 1: In the Beginning

1. Daniel J. Siegel and Tina Payne Bryson, *The Power of Showing Up: How Parental Presence Shapes Who Our Kids Become and How Their Brains Get Wired* (New York: Ballantine Books, 2020), 9–14.
2. Dietrich Bonhoeffer, *Creation and Fall: A Theological Exposition of Genesis 1–3*, trans. Douglas Stephen Bax, ed. John W. de Gruchy (Minneapolis: Fortress Press, 2004), 128–29.
3. Rabbi Yehuda Leib Shapira-Frankfurter, quoted in Rabbi Reuven Chaim Klein, "Fascinating Explorations in Lashon HaKodesh," *Jewish Review*, November 15, 2019, https://jewishreview.co.il/where-are-you-2446/.

Chapter 2: The Art of the Turn

1. Michael Card, *Inexpressible: Hesed and the Mystery of God's Lovingkindness* (Downers Grove, IL: InterVarsity Press Books, 2018), 9.
2. E. James Wilder, *The Pandora Problem: Facing Narcissism in Leaders & Ourselves* (Carmel, IN: Deeper Walk International, 2018), 16.
3. Michael Card, *Luke: The Gospel of Amazement* (Downers Grove, IL: InterVarsity Press Books, 2011), 29.
4. Bob Dylan, vocalist, "Bye and Bye," by Bob Dylan, MP3 audio, track 4 on Bob Dylan, *Love and Theft*, Special Rider Music, 2001.
5. *The Shawshank Redemption*, directed by Frank Darabont (1994; Burbank, CA: Warner Home Video, 2007), DVD.

Chapter 3: Come Let Me Love You

1. John Denver, vocalist, "Annie's Song," by John Denver, MP3 audio, track 15 on John Denver, *The Essential John Denver*, Sony Legacy, 2007.
2. C. S. Lewis, *The Weight of Glory* (1949; repr., New York: HarperOne, 2001), 29.
3. C. S. Lewis, *The Pilgrim's Regress: An Allegorical Apology for Christianity, Reason and Romanticism* (1933; repr., Grand Rapids, MI: William B. Eerdmans, 2014), 237.
4. C. S. Lewis, *Mere Christianity* (1952; repr., New York: HarperOne, 2001), 136–37.
5. John Piper, "Jesus Died for Her Beauty" (sermon, Bethlehem Baptist Church, Minneapolis, MN, July 6, 2018), You Tube video, 3:57, Desiring God, https://www.desiringgod.org/messages/an-impossible -covenant/excerpts/jesus-died-for-her-beauty.
6. John Calvin, *Commentary on Galatians and Ephesians*, s.v. "Ephesians 5:28–33," archived at Christian Classics Ethereal Library, https://www.ccel.org/ccel/calvin/calcom41.iv.vi.vi.html.
7. C. H. Spurgeon, *Evening by Evening; or, Readings at Eventide* (New York: Sheldon and Company, 1869), 86.
8. Thomas Watson, *The Godly Man's Picture* (Zeeland, MI: Reformed Church Publications, 2009), 189.
9. John Calvin, *Institutes of the Christian Religion*, ed. John T. McNeill (Philadelphia: Westminster, 1960), 2.8.18 (2:385).
10. Calvin, *Institutes*, 3.11.10 (2:737).
11. N. T. Wright, "What Is Marriage For?" *Plough Quarterly*, no. 6 (2015), https://www.plough.com/en/topics/life/marriage/what-is -marriage-for.
12. Paul E. Miller, *A Loving Life: In a World of Broken Relationships* (Wheaton, IL: Crossway, 2014), 24.
13. T. S. Eliot, "Little Gidding," *Four Quartets* (Boston: Mariner Books, 1943).
14. Denver, "Annie's Song."

Chapter 4: How to Be Known

1. Mihaly Csikszentmihalyi, *Flow: The Psychology of Optimal Experience* (New York: Harper Perennial Modern Classics, 2008), 2–4.

Notes

2. Helen Keller wrote, "There is joy in self-forgetfulness. So I try to make the light in others' eyes my sun, the music in others' ears my symphony, the smile on others' lips my happiness." *The Story of My Life* (New York: Dover Publications, 1996), 70.

3. Yang Bai et al., "Awe, the Diminished Self, and Collective Engagement: Universals and Cultural Variations in the Small Self," *Journal of Personality and Social Psychology* 113, no. 2 (2017): 185–209, https://doi.org/10.1037/pspa0000087.

4. David Elliot, "The Christian as Homo Viator: A Resource in Aquinas for Overcoming 'Worldly Sin and Sorrow,'" *Journal of the Society of Christian Ethics* 34, no. 2 (Fall/Winter 2014): 101–21, https://doi.org/10.1353/sce.2014.0044.

5. Paul G. Kuntz, "Augustine: From Homo Erro to Homo Viator," *Augustinian Studies* 11 (1980): 79–89, https://doi.org/10.5840/augstudies1980114.

6. "I do but touch the surface of this boundless sea as with a swallow's wing; happy are you if you dare to plunge into its depths . . . Christ has linked his destiny with thine, his honour with thine, his life with thine, his happiness with thine. Thou must be in heaven, or else he will be bereaved. Thou must be in heaven, or else he will be imperfect. Thou art a member of his body; and if he should lose one of his members, then his body would not be perfect, nor the Head either. Thou art joined unto the Lord, and thou art 'one spirit' with him, and thou mayest bravely say, 'Who shall separate us?' for such is this eternal union that there is no separation between Christ and the soul that is joined to him . . . What a marriage is this! Do you know, dear friend, what I am talking about? I cannot speak of it as I would, but it is true, and there is the wonder of it. It is no fiction, no myth, no mere figure of speech; but it is really so in deed and in truth. For this cause, Christ left his Father, and became one with his church, that henceforth they should no more be twain, but one; and now we who have believed in Christ Jesus are one with him in time and to eternity. His love has made it so, and we may paraphrase the words we read just now, and say, 'Behold, what manner of love the Bridegroom hath bestowed upon us, that we should be called the spouse of Christ!'" Charles Haddon

Spurgeon, "Christ's Love to His Spouse," in *The Metropolitan Tabernacle Pulpit: Sermons Preached by C. H. Spurgeon*, vol. 42, 1896, The Spurgeon Center, https://www.spurgeon.org/resource -library/sermons/christs-love-to-his-spouse/#flipbook.

7. Abraham Heschel, *The Prophets* (New York: Harper Perennial, 2001), 71.

8. "The heart of God is poured out into the Christian's heart, so far as the Infinite can disclose itself to the finite. And as we tell the Lord what we are, He is pleased to tell us what He is. Surely, dear Friends, as these intercommunications go on, it would be hard to say how richly the inmost secrets of God may become known to His privileged people. Shall I be understood if I say that man may know a great deal more than he thinks he knows? He may know more of God than he knows he knows, for it is one thing to know, and another thing to know that we know!" Charles Spurgeon, "Private and Confidential," in *The Metropolitan Tabernacle Pulpit: Sermons Preached by C. H. Spurgeon*, vol. 60, 1914, Christian Classics Ethereal Library, https://ccel.org/ccel/spurgeon /sermons60.xlii.html.

9. John Calvin, "The Work of the Holy Spirit and Faith," in *Reformed Reader: A Sourcebook in Christian Theology, Volume 1, Classical Beginnings, 1519–1799*, ed. William Stacy Johnson and John H. Leith (Louisville, KY: Westminster John Knox Press, 1993), 240.

Chapter 5: There's No Place Like Home

1. C. S. Lewis, *The Weight of Glory* (1949; repr., New York: HarperOne, 2001), 42.

2. John Calvin, *Commentary on Corinthians*, vol. 1, s.v. "1 Corinthians 1:4–9," archived at Christian Classics Ethereal Library, https://ccel.org/ccel/calvin/calcom39.viii.ii.html.

3. J. I. Packer, *Knowing God* (Downers Grove, IL: InterVarsity Press Books, 1993), 206.

4. Daniel J. Siegel and Tina Payne Bryson, *The Power of Showing Up: How Parental Presence Shapes Who Our Kids Become and How Their Brains Get Wired* (New York: Ballantine Books, 2020), 9–14.

5. Packer, *Knowing God*, 201–2.

Chapter 6: Your Kingdom Come

1. N. T. Wright, *Surprised by Hope: Rethinking Heaven, the Resurrection, and the Mission of the Church* (New York: HarperOne, 2008), 29.

2. Mary Oliver, *Winter Hours* (New York: Mariner Books, 1999), 93.

3. Jonathan Edwards, quoted in Douglas A. Sweeney and Jan Stievermann, eds., *The Oxford Handbook of Jonathan Edwards* (Oxford: Oxford UP, 2021), 170. Original quote: "Miscellany 332," in *Works*, vol. 13, 410.

4. Eugene H. Peterson, *God's Message for Each Day: Wisdom from the Word of God* (Nashville: Thomas Nelson, 2020), 48.

5. Timothy Keller, *The Reason for God: Belief in an Age of Skepticism* (New York: Dutton, 2008), 23.

6. C. S. Lewis, *Mere Christianity* (1952; repr., New York: HarperOne, 2001), 24.

7. Richard G. Tedeschi and Cara L. Blevins, "Posttraumatic Growth: A Pathway to Resilience," in *The Routledge International Handbook of Psychosocial Resilience*, ed. Updesh Kumar (Oxfordshire: Taylor & Francis, 2016), 324–33.

8. Viktor E. Frankl, *Man's Search for Meaning* (1946; repr., Boston: Beacon Press, 2006), 113.

9. A. W. Tozer, *The Pursuit of God* (Chicago: Wingspread Publishers, 1948), 77.

10. Peter A. Levine, *Healing Trauma: A Pioneering Program for Restoring the Wisdom of Your Body* (Boulder, CO: Sounds True, 2008), 11.

11. Matthew W. Bates, *Salvation by Allegiance Alone: Rethinking Faith, Works, and the Gospel of Jesus the King* (Grand Rapids: Baker Academic), 43.

Chapter 7: Red Sea Road

1. Charles Spurgeon, "Direction in Dilemma," in *The Metropolitan Tabernacle Pulpit: Sermons Preached by C. H. Spurgeon*, vol. 9, 1863, Christian Classics Ethereal Library, https://www.ccel.org/ccel /spurgeon/sermons09.lv.html.

2. Curt Thompson, *Soul of Shame: Retelling the Stories We Believe About Ourselves* (Downers Grove, IL: InterVarsity Press Books, 2008), 127.

3. Alastair J. Roberts and Andrew Wilson, *Echoes of Exodus: Tracing Themes of Redemption through Scripture* (Wheaton, IL: Crossway, 2018), 125.

4. Christopher J. H. Wright, *The Mission of God: Unlocking the Bible's Grand Narrative* (Downers Grove, IL: InterVarsity Press Books, 2006), 265.

5. Wright, *Mission of God*, 275 (emphasis mine).

6. "What the Starling Said," *Irish Times*, August 9, 2000, https://www.irishtimes.com/opinion/what-the-starling-said-1.301184.

7. Ann Voskamp, *One Thousand Gifts: A Dare to Live Fully Right Where You Are* (Grand Rapids, MI: Zondervan, 2011).

Chapter 8: Into the Storm

1. Elise S. Eslinger, "Shalom to You," in *United Methodist Hymnal* (Nashville: United Methodist Publishing House, 1989), 666.

2. Cornelius Plantinga Jr., *Not the Way It's Supposed to Be: A Breviary of Sin* (Grand Rapids, MI: William B. Eerdmans, 1995), 10.

Chapter 9: Pilgrimage

1. Saint Ignatius of Loyola, *A Pilgrim's Testament: The Memoirs of Ignatius of Loyola*, trans. Parmananda R. Divarkar (Rome: Gregorian Biblical BookShop, 1983), 44.

2. Eugene H. Peterson, *The Jesus Way: A Conversation on the Ways That Jesus Is the Way* (Grand Rapids, MI: William B. Eerdmans, 2007), 39–40.

Chapter 10: The Fear of Being Found

1. James K. A. Smith, *You Are What You Love: The Spiritual Power of Habit* (Grand Rapids, MI: Brazos Press, 2016), 25.

2. Saint Augustine, *The Confessions of Saint Augustine*, book 2, trans. E.B. Pusey (Salt Lake City: Project Gutenberg, 2002), https://www.gutenberg.org/files/3296/3296-h/3296-h.htm.

3. Saint Augustine, quoted in Saint Thomas Aquinas, *Summa Theologica*, part 1–2 ("Pars Prima Secundae"), trans. Fathers of the English Dominican Province (Salt Lake City: Project Gutenberg, 2006), https://gutenberg.org/cache/epub/17897/pg17897.html.

4. John Calvin, *Institutes of the Christian Religion*, ed. John T. McNeill (Philadelphia: Westminster, 1960), 1.11.8.

Chapter 11: Kin

1. G. K. Chesterton, *The Innocence of Father Brown* (New York: Cassell and Company, 1911), 6.

2. Matthew W. Bates, *Salvation by Allegiance Alone: Rethinking Faith, Works, and the Gospel of Jesus the King* (Grand Rapids: Baker Academic), 78.

3. J. I. Packer, *Knowing God* (Downers Grove, IL: InterVarsity Press Books, 1993), 194.

4. R. Michael Allen, *Justification and the Gospel* (Grand Rapids, MI: Baker Academic, 2013), 70.

5. "Lord's Day 1," Heidelberg Catechism, Christian Reformed Church, accessed November 15, 2021, https://www.crcna.org /welcome/beliefs/confessions/eidelberg-catechism.

Chapter 12: Clematis

1. Augustine, in R. Michael Allen, *Reformed Theology* (London: Bloomsbury T&T Clark, 2010), 17.

2. Bruce Perry, as quoted in Laurie MacKinnon, "The Neurosequential Model of Therapeutics: An Interview with Bruce Perry," *The Australian and New Zealand Journal of Family Therapy* 33, no. 3 (2012): 210–18, https://seminarer.dk/wp-content/uploads/2019/10 /MacKinnon_AusNZJFamTher_2013.pdf.

3. Todd W. Hall and M. Elizabeth Lewis Hall, *Relational Spirituality: A Psychological-Theological Paradigm for Transformation* (Downers Grove, IL: InterVarsity Press Books, 2021), 81–82.

4. Hall and Hall, *Relational Spirituality*, 82.

5. Sue Johnson and Kenneth Sanderfer, *Created for Connection: The Hold Me Tight Guide for Christian Couples* (New York: Hachette Book Group, 2016), 22.

6. Johnson and Sanderfer, *Created for Connection*, 52.

7. Curt Thompson writes of calling someone to "serve as an 'emotional regulator'" in *Anatomy of the Soul* (Chicago, IL: Tyndale, 2010), 132.

8. James Clear, *Atomic Habits: An Easy & Proven Way to Build Good Habits & Break Bad Ones* (New York: Avery, 2018), 17.

9. Philip J. Flores, *Addiction as an Attachment Disorder* (Lanham, MD: Jason Aronson Publishing, 2011), 218.

10. Augustine, *The City of God*, ed. and trans. by R. W. Dyson (Cambridge: University of Cambridge, 1998), 609.

Chapter 13: Open Heart Surgery

1. Chaim Bentorah, *Hebrew Word Study: Revealing the Heart of God* (New Kensington, PA: Whitaker House, 2016), 98.
2. Bentorah, *Hebrew Word Study*, 125.
3. Bentorah, *Hebrew Word Study*, 211.
4. C. S. Lewis, *The Great Divorce* (1946; repr., New York: Macmillan, 1946), 69.

Chapter 14: The WayMaker

1. Eberhard Jüngel as quoted by Matt Jenson, *The Gravity of Sin: Augustine, Luther and Barth on* homo incurvatus in se (London, UK: Bloomsbury T&T Clark, 2007), 191.
2. Augustine of Hippo, *Concerning the City of God Against the Pagans*, trans. Henry Bettenson (London: Penguin, 1984), 552–53.
3. Dane C. Ortlund, *Gentle and Lowly: The Heart of Christ for Sinners and Sufferers* (Wheaton, IL: Crossway, 2020), 97–98.
4. Kenneth E. Bailey, *The Cross & the Prodigal: Luke 15 Through the Eyes of Middle Eastern Peasants* (Downers Grove, IL: InterVarsity Press Books, 2005), 59.
5. Bailey, *Cross & the Prodigal*, 52–59.

Chapter 15: Sign

1. G. Campbell Morgan, *Hosea: The Heart and Holiness of God* (Eugene, OR: Wipf & Stock, 1998), 19.
2. John Flavel, *Keeping the Heart: How to Maintain Your Love for God* (Fearn, Scotland: Christian Heritage, 2012), 57.
3. Morgan, *Hosea*, 103.
4. Amelia Nagoski and Emily Nagoski, *Burnout: The Secret to Unlocking the Stress Cycle* (New York: Ballantine Books, 2020), 14.

Chapter 16: Moses Way

1. "Article 13: The Doctrine of God's Providence," Belgic Confession, Christian Reformed Church, accessed November 15, 2021, https://www.crcna.org/welcome/beliefs/confessions/belgic-confession.

2. Saint Thérèse of Lisieux, "Chapter III—Pauline Enters the Carmel," in *Story of a Soul (l'Histoire d'une Ame): The Autobiography of St. Thérèse of Lisieux*, Christian Classics Ethereal Library, accessed November 15, 2021, https://www.ccel.org/ccel/therese/autobio.xi.html.

3. Martin Luther, *The Annotated Luther, Volume 4: Pastoral Writings*, ed. Mary Jane Haemig (Minneapolis: Fortress Press, 2016), 77.

4. C. S. Lewis, *The Great Divorce* (1946; repr., New York: Macmillan, 1946), 69.

5. Curt Thompson, *Anatomy of the Soul* (Chicago: Tyndale, 2010), 65–67.

6. Thomas Moore, *The Church Hymn Book* (Columbia University, 1873), 356.

7. Andrew Stephen Damick, *Orthodoxy and Heterodoxy: Finding the Way to Christ in a Complicated Religious Landscape* (Chesteron, IN: Ancient Faith Publishing, 2017), 172 (emphasis mine).

8. Martin Luther, *Luther's Works, Vol. 24:31, Sermons on the Gospel of St. John: Chapters 14–16*, ed. J. J. Pelikan, H. C. Oswald, H. T. Lehmann (Saint Louis: Concordia Publishing House, 1999).

9. Avraham Arieh Trugman, "Mikvah: The Art of Transition," Mikvah.org, accessed November 15, 2021, https://www.mikvah.org /article/mikvah%2C_the_art_of_transition.

Chapter 17: Honeymoon

1. Curt Thompson writes, "When we trust, we risk the possibility of rupture for the payoff of repair and more deeply joyful integration within and between our minds." *Anatomy of the Soul* (Chicago: Tyndale, 2010), 248.

2. Gilbert K. Chesterton wrote, "But perhaps God is strong enough to exult in monotony. It is possible that God says every morning, 'Do it again' to the sun; and every evening, 'Do it again' to the moon." *Orthodoxy* (New York: John Lane, 1908), 108–9.

3. Charles Haddon Spurgeon, "The Marriage Supper of the Lamb," in *The Metropolitan Tabernacle Pulpit: Sermons Preached by C. H. Spurgeon*, vol. 35, 1889, The Spurgeon Center, https://www.spurgeon .org/resource-library/sermons/the-marriage-of-the-lamb/#flipbook/.

ABOUT THE AUTHOR

ANN VOSKAMP is the wife of a farmer, mama to seven, and the author of four *New York Times* bestsellers: *The Broken Way*, *The Greatest Gift*, *Unwrapping the Greatest Gift*, and the sixty-week *New York Times* bestseller *One Thousand Gifts: A Dare to Live Fully Right Where You Are*, which has sold more than 1.5 million copies and has been translated into more than twenty languages.

Named by *Christianity Today* as one of fifty women most shaping culture and the church today, Ann knows unspoken broken, big country skies, and an intimacy with God that touches tender places. Cofounder of ShowUpNow.com, Ann is a passionate advocate for the marginalized and oppressed around the globe, partnering with Show Up Now, Mercy House Global, and Compassion International. She and her husband took a leap of faith to restore a 125-year-old stone church into The Village Table—a place where everyone has a seat and belongs.

Join the journey at
www.annvoskamp.com
instagram/annvoskamp